ME, MYSELF & EYE

A MEMOIR

DAN JEFFRIES

◆Tangent Books

Me, Myself & Eye: A Memoir
First published 2015 by Tangent Books

Tangent Books
Unit 5.16 Paintworks
Bristol
BS4 3EH
0117 972 0645
www.tangentbooks.co.uk
Email: richard@tangentbooks.co.uk

ISBN 978-1-910089-22-4

By Dan Jeffries

Design: Joe Burt (www.wildsparkdesign.com)

A CIP record of this book is available at the British Library.

Printed on paper from a sustainable source

To engage with the additional content that accompanies this book, please visit **www.memyselfandeye.co.uk** with your smartphone, tablet or computer.

Other books by Dan Jeffries:

"*We are each of us special, unique, and for much of our short lives, most of us quietly consider ourselves immortal too. Even if you are born with a significant abnormality or develop a rare disease, it's surprisingly unusual for someone to ask 'why me?' These things become part of the person, part of the personality, part of the way of life and expectation for family and friends. For Dan Jeffries, not one but two rare — indeed exceptionally rare — conditions have occurred together and to some extent complicate each other.*

Rather than inhabit a well of self-pity, Dan has managed to almost embrace these conditions and despite the disabilities that they have conferred, extract a great deal of meaning and magic from life, which he has imparted in this book."

Andy Levy

Prof of Endocrinology and Hon Consultant Physician
University of Bristol and University Hospitals Bristol NHS
Foundation Trust

CONTENTS

Prologue		9
1.	Dan 1.0	13
2.	Win Some, Lose Some	23
3.	Eye of the Tiger	31
4.	QEH: The Early Years	41
5.	Best Friends and Bouncers	49
6.	Girls and Stuff	57
7.	Theatre, Shweetie!	65
8.	Go East!	75
9.	This Sentence is Twenty	83
10.	The Divine Daniel	89
11.	Hello Creativity	95
12.	Fruit	103
13.	Blind and Dumb	111
14.	Demons / Angels	119
15.	When the Chips are Down...	133
16.	The Temp from Hell	141
17.	Lord of the Ring	153
18.	OMG	165
19.	Love	171
20.	ATM	181
21.	Blood and Tears	189
22.	Solo	197
23.	Plums and Gums	201
24.	Rings, Fingers and Noses	209
25.	Woof	217
26.	From Slump to Salvation	221
27.	Hallelujah	229

28. Pictures, Pains and Polyps 241

29. Echo 253

30. 'I'm All In' 263

31. Showtime 267

32. Two Steps Forward… 277

33. CSF 285

34. Caught by the Fuzz 303

35. Eyes Right! 309

36. Hormones 317

37. Light Relief 329

38. Building Blocks 335

39. 'After the Break…' 341

40. The Fear, The Fame 347

41. Teeth and Tribulations 359

42. The Book of Clips 373

43. Super Sharp Shooter 379

44. Water and Fire 385

45. Life's Little Challenges 391

46. Highs and Lows 399

47. Heartbreak and Heartache 409

48. Love, Lust and Everything In-between 419

49. The Power of Words 427

50. So Long, Old Pal 433

51. Stress 443

52. 183% 449

Epilogue 457

Kickstarter Heroes 473

Acknowledgements 475

PROLOGUE

I STEP OUT OF THE SHOWER, REACH FOR A TOWEL, AND LOOK at myself in the mirror.

Meh.

On the sink is a bottle of Alpecin: hair revitaliser, half full now — must get a new one off eBay. I pick it up, squirt some into my thinning hair, and gently rub it in with my large hands. I glance back up at the mirror again, wince at my uncomfortable features, and contemplate how utterly pointless this is.

I lick my lips and examine my teeth. I like these. Thankfully, teeth don't thin.

A minute or so later I stop rubbing my head like a chimp with ADHD. I reach out for my glasses, missing them at first, groping around until I find them. I raise them up to my head and place them over my ears — a ritual I have performed a million times before. I look in the mirror once again. *Now* I'm in focus.

'Town, drinks, socialising, strangers,' I think to myself, and roll my eyes at my own self-doubt. I'm off to meet Ian, an old school friend, to celebrate his birthday. He's thirty-six. Just like me.

I cross my living room to the bedroom. House music blares from my speakers. Millie sits on the sofa, licking her paws. Her head pops up as I cross the room and her little eyes follow me intently. She's totally nonplussed by the noise — I hope it's because she's old and deaf and not because she thinks I have shit taste in music.

Inside the bedroom, I open my wardrobe and think about what to wear. Casual, smart casual, or impressive? I know old school friends will be there, some I haven't seen for years. I know they'll probably be married, or engaged, or have kids. I know that I'll be 'the single one'. Hey, maybe I'll find the love of my life there!

I go casual.

* * *

Bristol. Friday night. 8pm.

We're meeting down on the Waterfront, which means walking down Park Street and crossing the city centre. I weave my way through the drunken melee of short skirts and rippling torsos, conscious that I might do my usual trick of accidentally bumping into someone with arms like The Incredible Hulk. Thankfully — this time — I don't.

I arrive at the restaurant and scan the large open space. The common challenge of trying to see where people are now raises its ugly head. Are they here? Will they see me? Balls. I should have texted Ian to tell him to keep an eye out for me: something I'd normally do. I can't see them so I cross to the bar and order myself a vodka and diet Coke. Whilst there, I think I spot someone standing next to me that I went to school with. He doesn't recognise me. I'm not surprised — eighteen years can change a man.

Eventually Ian turns up. He shakes hands with the guy I'm standing next to, turns to me, and exclaims, "Hello Monkey!" I'm introduced to the chap next to me and of course we immediately recognise one another and it's, "How are you! God, has it been that long?" A few more people turn up and, as is the way with Bristol, we all start to realise that we already know each other through mutual friends. Phew. I can start to relax a bit.

I order another vodka.

* * *

A waiter comes and tells us our table is ready, and we casually wander over. Weirdly, there are not enough places at the table, but now that I'm buoyed up on vodka (or 'pissed' as it's more commonly known) and feeling part of the group, I grab a spare chair and seat myself at the head of the table, like I'm the Court Jester in residence. I'm sat next to Merv (the guy at the bar), and his girlfriend, plus another couple I don't know. I'm on good form, more comfortable now that I'm the centre of attention and not on the periphery.

"So Dan, Ian tells me you work in music?" asks Merv's girlfriend, Danielle.

"Yup. Music education. I write my own music, DJ a bit, and run my own label too."

"Really? That's pretty exciting. Have you been doing that for long?"

I reach out to grab my drink and knock hers over by mistake.

"Shit! I'm so sorry! My eyesight is rubbish. I can't always see what's around me."

Danielle smiles as we clean up the mess.

"Oh, don't worry about it. Have your eyes always been like that?"

And so it begins. I know that I'm about to tell 'the story' and tell it to a group of people that have never heard it before. I'll see their jaws drop, their eyes widen, their mouths curl in sadness, and ripple with laughter.

I order another drink and one for Danielle.

Thirty minutes later and the story is told. I see the emotions written across the faces of my audience: shock, surprise, pity, disbelief. Questions are asked, drinks are bought. We decide to skip dessert.

I turn to Danielle. "I bet you wish you'd never asked!" I joke.

She looks at me, thinks for a second, and then utters a phrase I will never forget.

"You should write a book!"

A smile creeps across my face like the sun at the dawn of creation.

"A book you say? Now *there's* a good idea..."

1. DAN 1.0

Phwoar! That was a bit good wasn't it?

Sorry. Probably shouldn't start off chapter one by boasting about my writing, especially considering this is the first book I've ever written. It's currently 2.30 in the morning and my brain has decided that this is the moment I need to start writing. I've been waiting weeks for a flash of inspiration, and those bloody Gods of Creativity decide to give it to me halfway through the night.

I wonder if the testosterone injection I had this morning has anything to do with it?

Hi, I'm Dan. And this is my book.

Firstly, thanks for buying it. Or at least testing it out before you decide if it's worth buying or not (it is). I thought long and hard about whether to go purely digital and just make an eBook, or whether to stick with the traditional. Actually, I've decided to go for both: I know how important leather bookmarks are to some. And I also thought long and hard about why anyone might be interested in my story. Sure, I can tell it over a couple of drinks and a chicken jalfrezi but that doesn't necessarily mean that it's going to translate into a book, does it? Well, I guess we're about to find out.

One of the reasons why I wanted to merge traditional with technology is that I have a lot of great pictures to show you, a few key documents, and the odd bit of music and video too. And in order to keep the cost of the book down (aren't I nice!), I thought — hello! — let's use technology and combine the two experiences. So you won't find any pictures in the book itself, but when it's time to 'engage', I'll let you know.

In fact, let's test this out now. At the end of this sentence is a number which is known as a footnote – it tells you there's some extra information at the bottom of the page.[1] Now jump on the Web and go to www.memyselfandeye.co.uk. You can do this on a smartphone, tablet or computer. Once you're on the website, find the link to view the book content and then locate chapter one. Make sense? Let's try it again.[2] Aww, how cute! Actually, maybe not that cute. How about... dashing. Or... um... seductive? Yes, that'll do. Seductive.

My mum would no doubt tell you that I look dashing in every photo I'm in, but that's mums for you. And don't we just love them for it. Talking of mums, this would probably be a good time to introduce you to the family and give you a bit of background.

I was born Daniel Jeffries on the 2nd March, 1977. I do have a middle name but you'll have to read more of the book

1 → Hello! I'm a footnote! The arrow tells you that I'm something to view on the website.

2 → All grown up.

to find out what that is (trust me, it's worth it). The loving parents who gave me that moniker are Chris and Sue. Dad hails from 'Laandan' town, Mum from a little village in the West Country. This may account for why I have an acceptable blend of urban cynicism and rural warmth. I was born in the delightful seaside town of Weston-super-Mare, believed to be the original settling place of the Romans.[3] The birth itself was a difficult one: I was born standing up! No, not really. It was definitely an interesting birth though. I took forever to make my appearance, and once ready, they had to use forceps to help me out. My mum even thinks that there were concerns about whether I would make it. Clearly I was demonstrating my ability to challenge the medical world before I had even popped out.

I've got a sister too: Alix. She's three years younger than me and where I may be the voice of reason, she is the roar of passion. It makes for a great combination: I douse her fires and she stokes my cauldron. Thankfully, we've got a very close and honest relationship — something I know siblings can struggle to develop. Yeah, we have our ups and downs but on the whole we're watertight. And it's this close relationship that got me through some very difficult times later on in my story. To her I am indebted.

So why am I writing this book? What is it about me that makes this book a candidate for Richard and Judy's 'Book Of The Year'?[4]

I was born with a very rare eye condition called Wyburn-Mason syndrome. In a nutshell, Wyburn-Mason syndrome

---

3   That might not be true.
4   Hint hint.

— also known as Bonnet-Dechaume-Blanc syndrome or retinoencephalofacial angiomatosis — is characterised by arteriovenous malformations that affect the retina, visual pathways, midbrain, and facial structures. It usually is unilateral and often is asymptomatic.

Now, I don't want to insult your intelligence by having to explain what all that means, but just in case you're not quite sure what a 'retinoencephalofacial angiomatosis' is, I'll offer my simplified explanation. Wyburn-Mason syndrome is where blood vessels do not form correctly around the brain. These are known as arteriovenous malformations or AVMs for short. These vascular defects are nonhereditary and congenital, i.e. present from birth. In my case, these deformed blood vessels affect my 'visual pathway'. It means I am totally blind in my left eye. Totally. No light, no shapes: nothing.[5]

It was actually my dad who helped in the diagnosis of my condition. Being partially sighted himself, he was naturally keen to make sure that my eyes were working as they should be. So, when I was four, Mum and Dad took me to an optician. The optician examined my eyes and discovered a mass of overly large blood vessels. They suggested that I should see a doctor.

The doctor, clearly concerned about the discovery, then referred me to Bristol Eye Hospital where I was seen by Mr Grey in May 1982.[6] He diagnosed that I had Wyburn-Mason syndrome. He also observed that, thankfully, I had no

---

5 → Here are some images of my eye showing you exactly what's going on.

6 → Have a look at the letter sent by my GP to the Eye Hospital. It's amazing to see the very first piece of communication about my condition.

neurological abnormalities.[7]

So, for as long as I can remember, I've only been able to see out of one eye.[8] Growing up, it didn't really bother me that much. I could still read, still play with toys, still watch TV. Perhaps worst of all came the realisation that I would never be able to watch anything in 3D. I still used to try on those awful paper glasses you would get in The Sun though, determined that if I squinted hard enough, it would work. But it didn't, and all I could see was a world of red whilst everyone else gawped at comic book heroes and man-eating sharks.

Some of my earliest memories are of visiting Bristol Eye Hospital for various tests and check-ups. Did I mention that I'm short-sighted in my right eye too? And because I've got an incredibly rare condition, I was always of great interest to the doctors and specialists at the hospital. Early on, we were told that about 1 in 3 million people have Wyburn-Mason syndrome. That's pretty damn rare. The Eye Hospital wanted to monitor my progress — make sure I was growing and developing properly. And there was also concern that the syndrome may have other effects on me. I think that they were worried that the condition could develop and affect my right eye as well, rendering me completely blind. Of course no one wanted that.

Besides going to the Eye Hospital, my earliest memories are when I started to go to school. It was called Wyncroft: a funny little place that was, in essence, the home of an elderly couple. It only taught about ninety children in total, and I was

---

7 → His original letter. I love how it's hand-typed and that the typist could spell incredibly complicated medical terms correctly but couldn't spell 'May'.

8 Even though my left eye is now totally blind, hospital letters suggest that there was some sight in my very early years, but this deteriorated rapidly. I don't ever remember seeing out of it.

there from four till eleven (that's age, not time). I remember in the very early days being taught by Mrs Mayhew. She once picked me up by my feet and swung me round, and I got to look up her skirt. Not sure why I'm telling you this.

At age five, after the diagnosis of my condition, the Eye Hospital gave me a pair of plastic sunglasses with a surgical plaster covering the right eye. The idea was to try and encourage the left eye to work. It didn't. Whilst you might think that wearing plastic sunglasses with a plaster over the eye would make me a source of mockery, you must be aware that these glasses were immune from ridicule for, on the side of each arm, there sat a plastic figure of Snoopy: my canine guardian angel. I was the height of cool fashion, and me and Snoopy knew it. No child dared to taunt my plaster-laden glasses, and if they did, Snoopy was there to send them packing. (In reality I wasn't really the height of cool fashion, nor did Snoopy act as my personal bodyguard. At least I don't think he did — this period is a bit of a childhood blur. I do, however, vividly remember the smell of the surgical plaster wrapped around the lens, and it's a smell I still love to this day. Ain't life weird?)[9]

Eye condition aside, I settled in pretty well at Wyncroft. Whilst I was good at reading and sums, what I was really, really good at was acting and music. Every year there was a school play, and almost every year I was cast in the lead role. One year, my entrance on to the stage involved skipping through the audience, whooping and cheering and saying "hello" to everyone as I passed them by. I don't think my parents could quite believe it. Looking back, I'm not sure I can either.

9   → My sister found another pair of glasses adorned with a plaster. Not the Snoopy ones, alas. Still cute though.

1982. Spain hosted the World Cup. Unlike most boys my age, I wasn't that interested in football and I didn't support a team. Dad didn't either, so I guess that gets passed on. For some reason, I did like Judo. I used to attend a weekly class in the Salvation Army hall, turning up every Saturday morning in my ill-fitting *Judo Gi*. I remember the Judo instructor treating me very kindly, ensuring that I didn't get the crap beaten out of me, or that some fourteen-year-old beefcake didn't throw me down on my head. I have a feeling Mum might have had a small word. But let's be honest — who in their right mind would attack such a frightening figure?[10]

Back at Wyncroft, I used to run about like all the normal kids, but if I got too hot from physical exertion, a red, blotchy patch would appear across the left hand side of my face. We found out that this was a 'Port Wine stain' and directly connected to the Wyburn-Mason syndrome.

[Port Wine stain] is the most common type of capillary malformation and is a congenital malformation of the superficial blood vessels of the dermis (skin). [11]

Rarely, acquired forms can occur at any age after birth. The cause has not been explained but trauma, chronic ultraviolet (UV) exposure, hormonal influences, infections, solid brain tumour and various internal vascular disorders have been suggested as possible associations.

10 → Sunloungers, beware!

11 Looking for pictures of Port Wine stains makes me realise how fortunate I am that this wasn't a permanent feature. I know my conditions are rare, but I still consider myself incredibly lucky.

Note that — not for the first time — I feature in a paragraph that starts, 'Rarely...'

Interestingly enough, whilst looking into Port Wine stains, I happened to scroll down and find a definition of Wyburn-Mason that I had not read before. It contained this observation:

> *Lesions may occur anywhere on the face and there may be facial hypertrophy or occasional involvement of the optic chiasm, the hypothalamus, the midbrain and the basal ganglia, with associated mental retardation or neurological features.*

Thankfully, mental retardation is not something I suffer from, though at times some may beg to differ.

Weston didn't always have a lot to offer, but one thing it did have was Mr B's Fun Factory. Almost every birthday party took place there and, after running round for hours, jumping into ball pits and unsuccessfully chasing girls, the Port Wine stain would start to appear, giving me a red, blotchy face. After a short time it would start to fade. I was conscious of it but it wasn't really a problem; it was just another 'thing' that made me a bit different. I was starting to learn to live with my ailments.

After realising I would never be a Judo master, I turned my hand to other sports. Once a week we would visit Weston Cricket Club where I would either play Soft Tennis or very basic cricket. I discovered that I was quite good at bowling — probably because I could target my sight on the wicket. I wasn't so good at tennis. Sure, I could hit the ball, but I had no real sense of the depth of the court, so pretty much every shot hit the back wall. My sister and I were occasionally entered into Soft Tennis tournaments but rarely got past the first round. We were both pretty rubbish. I had an excuse. The problem for my sister was that there were other children playing who were just better at it than her.[12]

It was becoming clear that sport was not my forte, and so I decided to focus my attention on activities that needed minimal exertion. Alongside learning the recorder at school, (standard practice, 'Three Blind Mice' anyone?) I also started to have private piano lessons with Mr Croft — a man so old you could see dew drops hanging from his ears. I loved playing the piano. Dad bought me a synth keyboard with a range of terrible noises and drum patterns, and every night I would practice the pieces that Mr Croft gave me, calling Mum and Dad in to listen when I had mastered the latest assignment.

Yet whilst I loved being creative, something was still missing. I somehow yearned for competition, to try and win, to be victorious — to beat my fellow man! I clearly needed a challenge.

So there I was: a young boy who was blind in his left eye, short-sighted in his right, and got a blotchy red face any time he did something sporty. I realised that I needed an activity that required far less sweating, took advantage of my wonky eyesight and, if possible, benefited from my narrow field of vision. My salvation manifested itself in the pubs and clubs of Weston — and that salvation was snooker.

---

12   → Notice how elated my sister looks at losing yet another tennis tournament.

2. WIN SOME, LOSE SOME

Now, let's be clear: it's not like I sat down one morning, got out a piece of paper, and said, "Right! What are the options before me that will take advantage of my blind eye and narrow field of vision?" and then whittled them down until I came up with snooker. To be honest, I'm not quite sure how I actually found myself there. It probably all stems from my dad.

My father, who has never been sporty, (does watching the horses count?) has always enjoyed snooker and he was pretty good at it too. He used to take part in a local league once a week, and I remember seeing the scrawled scoring cards on the mantelpiece, gradually getting more and more messy as the match went later into the night. But in most of the cards I saw, he was often the player that won. He had a genuine love for the sport. One of the first memories I have is of a nightclub contact card with a scrawl on the reverse:

'To Dan
Happy Birthday
Alex 'Hurricane' Higgins.'

Nice.

Snooker was one of the few sports that I loved watching on TV. It seemed to offer so many things: skill, ability, resilience, and a mild awareness of maths. Whether it was watching Cliff Thorburn cut a ball in from the finest of angles, or Kirk Stevens smash a red into a pocket from one end of the table to the other, I was hooked. World Championship finals offered the faint promise of a later-than-usual bedtime, making me feel part of a national family as we watched these two gladiators battle long into the night, fuelled by marmite on toast and hot chocolate.[13]

It wasn't long until I started to pester Dad for my own snooker table. So desperate was I to have one that I used to get some balls and a broom handle and just hit them along the living room floor. Dad, realising that we weren't quite this poor, finally relented and bought me my first ever snooker table. And this wasn't some cheapo job that you just rested on your dining table. Oh no. This was a *proper, actual* snooker table. It was 6x3 foot with a genuine slate bed, lush green felt, and pockets made from mermaid hair.[14] The spots were chalk marks, not plastic dots. It came with its own scoreboard for crying out loud! It was like being in my own little Crucible.[15]

---

13   Us, not them.

14   Maybe not.

15   → Look at that table! My OCD today wouldn't allow the pink to sit like that.

Alongside snooker, music was fast becoming the biggest thing in my life. Dad had bought me a stonking great ghetto blaster. It was massive: twin tape decks, FM stereo, and an aerial that reached to the moon. Michael Jackson's *Bad* was permanently on play, though I never really got past 'The Way You Make Me Feel'. I also had the latest Johnny Hates Jazz album, but let's not dwell on that.

Thankfully my music collection expanded massively when I won a competition on *Going Live!* One day in April, Phillip Schofield and Sarah Greene were showing off a revolutionary piece of technology: a gadget that stored music. Amazingly, when you spoke to it, it would play back whatever song you wanted. Of course, this kind of technology is something we accept as an everyday concept today, but back in the mid-eighties it was science fiction. And some lucky person had the chance to win it.

All you had to do was answer one simple question: what is the official name for Galki Day? I thought for a moment... Galki Day?! Never heard of it. I then remembered the date: April 1st. Ah, it must be another name for April Fools Day, I reasoned. I found a blank envelope, scribbled my name, address, and answer on the back and sent it off to Wood Lane.

A couple of weeks later there was a knock at the door. Mum answered it to find a postman standing there with a massive package... addressed to me! I tore open the box to discover an Ice Cube stereo, the Top 40 singles, and the hallowed device that would play back music. There was also a letter inside:

'Dear Daniel.
Congratulations! You won our Galki Day competition on

Going Live! As you are probably aware, that competition was aired on April Fool's Day and was, in fact, a hoax. But, because we had such an overwhelming response, we felt it was unfair not to give a prize. Your name was pulled out of the hat and so you've won all the goodies included in this package. Have fun!'

I couldn't believe it! I'd actually gone and won something, and won something big! My moment of glory was, however, tainted by the fact that I never heard them read my name out on TV. Oh well, the prizes were what mattered, and they were good'uns. The Ice Cube stereo had a tape deck, radio, and a lid you could take off to store cans of drink when you took it to the beach.[16] They also gave me the actual music player itself, with little memory cards to store the music. It didn't work, of course. I wish I still had it, but alas, it's lost in the sandstorm of time. What I do still have is that bundle of Top 40 singles, and what a bundle it was: Paula Abdul's 'Straight Up', Kon Kan's 'I Beg Your Pardon', and thirty-eight other smash hits I'm completely unable to remember.

My bedroom was slowly becoming my own little haven of entertainment. And so when friends came round (inevitably after spending hours on the Grand Pier playing *Double Dragon*), we indulged ourselves in music and snooker. I particularly enjoyed the snooker bit because I usually won.

As much as I loved having my own snooker table, nothing compared to playing on the full-size versions I would see on TV. When I was really young I would stand on a beer crate just to get my hand on the baize. Now I was a bit older and

16   → What a beaut!

I could fully immerse myself in these halls of quiet reverie. I loved the smell and the ambience: beer soaked bar cloths, the hushed tones of concentration, the soothing 'clack' of ball-on-ball. Add to that the simple delight of pushing 20p into a slot on the wall every time you wanted to keep the lights on over the table, and I was in my own little paradise. Even better, I was starting to beat my dad more and more. To celebrate my coming of age, a family friend gave me a professional snooker cue that had been cut down to size, perfectly fitting my diminutive form. Solid wood. A one-piece. My wand.

I was so into snooker that on a family holiday to Devon I was entered into a fancy dress competition. What did I go as? Dennis Taylor? Ray Reardon? A trophy? Nope. My parents put me in a bin liner, stuck a snooker cue in my hand, and taped a piece of paper to my chest with the words 'Pot Black' written on it. I didn't win.[17]

After a suggestion from Dad, I joined the 147 Snooker Club run by the brilliantly named Bruce Bernard (that's Bern*ard*, not Bernard). Every Sunday morning, groups of children would practice their techniques and play against each other in the best of three frames. I must have caught the eye of Bruce because, not long after I started, I was asked to play in the junior league. Sporting glory at last.

Okay, so I was no Alex Higgins, but I wasn't too shabby either considering I was blind in one eye and short-sighted in the other. Actually, I'm pretty sure that helped. It seemed to focus my line of sight on just the ball I was hitting. I won a couple of trophies in the league (and one from my mum), made some great long pots (thank you, eye) and generally did

---

17   → You can see why.

pretty well. And no one ever really knew about my sight. I think that made Bruce, my parents, and me a little bit proud.

Whilst I was doing my best to become the next Jimmy White (I actually wrote to *Jim'll Fix It* asking if I could have a game against him: it never happened), things had been developing with my health. In 1985 I underwent a CAT Scan and then an angiogram. The CAT Scan involved going inside a large tube ('the polo' as Dad called it), to take X-rays of the inside of my head — the angiogram involved pumping a coloured dye around my body in order to get a better look at the structure of my vascular system. The consultants wanted to look in more detail at these 'tortuous' blood vessels around my eye and brain that were caused by the Wyburn-Mason syndrome. How intricate was this network of engorged vessels? How far reaching were they? Could they start to affect the vision in my other eye? Their conclusions were that the AV malformations were severe but did not threaten the vision in my right eye nor pose any neurological threats. I can only imagine the huge relief this gave my parents. If I'm being honest, I don't remember this phase of my life that well (the medical records have helped fill in the gaps), but I do remember Mum and Dad buying me a Transformer toy as a reward, and that made everything okay.[18]

As if that wasn't enough, I had also been diagnosed with a systolic heart murmur. According to the National Heart, Lung and Blood Institute:

---

18 → I have a collection of letters from the consultants highlighting their discussions about my condition during 1985. There's even a reference to Mum asking if there was anything in the world that could improve the vision in my left eye. I was touched when I read that.

A heart murmur is an extra or unusual sound heard during a heartbeat. Murmurs range from very faint to very loud. Sometimes they sound like a whooshing or swishing noise.

Normal heartbeats make a 'lub-DUPP' or 'lub-DUB' sound. This is the sound of the heart valves closing as blood moves through the heart. Doctors can hear these sounds and heart murmurs using a stethoscope.

I don't remember hearing any extra 'lub-DUPPs', but obviously it was something that the consultants wanted to keep an eye on, especially given the complications I had with my vascular system. By the time I was nine the murmur had gone. It never really got in the way: I could still run and jump and do all the things the other kids could do — even if my face did get a bit red and blotchy whilst I was doing it. The only thing I couldn't do now was wee properly.

Now at this point you might be thinking, Whoa, Daniel! Do I need to know this? Well, maybe you do and maybe you don't, but I would be doing you a disservice if I *didn't* tell you about my circumcision. And besides, there are some cracking snip-based euphemisms coming up.

For some strange reason I was finding it hard to wee. It was painful and I didn't like it. Mum took me to the doctor and after some investigations it was decided that the best course of action was to say bye bye to 'Robin Hood' and hello to 'Little John'. The circumcision itself was fine — I had a shiny new winkie, albeit a little sore. The hospital sent me home and Mum put me to bed, replete with copies of the Beano and a bottle of Lucozade (crinkly orange wrapper intact).

The next morning I awoke, went to get out of bed... but

couldn't. I lifted the blankets and, to my horror, saw that my cocktail sausage was stuck to the sheets. And I mean properly stuck. During the night, pus had leaked from my ding-a-ling and formed a natural glue, welding me to the crisp, white bed linen.

"MUUUUUUUUUUMMMMMMMMMMMMMM!!!!!"

She raced upstairs to see me like a rabbit in the headlights, sheet in hand and pointing down to my joystick. She knelt by the bed, evaluated the situation, and looked me deep in the eye(s). I knew what was coming.

"We're going to have to rip it off."

I gulped, accepted my fate, gripped Mum's hand, and — WHOOSH — it was off. Tears formed. Lucozade was spilt. But I was free.

For some unknown reason the Hospital had neglected to tell us that this was likely to happen. Mum, who rarely gets annoyed, took me to the doctor's surgery to explain what we'd had to do, practically thrusting my crust-laden todger in his face. They quickly provided us with a plastic stool that I had to put over my lap to keep the sheets from touching. Oh, how the simplest things can help! With the exception of waking up one morning and weeing all the way down the stairs, this little snip caused minimal problems. Looking back, I'm glad I had it done.

Foreskins are *so* last century.

3. EYE OF THE TIGER

BY THE TIME I WAS EIGHT, BRISTOL EYE HOSPITAL FELT LIKE a second home. Oddly, I used to look forward to my visits there. It made me feel a bit special, knowing that I would be the focus of everyone's attention. I did have an incredibly rare eye condition after all, and the specialists clearly wanted to follow its developments. You could say they wanted to keep an eye on it (groan).

So every six to twelve months we'd make the hallowed trip to Bristol. My visits there usually went something like this:

Get to the hospital with Mum, pick up a ticket (like you're at the meat counter), wait a while, see a nurse, have some eye drops, then read the chart with all the different letters. Right eye fine, then get asked to do it with my left eye. Point out it was blind, have a chuckle, try it anyway, chuckle again, give up, then go back and wait. And wait. And wait a bit more.[19] Realise eyes were reacting to the drops, ask Mum to have a look. "They look like saucers!" Finally hear my name being called, head off for a Field Test. Follow the lights, press the buzzer, finish the test, go back and wait for my specialist. See my specialist, then see more specialists, then get asked if it was okay for other specialists to come and see my eye. Of course it was: I was famous! Once it was over, go to the shop, get a KitKat, call Dad, tell him the news, and go back home.

For me, visiting the hospital was fun. I liked the procedure. I liked the technology. I liked the nurses. But for Mum and Dad I can imagine it was an ordeal every time. Mum would always be the one to come with me whilst Dad would stay at home — one of our few family superstitions. I think, sadly, that Dad felt possibly responsible for my eyes, because he's partially-sighted himself. I once joked that if you held his glasses up to the sun you could burn a hole direct to the Earth's core, but there's no link between our conditions. None. So Dad, if you're reading this (and you bloody well better be!), absolve yourself: it's nature and nothing more.

Right. Enough schmaltz. Let's play a game.

I want you to close your left eye. Look straight ahead with your right eye and, with your right hand, slowly bring one of your fingers in from the top, then the sides, and then the bottom. Keep looking dead ahead. Make a mental note when you see your finger. As soon as you do, take your finger out and bring it in again, but this time from a different angle. Make a buzzing noise when you see it if you like, though you probably shouldn't if you're sat on a bus.

---

19   Love you, NHS!

This, ladies and gentlemen, is a very crude version of what is known as the Field Test. This method is, unsurprisingly, not the system used in hospitals but it gives you some idea of the concept. The test is designed to assess your peripheral vision. Here's a more thorough explanation from *www.medicinenet.com*:

> *A visual field test is a method of measuring an individual's entire scope of vision, that is their central and peripheral (side) vision. Visual field testing actually maps the visual fields of each eye individually. The test is a subjective examination, requiring the patient to understand the testing instructions, fully cooperate, and complete the entire test in order to provide useful information.*

'Fully cooperate.' That's the clincher.

Undergoing a Field Test was quite an exciting experience: I'd go in to a darkened room to be confronted by a big piece of equipment with a large dish facing towards me. I'd sit on a chair, have it adjusted, and then rest my chin on the chinrest. My eyes would dart about the dish, taking it all in: thin, mysterious etchings, faint black lines, numbers and symbols I didn't understand and, right in the centre, the ominous black dot — looking at me, teasing me, beckoning me.

The specialist would then guide a small white light around the dish, coming in from all manner of angles: sometimes from the side, sometimes dead centre. In my hand I held a little black buzzer, my thumb nervously hovering over it, poised in anticipation of pressing it as soon as I saw the dot. The trouble was, it was very tempting to cheat. My eyes would naturally flick away, trying to find that little dot of light coming in from the side, panicking when I couldn't see it. But that was the point: to gauge what I *couldn't* see. And I'd always get caught. "Look straight ahead," a voice would boom. The temptation to press the buzzer when I couldn't see the dot was heavy, but I tried my bestest not to. What was the point in giving inaccurate results?

'Fully cooperate.' I come back to it again.[20]

Thankfully, my childhood didn't consist entirely of eye tests and visits to the hospital. I had taken it upon myself to try and help out in the community: more specifically to help those who had visual impairments, just like me. When I was about six, I organised a jumble sale outside my house to raise funds for the Lauriston Hotel for the Blind. I found some old toys and books and even went round to the local newsagents to see if they had any stock they could give me (they did: out of date Space Raiders), which I sold for 5p a pack. All in all, I raised the grand total of £9.43 and a half (yes, half pennies were an important addition to any charity fundraising total). The Lauriston was so pleased with my efforts that I was the honorary guest at the grand opening of their new annex, and was even interviewed by BBC Points West for my efforts. I didn't do it for the fame of course — I did it because I wanted to help those who really couldn't see, who relied on guide dogs to get them around. I would visit the hotel regularly to spend some time with the elderly residents, holding their hands and just talking to them about everyday things. I guess when I'm old and grey, that kind of communication with the younger generations will be just as important for me too.[21]

20 → Here are two field test results from 1985, fascinatingly drawn by hand. Notice the left eye in particular.

21 → What a star!

I had also decided, primarily thanks to HTV News (ITV's regional news programme), that I wanted to learn sign language. HTV News had a regular 'signer' on their show, a lady called Sherrie Eugene. My sister and I would try and copy her signing, mimicking her hand movements and usually ending up in fits of laughter when we couldn't keep up. Mum, realising that I was clearly showing an interest in this, looked into local sign language groups and one evening we went along to this tiny little place where a group of deaf residents met once a week. I was welcomed by the group, mostly senior citizens, and over the next few weeks I started to learn the alphabet and a few words. I even discovered that there was a sign language for those who were deaf *and* blind: a language that relied upon tactile hand positioning and gestures. It was amazing to watch and I only tried a few letters — it was that complicated. After a couple of months I stopped attending the group, and to be honest I can't really remember why. Maybe I was finding it too difficult. I'd learnt the alphabet and could recite that at lightning speed, which was good enough for me and my dad, who would ask me to show it off when we were out with friends and family.[22]

And my small contribution to entertaining the elderly didn't end there. Along with Mr Croft and a select group of his pupils, I would visit old people's homes and community centres and perform for them. I enjoyed the spotlight — the applause at the end, the free squash and biscuits. Alix, who would do a bit of singing, wasn't quite so keen.[23] But me, I loved to entertain: whether it was playing the piano, the recorder,

22   → I can still do it now.
23   → If looks could kill. And check out my socks!

or singing old-time songs. The piano gave me an opportunity to show some skill and dexterity, demonstrating how nimbly my fingers could move over the keys. When it came to singing I had no fear of hitting the high notes. You'd often find me warbling 'O For The Wings Of A Dove' or, if feeling a bit more theatrical, 'The Phantom of the Opera'. That all changed once the plums went southwards.

* * *

A key moment in my early life was getting my first pair of glasses. I had, of course, experimented with the Snoopy sunglasses and other plaster-covered frames, but these were merely a device to see if we could get my left eye to respond properly. Accepting that my left eye was a lost cause, it was time to focus on my right eye. It was becoming clear that, upon every visit to the Eye Hospital, the sight in my right eye was degrading year-by-year. Nothing too serious, but serious enough to warrant my first pair of prescription glasses. I vividly remember the excitement of going to the optician, having my eyes tested and watching them scratch their head as they tried to figure out what was wrong with my left eye. Then I had to choose the frames. Back then they looked horrendous. Today, they'd go for a fortune at Camden Market.[24]

I was, of course, still going to school. I enjoyed most subjects but English was a definite favourite. I thrived on creative writing, and thoroughly enjoyed demonstrating my ability to spell. Now that I was wearing glasses, there was no doubt that they gave me an air of geek-chic which, in turn,

---

24 → I'm not sure which is worse – my glasses or Alix's fringe.

raised awareness of the fact that I had something wrong with my eyes. When fellow schoolmates enquired as to what was wrong, I would take great delight in covering my good eye and asking them to hold up some fingers in front of me, knowing I wouldn't be able to see them. Realising that I couldn't see, they would naturally then try to flick their fingers really close to my eye or, no doubt, give me the middle finger. I never saw it, so I was none the wiser. Ignorance really is bliss.

Wyncroft was a funny old school. First off, it had no playground so you can imagine the mischief we got up to at break time. We would dare each other to climb out of the window into the garden. That might not seem like a big deal to you, but trust me, it was. The fear that we might get caught was immense. I also remember daring each other to climb the stairs of the house, to explore rooms that were out of bounds. It was a frightening adventure because Mrs Thorn, the Headmistress, truly lived up to her name. I was particularly naughty because — and I can't believe I'm going to confess to this — I would pretend to go to the toilet, but actually sneak into their dining room and steal a piece of chocolate. Oh, the shame.

Worst of all, Wyncroft used a weapon of torture called 'The Mat'. The Mat would put the fear of God into the bravest of children. Positioned in the main hallway, The Mat was where you were sent if you had been naughty. *Really* naughty. As if it wasn't humiliating enough to be on display in front of the children, you could also be seen by *all* the parents as they waited outside. Children would bury their faces into their dirt-covered knees to avoid the utter embarrassment of being spotted, but there was no escape. If your parents saw you sitting there as they waited in line, you could guarantee the car ride home wouldn't be much fun.

Thankfully, I didn't get to sit on The Mat too often. My chocolate stealing was never discovered, nor did it lead to a life of crime. My form teacher, Mrs Gill, was superb. She kept us all on the right path, helping us to develop our skills and pushing us into the areas we loved: which for me was still music, writing, and acting. I often wonder where this artistic confidence came from. It can't be ignored that my great-granddad — a magician working under the name of Educated Hands — performed at Windsor Castle under Royal Command. Both my granddad on my father's side, and indeed my dad himself have the ability to entertain at the drop of a hat. I guess this is why I felt more than comfortable singing 'The Phantom of the Opera' to a room full of octogenarians. I was, you might say, a confident little boy.

* * *

When I wasn't singing songs to OAPs, I was usually found playing computer games. Dad had first introduced computers into our lives when he bought an Atari 2600: one of the very first home computers ever produced.[25] The cartridges were the size of books, and the controls — along with the graphics — were awkward and clunky. It was amazing.

And then in 1982, a new computer was born. It was the Spectrum 48K. The advert promised the world.[26] And, getting bored of Pong and Space Invaders, I asked Dad if I could have it for Christmas.

25 → So revolutionary, even Morecambe and Wise put their name to it.

26 → Almost Orwellian in style. Well, compared to Morecambe and Wise it is.

"Only if you've been a good boy!" was the stock reply I was given. Of course I had been — I was always good! I pleaded some more. "Let's see what Father Christmas brings!" Gah!

I knew that Father Christmas probably wasn't real but not being entirely sure I decided, that year, I would try and catch him in the act. To do so, I tied a bit of string around my big toe and sellotaped the stocking to the end of the string, so when Father Christmas filled it with presents it would tug at my foot and wake me up. I awoke on Christmas morning to see that Santa had managed to bypass my system and had filled my stocking full to the brim with brightly wrapped presents. He's a clever one.

I ran into my parents' bedroom, whooping with joy at the goodies Santa had brought me. I climbed into their bed and started to unwrap my presents. One of them, confusingly, was a power lead. Eh? But then I opened another present to find a cassette player. I suddenly remembered that the Spectrum 48K needed a tape player in order to load the games! This was looking *very* promising.

I was so excited I could barely breathe. We went downstairs and opened the rest of our presents, and I was almost wetting myself in anticipation at the arrival of my brand-new computer. The huge pile of presents slowly started to dwindle until there were only a couple left. Alix opened her big present and got exactly what she wanted: a Big Yellow Teapot. And that was it — no more presents left. I ran around the back of the tree and checked with my own eye(s). It was official: there were no more presents left. I was horrified. Had Father Christmas forgotten my computer?!

I stormed out of the lounge and hid in the toilet, tears streaming down my face. I stayed there for the next ten minutes, refusing to leave, distraught that Father Christmas had forgotten the one present that I had wanted. When I finally emerged — face all red and blotchy — Dad asked what was wrong, a sly smirk evident on his lips. I glared at him and Mum. And then, from behind his back, he produced a large box. I suddenly stopped crying. Could this be it?! I ripped open the wrapping paper to see the letters '48K' emblazoned on the side. I ran over to them and hugged their legs with all my might. And as soon as *Horace Goes Skiing* had loaded up I had forgotten all about my traumatic morning.[27]

I don't think my parents ever forgave themselves for that ill-judged prank, and rightly so. However, I am happy to say, here and now, that Mum and Dad — I forgive you. But may it be burnt upon your souls from now until the end of time.

---

27 → As you can see.

4. QEH: THE EARLY YEARS

WHILST I WOULD HAVE BEEN PERFECTLY CONTENT TO live in a world of badly-pixelated ski slopes, the cool hand of reality was about to place itself on my shoulder. I was reaching the dizzying heights of ten, and that meant only one thing: 'big school'.

It was becoming apparent that I was, academically, reasonably bright. Wyncroft was very good at giving its pupils the opportunity to consider an education outside of Weston and so we started to look at schools in Bristol. It's not that Weston couldn't offer a decent state education, but my parents were in a position where they could give me the chance to experience something new, something they hadn't experienced in their formative years. And that experience was QEH.

QEH — or Queen Elizabeth's Hospital to give it its official title — was almost 400 years old and located right in the heart of Bristol. As you approached its blue wrought iron gates you were greeted with a set of steps Harry Potter would gawp at.[28] The interior was just as impressive: huge, imposing rooms, a massive dining hall, decades-old boards listing previous Captains of School. It had an excellent reputation and great facilities, even if the sports fields were located a few miles away in Failand — something I wasn't particularly concerned about. Both Mum and Dad knew this was the right school for me, even if Dad couldn't help but remind me that he used to call it 'Queen Elephant's Hospital' when he was growing up in Bristol. They were simpler times back then.

QEH was a boarding school. It had around 90 boarders that would sleep there during the week and around 400 day boys who were located in Bristol or nearby. Leaving home that first night was a real mixture of excitement and emotion. You think it'll be like a sleepover at a friend's house, but the reality was very different. Knowing it would be six days until you saw your family again was difficult, and I won't deny that I cried a fair bit for the first few weeks. I'm sure Mum did too. It was tough but looking back, I know it made me stronger — something I would need to call on in later life.

Our dormitory consisted of about 12 boys spread over three floors. Walking into my dormitory for the first time was an incredibly daunting experience. Thankfully, Justin Hawksby slept opposite me. And he made me piss myself.

Literally.

Our beds were wooden blocks with mattresses (god, that sounds terrible). Okay, let's try that again. They were beds, and these beds had drawers where we would store our clothes

---

28   → The first time I visited the school we were allowed to walk up those steps. That privilege wouldn't be granted again until I was in the Sixth Form.

and 'tuck' and letters from Mummy and Daddy. It was the first night and Justin Hawksby, no doubt wanting to impress the rest of us, decided to see if he could fit himself into one of these drawers. He looked about for a teacher, saw that the coast was clear, and — to the delight of the rest of the dorm — stepped into the drawer and curled himself into a ball. A perfect fit. There were cheers and laughter all round, but the *piece de resistance* came from Jim Parkes who, in a moment of inspired madness, stretched out his legs and pushed the drawer shut. I was in fits. Justin was completely trapped in his own bed, banging like mad to get out. I laughed so hard I wet myself. And to make it worse, I was wearing light blue pyjamas. From that day on I would be known as 'Wet Patch'.

Embarrassingly, that wasn't the only time that I wet myself through laughing. Near to our school was a shop called Oriental House that sold a plethora of jokes, gadgets, and comedy paraphernalia. One time, a friend of mine bought a green, sticky hand that you could fling at things — a bit like those sticky Octopus toys you could throw at a wall and watch them slide down (they used to creep the hell out of me). Anyway, we were in the common room one day and some lads were playing table tennis. The boy with the green, sticky hand was flinging it wherever he could find space. He flung it towards the table and — completely by fluke — caught the table tennis ball mid-air. It seemed to freeze in time and space for several seconds before it fell down to earth. This was the funniest thing I had ever seen, and I found myself bent double on the floor. In fact it was so funny my bladder decided to let things go, and I had to make a mad dash to the toilets, covering my now-damp crotch as I ran. Thanks a lot, Mother Nature.

Wetting myself with laughter wasn't the only character-building aspect of boarding school. We studied six days a week, and that meant Saturday school, with sports (for those who were inclined) in the afternoon. When it came to Sunday morning, the boarders would parade down Park Street to attend a church service at the Lord Mayor's chapel, replete in full boarders uniform: knee-length yellow socks, moleskin breeches, and gown with white collar.[29] Once service was over, we'd walk back to school, pack a bag, and then wait in anticipation for 10.30am, when our parents would come and pick us up. The sight of the family car swinging its way through those huge iron gates brought about a wonderful sense of familiarity. It wasn't easy being away from home at such a young age so I would treasure these Sundays like they were gold. What could beat Mum's Sunday lunch? Nothing. What could be better than a family walk around town? Nothing. And then, just as I was getting comfortable, it was time to head back. 6pm seemed to arrive far too quickly, and I remember the silent car journeys back to Bristol and the teary goodbyes as Mum hugged me tight by the gates. I know that she and Alix used to listen to Elton John's 'Daniel' on the way home and quietly weep.

After three years of doing this, Mum asked if I would prefer to stay at home on Sunday nights and return back to school on Monday morning. Would I? Hell yeah! I can't tell you the difference this made — to spend a night in my own bed having been fed like a king all day. By 8pm I was snuggled under the duvet, marmite on toast and hot chocolate next to me, *The Inspector Wexford Mysteries* quietly streaming from the TV. It didn't matter that Mum and I had to wake up at 6am

---

29   → We also had to wear this if ever we wanted to go into town after school. I don't think I left the grounds for the first three years.

to make it back in time for assembly — I'd spent the night in my own bed, and I was all the better for it.

* * *

Every child faces challenges at school. The first obstacle for me to overcome contained two of the most terrifying syllables in the English language: rugby.

For the first time in the school's four-hundred-year history, a boy was exempt from playing rugby: and that boy was me. Doctors at the Eye Hospital felt that the vascular activity around my eye and brain was a serious enough issue that I shouldn't engage in any contact sport. The fear was that this arteriovenous malformation (or 'the worms' as our family called them) could become damaged if I took a hit, and potentially cause bleeding in the brain. I think there were also concerns that somehow the syndrome could pass over to the other eye, or in some way damage the eye. I didn't really understand — I just knew I would never experience the joy of a sticking my head between another boy's legs.

And, if I'm being honest, I was pretty happy about this. I couldn't think of anything worse than humiliating myself on a cold, wet field pretending to be rough and tough and like I could see what I was doing. I remember Dad telling me he had to play rugby at school and that, if anyone ran towards him, he'd simply throw the ball in the air to get it as far away from himself as possible. I think we're both cut from the same rugby cloth.

So, for the first two years of school my sport of choice was badminton. Yes, hurly, burly badminton. Twice a week I would head down to the gym, clad in shorts and white t-shirt, to play against boys in the 3rd and 4th form who had fulfilled their rugby duties for the past two years and had wisely decided to seek sporting glory elsewhere. Surprisingly, I was quite good at badminton, but it's just not rugby, is it? And there's no doubt that when you're in an establishment that recognises sporting achievement so highly, someone scoring the winning try in the dying seconds of a game will probably grab the limelight over me beating Kev Morgan 21-18. Thankfully, there was always drama.

Starting the same year as me was a teacher called Mr Brown. He was very nice but unfortunately had the biggest chin you'd ever seen. It didn't take long for him to gain the inspired nickname 'Chin' or, more creatively, 'Roger Ramjet'.[30] I once stupidly muttered, "Here comes Roger Ramjet!" under my breath as he came to teach us Geography. I clearly didn't mutter it very well because he heard me and, needless to say, he wasn't impressed. Anyway, as well as being a Geography teacher, he was also one of the new boarding house masters and — much to my delight — would be running the Drama Club. So in the first year he put on a couple of different productions, one of which was called *A Day in the Mind of Tich Oldfield* and I, dear reader, was cast as Tich.

Tich was a dreamer. He lived in his own little world, fantasising about being on television and losing himself in a myriad of whacky thoughts and ideas. The very start of the play involved a dream sequence where Tich was in a talent show. The script was vague enough to allow the actor to come up with what the talent might be. After realising that physical trickery was not my thing, we decided that I would do a routine

---

30 → Who looks like this, in case you were wondering.

of impressions instead. It started off with David Coleman, ("err... quite remarkable!") who morphed into David Frost, ("who would live in a house like this?") who handed over to Lloyd Grossman, ("let's look at the evvvidennce..."), who went on to reveal it was the house of Prince Charles (plastic ears included). The whole skit was devised by me. It was my equivalent of scoring a match-winning try.

That same term, I was asked to be in a production of *The Christmas Carol* at the Old Vic Theatre, playing Tiny Tim. Now *this* was more like it! I can't quite remember how it all happened, but I know that the father of one of the boys in my year worked as a set designer at the Theatre — reaffirming the adage that it's not *what* you know but *who* you know. A very lovely lady would pick me up from school three times a week for rehearsals, all building up to the full production at Christmas. It was a pretty magical experience, and I loved hobnobbing with the cast and crew, all of whom were students studying at the Theatre School. I felt important — a part of the creative process. When the production ended, the cast signed a specially printed t-shirt. I still have it to this day and it's never been washed.[31]

A pretty involved first year at school was topped off when I was awarded the Stephen Holmes Prize for Endeavour, given to an individual who had 'triumphed over adversity'. I was both humbled and surprised. What had I done to deserve *this*? I could only assume it was because I had coped with my eye condition, but in my mind I was merely existing and making the most of the opportunities afforded to me. But a prize I had won, and who was I to argue? This wasn't a shield, or a

---

31   → And, suffice to say, it no longer fits.

trophy, or a cup: it was book tokens and the books would be presented to me at the end of year prize-giving ceremony in the magnificent Wills Memorial Building.

I was now faced with a dilemma. What should I buy? I was conscious that, when awarding the prize, the honoured guest would announce in booming tones the title of the chosen book, and I was highly concerned that my choice of *Five Go to Smuggler's Top* probably wouldn't sound very academic. So, wanting to impress the school, I chose *The Iliad* and *The Odyssey*.

They never announced the names of the books. I wish I'd just bought the Famous Five instead.

5. BEST FRIENDS
AND BOUNCERS

E VERY BOY WHO STARTED LIFE AS A BOARDER AT QEH HAD A
'Guardian Angel': someone in the second year who looked
after you, showed you the ropes, and kept you out of trouble.
Mine was a boy called Andy. I met him outside my dorm. He
was wearing a jumper with a moose on it that had a tiny pair
of plastic sunglasses over its eyes. I was mega-impressed.

Now I was in the second year, it was time for me to be
an 'Angel'. Luckily, I knew who I would be looking after. His
name was James, and we were best mates.

James and I had known each other for years. We both
went to Wyncroft, and almost every weekend I would stay at
his house or he would stay at mine. Staying at his was much
more fun as he lived on a farm. This meant acres of space,
shooting air rifles and — best of all — riding on his quad bike.
Well, trying to: I was more inclined to watch him race around
the fields. I preferred going into the woods, climbing trees,

and struggling with nature. I was no good at any of this 'boy' stuff, but that made me all the more determined to give it a go.

One afternoon, his mum called us in for tea and we raced down from the woods.

"Bet I can beat you!" he yelled as he split off to take the path back to his house.

"Bet you can't!" I shouted back.

I was determined not to be beaten. He was going the long way round — I was going to cut straight through and reach his front door first. And I might have won had I not run straight into a line of barbed wire. I screamed with pain as I sprung backwards, my right leg snared by the twisted knots of metal.

Seconds later I awoke to see his mum standing over me, mild panic etched across her face. She tried to pull the wire out and I yelped in pain. She told James to go back to the house and get the wire cutters. I closed my eyes in anticipation.

Minutes later and he returned. His mum steadied her hand and snipped one side of the wire, then the other. Jolts went through my body with each torturous cut. I slowly stood up, the lone piece of metal still wedged in my leg. It actually looked quite cool. I hobbled down the hill and his mum guided me towards the car. She told James to stay home and look after his little brother — we were going to the hospital.

As I sat nervously in the passenger seat, James' mum drove as cautiously as she could to Weston General, doing her utmost to avoid the bumps and cattle grids of the countryside. As we turned into the hospital car park, the wire suddenly fell out of my leg and into my hands. No pain, no blood, no reaction. She parked up and told me to wait whilst she went and found a nurse. I wasn't going anywhere. A minute later she returned with a wheelchair, and I perked right up: I'd never been in a wheelchair before.

An hour later and I was back in the car, heading for home. My bum ached from the tetanus. As this was the mid 80's and well before the advent of mobile phones, it was no doubt a moment of joy when my mum opened the door to see my leg wrapped in bandages. I explained I hadn't done anything wrong, I just hadn't seen the wire. Not seeing things and the perils that could bring was something I was going to have to get used to.

Back at QEH, I was eagerly awaiting the arrival of my best mate. I'd made some good friends at school, of course I had, but this was going to be amazing. Having been there for a year now, I felt somewhat proud that I could impart my knowledge of the school, and I was determined to make James feel safe, secure, and comfortable.

A week after his arrival, I was walking back from the gym when the boarding master ran up to me.

"James has run away!"

I looked at him in disbelief. During rugby practice that day, James had called for a taxi and simply gone home. I had no idea he had been *that* homesick and now the boarding master wanted me to talk to him, to encourage him to stay and continue his education at QEH. He'd be coming back later that night.

That evening, I was having a shower when I heard someone shouting my name.

"Dan? You need to get dressed. James is outside."

I put on my dressing gown and was escorted to the boarding master's flat and then straight outside to a parked car where James was sitting on the back seat. I opened the door and climbed in next to him. I had no idea what to say.

How do you convince someone to stay when they're clearly unhappy? His mum sat in the front seat, visibly biting her lip as she fought back the tears. I asked him what was wrong, but got little in return. And after a few minutes I could tell this was a lost cause. I climbed out of the car, and made my way back to the showers. I stood under the warm water and closed my eyes.

* * *

It was a shame that James had decided to leave, but I wasn't going to let it bother me — school was a difficult enough adventure as it was. As with all institutions, there was an element of bullying and being blind in one eye with special allowances to miss rugby made me a bit of a target. Well, for one boy in particular. He seemed to pick on me quite a bit, and I wasn't sure what to do. Calling home one evening I started to cry, explaining that I wasn't happy because this boy was teasing and tormenting me. The next day that boy came up to me and apologised, promising never to do it again. I found out a few days later that Dad had called the school and demanded something should be done. Thanks Dad.[32]

Whilst I tried to immerse myself in all things creative, I still needed to be active. I played squash, kept up the snooker a little bit, and even got to do fencing and archery. I found that any activity with a straight line or a target, or one that required hand-eye coordination, I could cope with. If it required some

---

32 Whilst I didn't like the boy that much, I had great admiration for him when, one hot and sultry day in the dorms, he killed a wasp by hitting it with a badminton racquet. That takes some skill. Sadly, he got expelled in the Third Year for dealing drugs. He should have stuck with pest control.

sense of spatial awareness, I was scuppered. And happily, off the back of this, shooting guns came naturally.

I should probably explain that. At age thirteen, I decided to join the ATC: the Air Training Corps. Why? I don't know. Probably to get out of playing badminton again. And also because of the uniform. [33] The ATC was like a mini army for the school. Every week we would parade around the schoolyard, learn how to line up, salute, march time and all that nonsense. Writing this, I am chuckling to myself about why I even bothered: it really must have been the guns.

At the back of the yard and through a small cloister, lived the ATC hut.[34] It was where the troops met, shared stories, and read articles about flying. We could also shoot air rifles too, and the ATC hut had its own shooting range. I call it a range: it was more like a wooden box, but there was something deeply exciting about it. And — because I could barely see the target — if I hit it, I was overjoyed. We even got the chance to fire some real heavyweight rifles at the Territorial Army centre on Whiteladies Road. It was a 25-metre distance to the target. I don't think I hit it once.

I tried my best to get involved, I really did. We got to fly planes — known as Chipmunks — but I was always sick on the way down (nothing makes you look more manly than walking back into the barracks with a bag full of sick). I went on a two-day night exercise activity but ended up running for my life when I was chased by a cow at two o'clock in the morning. It didn't really cut it for me, and I soon realised that my dreams of saving the country were fruitless. So I took up

33 → Oooh, the uniform!

34 I'd only really known the cloister as a place to clean your shoes and discover well-worn girlie mags.

cricket scoring instead.

Now, I recognise that's quite a leap. I had ditched the guns in favour of the 'thwack' of willow on leather and the promise of salmon and cucumber sandwiches. Cricket wasn't a totally alien sport to me. I'd enjoyed watching it on TV when I was younger (I remember a ferocious fight between me and my sister because she wanted to watch *Neighbours* and I wanted to watch the end of the match), but never in my wildest dreams did I expect to be one of the official scorers for the school cricket team. Of course, I'd have preferred to be standing at the crease than just watching it, but I wasn't allowed. Once again, the fear that the ball might hit me on the head and, as with the rugby, cause more damage to my sight was too big a risk. However, it was with genuine pride that I was told that the school had invested in a cricket helmet, just for me. And even better: I was going to play in a match. To represent my school! Oh my! Okay, so it was the Under 13s v the Under 12s and I was eleventh man. And I didn't even get to bat or bowl. But my name and photo appeared in the end of year book and that was good enough for me.[35]

Some small part of me thought I might get picked to play for the team again, but it wasn't to be. So by the Third Year I was under no illusion that I was going to achieve the glory of being a professional sportsman, so I did the next best thing and became a scorer instead. Every Saturday during the summer I'd score either at Failand or travel with the team to different schools. My job was to note down every ball bowled, every wicket taken, and every leg bye earned. Or at least I would try. The trouble was, I couldn't see very well. So, when

35   → I'm the one not wearing whites.

the other school's scorer would ask, "Who just caught that?" I would squint across the field, analyse the form of whoever was being patted on the back and take a wild guess at their name. I was probably the root cause of the most inaccurate cricket statistics in years.

6. GIRLS AND STUFF

Aඵ WOULD BEFALL ALMOST ANY THIRTEEN-YEAR-OLD AT AN all-boys boarding school, the introduction of girls into our lives brought about an immediate stirring to the nether regions of our moleskin breeches.

It all started in the Third Year. We were told that we would be doing a play called *The Golden Pathway Annual...* with The Red Maids School for Girls.

Maids? Girls? Really? What... *real* girls?!

So once a week, a small group of girls from Red Maids would visit the school and we'd rehearse the play together. There was a natural air of embarrassment and giggles as we got to know each other, but we all quickly formed friendships that would carry on for the rest of our school days. *The Golden Pathway Annual* was lots of fun: Ben Fortune had to wear a dog mask and we mimed eating a picnic to a cacophony of massive burps. It was great.[36]

Working with the opposite sex was a revelation. I hadn't really had any contact with girls since I'd left primary school and now I was surrounded by them. And I felt like I was in my element. I far preferred the warm, accepting company of girls over the testosterone-fuelled machismo of boys. It gave me a chance to shine: I was funny, witty, spontaneous. Rehearsals gave me the opportunity to let myself go, to play the fool, to let my creative mind flourish. I was beginning to find my funny bone.

It was at this time that I was also introduced to improvising — and I couldn't get enough of it. I could respond to my surroundings, make wise-cracks about the smallest of things, be physically silly and get away with naughty jokes too. I came to realise that there's no greater satisfaction than entertaining an audience and making people laugh, a weapon I knew I could harness in the light of the fact that I was neither particularly buff, sporty, or good-looking.

It was during *The Golden Pathway Annual* that I had my first taste of love. Her name was Nancy. Rumours had been going around that we both fancied each other and it was with typical teenage awkwardness that we declared we were boyfriend and girlfriend. We made each other laugh in that way thirteen-and fourteen-year-olds do. We'd write stupidly long letters to each other, hers always adorned with the manic scribble of other girls, interjecting her stream of consciousness. Breakfasts were always a thrilling experience as you scrambled to the table to see if you had a letter from someone — made even more exciting if the envelope looked

36   → The three of us on stage. But who's the ghostly figure in the background?!

like a toilet wall and emitted the wonderful aroma of cheap perfume (usually a sign it wasn't from your parents). From then on, unless you were being dumped, it didn't matter what the rest of the day had in store. Plans were hatched to meet up at the weekend, find some secluded spot up on The Downs, play and fumble, usually apologise (especially me), share a cigarette (badly), and then head back to our respective schools. These became the most exciting of times and suddenly going home at weekends to see the family didn't seem to matter quite so much any more.

And then there were the social events. Every couple of weeks, a minibus packed with boarders would visit Red Maids to play tennis or badminton, depending on the weather. Well, I say 'play': it was more like swap letters, gossip like mad, and try and get a cheeky snog where possible. It wasn't just Nancy I went to see. I had forged really good friendships with other girls too: particularly Vicki and Faye, two wonderful ladies who are now doing brilliantly for themselves as an actress and entrepreneur respectively. And during my Third and Fourth Years at school I had — for good or bad — made a bit of a name for myself. When I used to call the school in the evenings, the Housemistress would immediately know it was me.

"Who do you want this time?"

When I used to wait at the school gates to meet someone, girls I had never met would point at me and whisper — presumably because they knew who I was and not because I was a source of comedy. But even if they did, I didn't care: I was in the spotlight. I can't deny, I still yearn for that attention, attention that has been somewhat missing from my life of late.

* * *

A few months after we got together, Nancy and I split up. I think she dumped me. She probably did. It was pretty rare for boys to dump girls. Guns N' Roses' 'November Rain' (our song) was on permanent repeat. I re-read the letters she had sent me over and over again. But there was no getting away from it: it was finished. It didn't take long for me to change the CD though and I was back in the game, chasing someone else to kindle a new relationship with. And then another. And then maybe another.

I won't bore you with every relationship I had. Some were good, others were great, none of them lasted. But there was one relationship that ended in a particularly hilarious way and, if you'll permit me, I'll share this little story with you before we move on.

It was 1994. Rave music had taken over the world — much to my utter delight — and being sixteen, we were allowed to attend the annual Redland High School disco. This was another opportunity for girls and boys to get together and, having infiltrated Red Maids for a few years, it felt like pastures new. Eugh. That is such a sixteen-year-old thing to say.

Being sixteen, I felt more confident than ever. GCSEs would soon be over, and it was only a few months before I would be moving on to A-Levels. I had immersed myself in a culture that I loved and took pride in my Joe Bloggs tops, baggy jeans, and especially my rave-infused Zippy t-shirt (bought from the back pages of *Viz*).[37] The Prodigy's 'Everybody In The Place' was at No. 2 in the charts, only beaten by a re-release of Queen's 'Bohemian Rhapsody'. Regardless, it felt like a victory for dance music. Life was good.

---

37 → I stumbled across a picture of Alix wearing it in her teens, the cheeky sod. I've still got it. Rather threadbare now.

A gang of us rocked up to the disco, full of vim and swagger. As soon as we arrived, we heard the pounding beats of Altern-8 and immediately took to the dance floor. My arms and hands made the most incredible shapes ever seen, so much so that the next day I could barely lift them. After a good stomp, I decided to get myself a drink and take a breather. A friend of mine, Chris, was talking to a rather lovely-looking girl and, seeing as the only free space was next to him, I sat myself down. It looked like he was trying to get to know her better but with little success. Once defeated, he got up, leaving a spare seat for me. I moved over to say hello. She was gorgeous and — to my surprise — a full-blown goth: long black hair, black nails, full black clothing, and pasty white face. But the biggest ruby-red lips I had ever seen. I don't know what I said or did but within seconds those lips were clamped to mine. I left that night with her home number and promised I would call.

And true to my word, I did. A few days later we arranged to meet up. In fact, we met up almost every weekend down on College Green, and I'd often go back to her parents' house who were both Buddhists and incredibly relaxed. This was great! However, I was starting to realise that my dress sense was in stark contrast to hers. While she worshipped The Cure and the undead, I worshipped Sonz of a Loop Da Loop Era and smiley faces. Something had to change.

So one weekend I decided to have a complete makeover. I bought a pair of purple Doc Martens, some tie-dyed tops, and trousers that verged on the ridiculous.[38] I had totally bought into the 'crusty' way of life, albeit that I went to a private, fee-

---

38 → Well I liked them — even if they did look like tablecloths.

paying boarding school. I don't know why but I thought that I needed to do this — I needed to impress her, I needed to fit in with *her* cultural identity. All I had to do now was find a free afternoon to see her. And so it was on a Saturday morning that I approached Mr Broadley, the boarding master in charge of cricket.

"I can't do the scoring today."

"Why not?"

"I… er… I just can't."

He agreed to let me have the day off, but I could tell that he knew I was up to something, and being sixteen, it probably involved girls.

Once lessons were over, I made my way down Park Street towards College Green to meet the love of my life, glancing in every shop window I passed to check out my new attire. It was a lovely, warm day and as I approached my destination I could see that College Green was heaving. I walked around trying to find her, seeing if she was huddled with a group of friends, but as hard as I tried I couldn't see her anywhere. I hung around for a good hour, hoping she might be late and that she'd run up to me out of the blue, throwing her arms around me, elated to see me. But it didn't happen. If only we had had mobile phones back then! I made my way back up the hill, saddened by the fact that my eyes had failed me and that I couldn't impress her with my new clothes.

When I got back to school I decided to give her a call at home, just to make sure she was okay. Her mum answered.

"Hi. Is Tia there?"

"Hi Dan. Tia doesn't want to speak to you right now."

"Why? What's wrong?"

"She says that she waited for you at College Green, and

you didn't show up."

"But that's not true! I was there on time and waited for ages! I couldn't see her anywhere! Can I talk to her?"

Her mum sounded sad.

"No, she doesn't want to talk to you. In fact, she doesn't want to see you any more. Sorry Dan."

And with that she hung up the phone and I never saw or heard from Tia again.

Dejected and upset, I made my way down to dinner. Mr Broadley was on duty that night. As I walked past him, he put his hand on my shoulder and stopped me in my tracks. He looked me up and down, analysing my newly acquired threads. He chuckled to himself and quietly shook his head.

"I bet she didn't miss you in *those* clothes!" he quipped.

I just stood there and looked at him. How little he realised the gut-wrenching irony packed into that one sentence. I walked over to one of the dining tables, my Doc Marten boots rubbing against my feet, and ate my chicken pie and chips in silence.

7. THEATRE, SHWEETIE!

WHILST GIRLS HAD BECOME THE NEW HORIZON, WRITING music was fast becoming the biggest love of my life. I had outgrown the Spectrum 48k long ago and upgraded to an Amiga 500. Whilst it was great for games, it wasn't powerful enough for music and — after much pleading and begging - Dad bought me an Amiga 1200. I used a programme called Octamed which could play up to eight sounds at the same time (my Amiga 500 before it could only handle four!). Not long after, school bought an Atari ST with a software package called C-Labs. Alongside it sat a synth keyboard that had leads, pads, basses, whiny flutes, and the obligatory terrible drum sounds. But now I could play up to sixteen sounds at the same time, allowing me to create more complex songs. Whilst I loved rave and hardcore, I found it very difficult to write, and so I turned my hand to house and garage, a genre I was slowly falling in love with. All of a sudden, I was sacking off piano practice and choir rehearsals in favour of sitting in front of a computer and making my own sounds.

I was now seventeen. I had, over the years, amassed a nice little collection of records. Every time I went record shopping, I'd leave with handfuls of brightly coloured flyers, promoting the next big DJ coming to Bristol. These were my new idols, and it didn't take long for me to realise that DJing was next on my list of things to learn. And so — after convincing him that they would earn me my fortune — Dad bought me my first set of decks: a pair Disco 2000s. And they were bad. *Really* bad. So bad that I can't seem to find any reference to them online! But they were mine. I could have easily asked for Technics, the 'Daddy' of record decks, but I didn't want to: partly because of how expensive they were, but also because I didn't think it was the right way to learn. The way I saw it, you didn't learn to drive in a Ferrari. Start small, make sure you want to drive, and then — when you're good in your crappy little car — get the best car you can. I saw DJing very much like this: I wanted to 'earn my chops.'

My musical tastes had changed dramatically over the years. Adam and the Ants to Shakin' Stevens to Queen had been the pre-teen journey. Now it was Bomb the Bass, 4 Hero, Ruffige Cru and SL2. I was exploring more underground labels like Reinforced Records that offered sounds and textures that I had never heard before. And — of course — The Prodigy. Tunes like 'Your Love' and 'Everybody In the Place (Let's Go)' were revolutionary for me, and undoubtedly change my direction in music.[39]

Whilst I owned all these brilliant records, I found that rave

---

39 ♫ Here's my Top 10 rave tunes that shaped my teenage years.

was really hard to mix. It was choppy, messy, oddly structured, and I wasn't skilled enough to combine those types of tunes. So I went hunting for 50p records that had B-side house remixes on them by the likes of David Morales and Roger Sanchez. This helped me develop my 4/4 beat-mixing skills that I would later use in mixing rave. It took a lot of months, and a lot of terrible mixes but I finally got there. That moment when you mix your first two tunes together is something you never forget.

Meanwhile, back in the real world, GCSE results-day had arrived. I had already taken R.E. (Religious Education) in Fourth Form and managed a C, but now it was the big ones: Maths, English (Lit and Lang), Biology, Music, Latin, Geography, and French. And I did okay: 2 B's, 5 C's, a D, and an E (Geography), but I didn't care about that one, I knew I was never going to study rocks. More importantly, what was I going to do for A-Levels?

To progress into the Sixth Form, you had to choose three subjects. The trouble was, there were only two that I was interested in: English and Classical Civilisation. I knew what I wanted to do for the third, but the school didn't offer it. It was time to talk to the headmaster.

"Sir?"

"Yes?"

"I have an issue with my A-Levels."

"Go on..."

"Well, I know I have to do three, but there's only two that I want to do: English and Class Civ."

"Why, what else is it you want to do?"

"Theatre Studies."

Pause.

"Theatre Studies?"

"Yes."

"Leave it with me."

I had a good relationship with Dr Gliddon. He had seen me go from being a slightly timid boy (probably the lack of rugby) to someone who was well involved in the school. I often read at church services, public events, and school assemblies. I knew I could approach him about my predicament but I still left his office nervous with anticipation.

A week later and I was back.

"Well Daniel, I've been looking into this and you've got two options. You can go to St Brendan's Sixth Form College for a couple of days a week... or you can go to Clifton High School for Girls."

Silence.

Well, this WAS a dilemma. St Brendan's Sixth Form College or Clifton High School for Girls? Let me see...

"I think Clifton High sounds good, Sir. It's nearer."

He looked at me with a knowing smile.

"Clifton High it is."

I left his office in a whirlwind of excitement and fear. My sister went to Clifton High. It'd be full of girls! Would I have to wear my uniform? Would I have to sit in assembly?!

A week later I found out.

* * *

The build-up to my first visit to Clifton High was excruciating. I was pretty confident around girls by now, but walking into a school of four hundred of them was a whole new ball game. Thankfully, by the time we got to Sixth Form, we no longer had to wear our daytime boarder's uniform (long yellow socks, knee length breeches, and a jacket) and could instead wear our usual day uniform: a plain black suit. I set off for Clifton High, bouncing down the main steps, steps that had been out of bounds for the past five years. As I approached Clifton High, I was presented with a dilemma: do I make a grand entrance via the main front gates, or do I sneak in from the side? Unusually for me, I took the side entrance.

As I made my way into the old, beautiful building, I could hear the muffled tones of discussion behind a thick pair of doors. I cautiously opened them to see if I was in the right place and as I popped my head round the door, I was greeted by a "hello!" from about fifteen girls. They were dressed in leotards, jogging bottoms, and t-shirts — I was in my school uniform. Immediate fail. However, everyone made me feel welcome and, after the introductions and chat about the course, we immediately got into some improvisation work. Bliss. This was a highly unusual situation. No boy from QEH had ever done Theatre Studies A-Level, let alone gone to an all-girls school to do it. I left that day feeling elated. I went to see the headmaster to feedback on how the day had been.

"There is just one thing."

"Yes?"

"When I got there, they were all wearing casual clothes. I was in my uniform. Can I do the same?"

A brief pause and then agreement. I could change into casual clothes after my lesson, go to Clifton High, come back, and change into my usual uniform. I felt like a free man.

* * *

During that first year of Sixth Form I studied both A-Level Theatre Studies and GCSE Drama. The GCSE was to be completed in one year and the A-Level over two. I worked with two different sets of girls, but there was some crossover between the GCSE and A-Level. The GCSE, for example, was more focused on producing a group piece that we had all collaborated on. After a couple of sessions of exploring ideas through improvisation, I came up with an idea for a piece called *Doomsday.* It was — bear with me here — set inside the mind of a film buff, and the characters were all facets of his psyche: Confidence, Destruction, Reason, Guilt, Insecurity, and Compassion. Every time they watched a film they would come together to talk about its impact and, healthily, would always disagree on the verdict. But now they had just watched *Superman III* and found themselves in utter despair at the moment when Superman turns evil after he's given a piece of Kryptonite. For the first time ever, they were all in agreement about the impact of the film. And that could only mean one thing: the death of themselves.

Okay, so it sounds like utter nonsense, but it actually worked really well. I wrote the script and our teacher directed it. I was very proud of it, and it earned me an 'A' at GCSE. Thank you, Superman![40] As for the A-Level, well this was a wholly different experience. We studied Berkoff's *Metamorphosis,* explored the techniques of Stanislavski and Brecht and watched numerous theatrical productions, honing our critiquing and analytical skills. We also, somewhat scarily, started to prepare our audition pieces for university, or for those that were very brave, drama school.

40   → When you've got a spare twenty minutes, why not have a read.

QEH was also starting to enter the 21st century by appointing a dedicated Head of Drama. Yes, a HEAD OF DRAMA! Suddenly the school was taking this acting malarkey seriously. Mr Straun — who had appeared in *Grange Hill*, no less — grasped the nettle and dived straight in. To be fair, QEH had had its own theatre since 1990 and it always used to tickle me to think that the sporting types had to travel miles just to see a patch of grass, but here was a theatre on our own doorstep. I remember an early discussion with Mr Straun about what our first production might be. I had always thought Dennis Potter's *Blue Remembered Hills* would make a fantastic school play. Three months later, *Blue Remembered Hills* was under production.[41]

Blue Remembered Hills was a unique play in that adults played the roles of children, giving it a wonderful innocence. A collection of budding actors from QEH and Clifton High were cast in the various roles, something that feels slightly odd when you're seventeen yourself. I played the part of Raymond, a quiet boy with a stutter. I had no problems with a stutter, but I did have problems with — when dared to — having to stand on my head. There was no way I was going to do that, so we changed it to holding my breath instead. It was a brilliant play and immense fun to work on. I got to wear a cowboy hat the whole time too.[42]

My final year at QEH saw me involved in numerous productions, both in and out of school. We produced another play with Clifton High called *My Mother Said I Never Should* by Charlotte Keatley. It was about the difficult relationship

---

41 → During rehearsals.

42 → And still one of my favourite pictures in existence. I have shape! And hair!

between mothers and daughters and, in light of that, there wasn't much scope for male parts. None in fact. But under the watchful gaze of the marvellous Mr McPherson, I helped out with stage management and some directing. I got the opportunity to try my hand at directing too with a play called *The Do It Yourself Frankenstein Outfit*, working with the Fifth Form. I was also cast as the lead male role in a production of Anthony Minghella's *A Little Like Drowning* — a play based around the reflections of Nonna, contemplating her life, loves, and losses. My character was a full-blooded Italian and it was a part I really wanted to play, so much so that when the director asked me to cut my hair, I agreed. In hindsight, I kind of regret making that decision. I had a really good head of hair — a wonderful pair of curtains that were thick and buoyant, so getting rid of them was a real sacrifice for me. Sadly, my hair would never be the same again.[43]

The last school play I was involved in was *Whitson's Will*, written by the Deputy Headmistress of Red Maids. The play was a two-hour epic about the founder of the school, John Whitson, and it was an honour to be asked to play the title role — the only male character in the entire production. Needless to say, that was a challenge in itself but one I was willing to undertake. Much to my shame, however, I wasn't particularly well behaved during this time. I started to date one of the girls I was acting alongside: a lovely, sweet girl who was a little bit new to relationships and probably didn't need a Lothario like

---

43   → It would change even more radically when, a few months later, I decided to dye it peroxide-blonde. It was going well until Avril, a friend of Mum's, stuck me under a hair dryer for thirty minutes. The result was hair that resembled straw. I returned to QEH that Sunday night to a room full of gasps and laughter. School was not impressed and I had to dye it the next day or face suspension. The result was a delicious copper brown.

me entering into her life. I thought I could pick and choose and play the field, but I was sorely mistaken and ended up losing out on all counts. I wasn't particularly professional on stage either. At one point during the performance I was chatting to some girls backstage when someone ran up to me and shouted, "YOU'RE MEANT TO BE ON STAGE!" I rushed on to see a group of girls looking awkward, not sure what to do. "Why are you just standing around?!" I blared at them, then dived into my lines. Improvisation saved me, but I knew the director wouldn't be impressed. If that wasn't bad enough, I didn't even manage to learn all my lines for the final scene of the play. To be fair, I was studying my A-Levels, and as my character was in almost every scene the amount of lines to learn was huge and I just didn't have the capacity to do it. I managed to conceal my script under a mound of paperwork as I uttered my final, poignant lines. Thankfully nobody noticed. It was not my finest hour.

However, being awarded the Dodd Prize for Drama probably *was* my finest hour. I didn't buy *The Iliad* this time, nor did I buy *The Famous Five*. I think I chose a collection of plays. And, more importantly than any prize, QEH announced they were to introduce GCSE and A-Level Drama to the curriculum with immediate effect. I may not have scored the winning try or had my name etched upon the Captain of School honours board but I had left my own little legacy, and that was good enough for me.

QEH was over. It was time to go to Drama School.

8. GO EAST!

O R SO I THOUGHT.

During my final year at school, I had spent a lot of time preparing a couple of really strong audition pieces, aiming to give myself the best chance possible. I had applied to a mixture of drama schools and universities: Warwick Uni, Manchester Met, Darlington College of Arts, Middlesex Uni, and four others I can't remember — all of them offering a three-year degree in drama or theatre studies. Manchester Met was probably the most prestigious as it offered a serious acting degree and was an institution a couple of my heroes, Steve Coogan and Julie Walters, had attended. When I arrived, there were hundreds of people waiting to audition. I knew my chances were slim.

What I didn't expect was eight straight rejections. EIGHT! Actually, that's a lie. Middlesex kindly offered me History. I hadn't even done it at GCSE.

"It's an offer Dan," urged my dad. "You really should consider it."

For Dad, an offer was an offer. And seeing as though I was the first member of the family to go to university, I could understand his motivation to want me to take a place, whatever it might be. My internal eyebrows, however, raised themselves to new heights. There was no way on earth I was going to study history. So it was time to play the 'Clearing Game'.

A-Level results-day arrived and I visited both QEH and Clifton High, nervous at what these little bits of paper would tell me. It was actually better than I expected: B in Theatre Studies, B in Classical Civilisation, and a C in English (metaphysical poetry was never my strong point). I was pretty pleased with that considering I hadn't really done a great deal of work, but it felt somewhat hollow with no drama school or university to go to. The plan now was to call those institutions that offered a degree in theatre or drama, and see if I could get a place based on the grades I had just been given. The most important thing, however, was to find out if I could defer my place — I had decided that I fancied a year off from education.

During that summer of '95 I had made a really good group of friends in Weston. We loved our music, we loved DJing, and we loved going out and partying. I had great friends at school, but I knew everyone would be going off and doing their own thing. Most of those friends also lived in Bristol or other parts of the country — there was no one in Weston. And if you went to a school in your area, you formed your friendships as you were growing up. I formed mine when I was 18 and about to go to uni. I didn't want to lose this and had therefore made the decision to take a year out. What I was going to do with that year, however, had yet to be decided.

That afternoon I got the newspapers out, scanned the clearing lists and started to make some calls. It's the educational equivalent of haggling for a vase and it felt dirty. "Needs must," I muttered to myself as I hung up the phone — rejected once again — and looked for more numbers to call. In many ways I was grateful that the whole process took place over the phone. Using the phone had become an instinctive way of communicating for me. Unlike my parents, I wasn't scared to leave a message on an answering machine. I had a strong voice with barely any regional inflection. I could humour, beguile, and flirt with confidence. Maybe this was because I felt faceless, boosted by the fact that you couldn't see me and therefore — in my mind — judge me. Now my voice and brain were my weapons in this battle of underachievers, and hence it was time to pull out the big guns. Guns I had, thankfully, primed and fired during my final year at school.[44]

QEH was involved with an organisation called The Gabblers Club, an idea conceived by a conglomerate of Bristol hoteliers keen to promote the skills of after-dinner speaking in Bristol's shining school children. Fancying the experience and the opportunity to get out of school once a week, I decided to put myself forward. After a brief 'speak off' between a handful of boys, I was chosen to represent my school. Every month, myself and another boy would go to the best hotels in Bristol, have a three-course meal, and then make a speech. It was a tough life.

I'd always been comfortable speaking after a meal. Growing up, Dad liked to encourage everyone to say a few

---

44   Contender for Worst Analogy Ever.

words, even if it was just "thanks for being here." My speeches round the dinner table were slowly gaining notoriety and there were often hushed tones as I stood there, thinking of the next soft insult to hurl at a family friend. But this was different — you couldn't wing this.

After a term of dinners and speeches, The Grand Final was drawing near. I had been given my subject: Rupert. Immediately I thought of Rupert the Bear, but I also thought of Rupert Pupkin too, the brilliant character played by Robert De Niro in *The King of Comedy.* I somehow wanted to merge these two subjects together.

The final had arrived. A lavish dinner was served, and then the speeches began. Sweaty palms ensued as I waited for my turn.

And soon enough, it was my turn to perform. I slowly walked to the stage, surveyed my audience (which included the Lord Mayor of Bristol), cleared my throat, and pulled my hands out of my pockets to reveal two socks, one on each hand. A nervous giggle, a brief pause, and I began.

If I'm being honest, it wasn't my finest hour. I probably came at it from too much of an obtuse angle. One sock was there to represent Rupert the Bear. I spoke about his early years and how he broke into mainstream comic strips ("His real name is Rupert Theodore Bear but his agent didn't think this would work, so they shortened it to Rupert The Bear" — that got a good laugh). On the other hand (literally) was Rupert Pupkin, the self proclaimed King of Comedy: a delusional stand-up comedian who kidnapped Jerry Lewis just to get his five minutes of fame. My aim was to interweave a story about celebrity, biography, and the yearning for stardom but it was probably a bit too clever for its own good. I didn't win the

Final, but I did come second overall, and I was pretty pleased with that.[45]

Upon reflection, coming second in a regional after-dinner speaking competition was like winning an Oscar compared to getting eight straight rejections for a place at university. I'm pretty sure my UCAS form emphasised that I was a proficient after-dinner speaker but, puzzlingly, that didn't seem to carry quite as much weight as getting good grades in your A-Levels.

Back on the phone and I was still rattling through the list of possible universities, with each of them telling me my grades weren't good enough. I was starting to give up hope when I got through to the University of Kent at Canterbury, who offered a four-year degree programme in Drama and Theatre Studies — with the opportunity to specialise in a chosen area in the final year. This sounded great. Canterbury conjured up images of spiralling towers and intellectuals discussing Chaucer. My A-Level grades were no problem and, yes: I could take a year out. Amazing! It was time to pay them a visit.

* * *

The next day I jumped on the train with Beccy, my best friend at the time, and we set off for the South East of England. I think it was the longest train ride I had ever been on, well over four hours. On arrival at the University we met with the course leader who explained that the four-year degree was very much about exploring all facets of the theatrical world — from stage design to lighting, to sound and radio production,

45   → Here I am collecting my prize.

writing and more. It wasn't an acting degree, though of course there would be the opportunity to perform. I had a positive feeling about the place. Plus, it was the only offer that I'd had. After a good look round the rehearsal spaces and facilities (it had its own theatre too — The Gulbenkian), we started to make our way back home.

As we strolled down the great hill that led back to the station, we passed a shop called Canterbury Rock. Never one to resist a bit of crate digging, I tapped Beccy on the shoulder and beckoned her inside. The place was empty, save for the bedraggled owner smiling gently as he sifted through a pile of vinyl. I looked around and all I could see was classic rock, prog rock, death metal, and worse. I guess the name of the shop should have given it away. I asked if he had any dance music, and he pointed to a small section on the left. I licked my lips and started to fondle.

I flicked through the records, not finding anything particularly great. As I was just about to give up hope, something caught my eye. I picked it up and pulled it out: blank. Hmmm, a dubplate. I flipped it over and saw 'Song to the Siren' in big letters. I knew this tune — it was part of The Chemical Brothers' album *Exit Planet Dust*, one of my favourite albums at the time. I looked at the price — £2.99 — flipped it over again, pondered for a few seconds, and then put it back. It was okay but I didn't really need it.

We left the shop and as soon as I closed the door, I stopped.

"I'll be back in a minute," I said to Beccy and turned around, went back in, and bought it. And I'm glad I did. A few months later I discovered that this was The Chemical Brothers' first ever release, and only 500 copies had ever been made. Fifteen years ago it was worth £150, so who knows what it's worth now.[46] I came back to Weston and reported on my visit. Mum and Dad were fully behind me doing this, although I knew Dad had *some* reservations about me studying drama when there were doctors and lawyers and forensic scientists out there earning a small fortune. What job could a drama degree guarantee? I couldn't answer that, but I still knew it was the right thing to do. I also had to consider the fact that it was on the other side of the country. Was I okay with that? I had to admit that it wasn't ideal but I'd been at boarding school for seven years — being apart wasn't going to be a problem.

I called the University back to confirm the place.

"Okay, great," they said. "We'll see you in September."

"Err... no, I thought I had a year off?"

"Oh no, sorry, these places are for this coming year. Do you still want it?"

Arse. Big arse. I was now in a quandary. Do I take the place now, or wait a year? I knew what my parents would say and, as much as I fancied a year off, I was also beginning to worry that I may not want to get back into education twelve months later.

"I'll see you in September," I conceded, and hung up the phone.

---

46 → And no, it's not for sale.

9. THIS SENTENCE
IS TWENTY

IT WAS DIFFICULT MAKING FRIENDS IN WESTON BECAUSE I was pretty much always at school in Bristol, so when I did finally discover my own little group, it was hard to let them go. Beccy had become a particularly good friend. We used to hang around together all the time, babysit her little nephew, chat and put the world to rights. I was a shoulder for her to cry on when boy problems raised their head, or if the world was becoming a bit too much. I even let her use my arm as a punch bag. The things you do, eh? But we never became an item. Thinking back, it's hard to deny that this was the start of a 'friendship template' that would become the backbone of most of my relationships with women.

And so, after a summer of clubbing, DJing, and late night house parties, the time had come to leave Weston behind and make the move to Canterbury. I got on the train with Mum and Alix, laden with pretty much everything I owned (except my decks and records: they would be sent up another time), and four hours later I was in my halls of residence: Keynes, named after the famous economist, which, being a drama student, meant nothing to me whatsoever. Dad had kindly agreed to pay for me to have my own private room, and moving into my own space for the first time was great. These rooms were like little pods, replete with desk and a walk-in bathroom. And, for the first time in seven years, I was in a room on my own. At QEH I had always shared: fifteen-plus boys for the first few years, then a dorm of three to four in the Forth and Fifth Form, and then just me and one other in the Sixth Form. But now I was on my own — a perfect little palace in which to work, learn, and study.

Actually, my first year was more play, sleep, and party. I had fortunately found a group of friends who loved their clubbing and dance music, and they all lived on the same floor as me. My drama colleagues, whilst lovely, were generally loud, brash and — for want of a better word — 'luvvies'. I saw so many people turn up exclaiming, "THIS IS ME!" only to be left by the wayside months later. I favoured the 'softly-softly' approach: you didn't really know who I was, but at some point you realised I was an intricate part of your life. Like mould.

One of the great things about UKC was that it was one of the first universities to have a campus fully set up for the Internet. UKC part-owned one of the main pipes that ran through to Europe, so their speeds were lightning fast, even compared to today. I remember sending an email for the first time and — not understanding quite what was going on or what to expect — assumed the reply would be immediate. It wasn't. And, being a single boy on my own and left to my own devices, I can't deny that I spent some evenings looking at 'lady pictures'. I was like a kid in a sweet shop but one that only stayed open between midnight and 6am. I also discovered chat rooms, the pre-cursor to MSN Messenger, Facebook and Skype. Chat rooms were great fun and I spent many an evening conversing with people from all over the world.

At times I had to remind myself that I was here to do a degree and that there was actual work to do. I was terrible at organising my time and could always find something to do other than what needed to be done. I remember one night waking up at midnight (yes, midnight), going to get breakfast (crisps and chocolate from the vending machine), making my way to the computer room and surfing the Web until about 6am. I stretched. "Time to start my essay," I mused.

By 9am it was printed off and sitting on the tutor's desk. 2,000 words on Ibsen's *Ghosts*, done. I got a B+. Result.

Now, you might think, Daniel — how is it that you can type so fast? 2,000 words in under three hours? That's amazing! Did you go to secretarial school?

Let me enlighten you.

Growing up, I always had a really overactive mind. I would avoid the cracks in paving stones (not unusual), I would remember how many steps there were in a flight of steps so I could always finish on my left foot (slightly unusual), and I would count words (WEIRDO ALERT!).

I don't really know how or why I started doing it. Before counting words, I was slightly obsessed with the layout of the QWERTY keyboard. Every night I would lie in bed, and my mind would recite it over and over until I fell asleep. The top line — QWERTY — well, that's pretty easy. But it was the second and third rows that proved more difficult, especially the bottom line. Z and X are the first two letters, but what comes next? See if you can remember. I can, and I had memorised this layout by the time I was eleven, hence the fast fingers.

My love of letters, words, and sentences actually goes back a stage further. When I was very young, Dad bought a new piece of technology into the home: a VCR. I was mesmerised. This machine felt like it was something from the future. Pressing the eject button to load in a tape was like navigating the shuttle launch. But, most interesting of all, it had a digital display.[47]

For some reason — and I have no idea why — I was infatuated with the way numbers were made up of lines. So, for example, a '1' is made up of two small lines. A '7': three lines. '0': six. I also started to notice this on calculators too (remember spelling out 'BOOBIES'?). There was something about those straight lines that I liked. Was it the sense of order?

I then took this obsession with digital letters one step further. As well as converting numbers into values represented by the amount of lines they had on a VCR, I had now developed a constant need to add up sentences. I'd better explain.

If someone said a sentence, I would picture it in my head and count the letters. Let's say that sentence had twenty-two letters. That wasn't good enough: I had to round it up to thirty. So this meant adding extra words, (usually "He said…" or "She meant…"), words that would extend the sentence, but wouldn't alter the meaning. So, for example, if someone said, "The sun is really bright today," I would instantly calculate that as twenty-five, so "I said" would go in front of it, making it thirty.

---

47   → Like this. Stick with me.

To make it even more interesting, those digital numbers came into play. So if the word 'to' appeared, that could now take the value of five: because a '2' on a VCR display is made up of five lines.

Make sense? Of course not.[48]

It actually got to be such an infatuation that I wrote to an OCD specialist asking if I was in trouble. She said, "Does it affect your life?" Not really, I thought. "Then it's a mild OCD. Don't worry about it." I'm still not convinced saying 'don't worry' to someone with OCD is the most sensible thing, but there you go.

So that was my active brain. I still add up sentences to this day and am happy to showcase my talents at parties, weddings, and Bar Mitzvahs. People are initially amazed but after a couple of sentences it loses its appeal — for them at least. Or they give me a ridiculous stream of words, which of course, nobody can do.[49]

48   → Watch me in action. That might help.
49   60.

10. THE DIVINE DANIEL

A LOT OF IMPORTANT EVENTS TOOK PLACE DURING MY time at University, but perhaps none were as important as losing my virginity.

(Mum, Dad — this is probably the first moment in the book where you might want to look away. I think there's a good Norman Wisdom film on Channel 4.)

Virginity is a funny thing. You're desperate to lose it, but only desperate to lose it right. Well, at least I was. I didn't want my first experience to be an anonymous fumble behind a wheelie bin, nor did I want to wait till I was sixty.

Typical of most people's experiences, my first year at Uni was full of drinking, smoking, and late-night shenanigans. My decks had at long last arrived, so more often than not people would congregate in my tiny room to listen to what I was currently into at the time: angry German techno. Unsurprisingly, the University didn't offer much in the way of techno during Freshers' Week, and the only event that came anywhere close was a performance by Sunscreem, made temporarily famous by their Balearic hit 'Perfect Motion'. Myself and a couple of newly acquired friends bought tickets to see them, and it was whilst we were hanging around outside that we started talking to some girls. It was pretty obvious that they were not in the most stable of states, and sadly one of them had gotten so drunk that she ended up puking everywhere, including in her hair. We escorted them back to their room, whereupon the girl with the puke in her hair (that sounds like a Stig Larsson book) threw her arms around me and — to my surprise — started snogging my face off. The others had all disappeared, except her friend who had passed out on the bed next to us. This was new terrain for me, made all the more complex by the fact that I knew she was drunk (although she had sobered up somewhat, promise), and that all I could smell was the delightful aroma of vomit. I decided not to run my hands through her hair. We got on the bed and started snogging some more, and things quickly got more intense as she seductively encouraged me to move downwards towards her 'lady-garden' and help myself to her fruit. As I reached the forbidden land, the smell of sick filled my nostrils once more and I quickly made my way back up for air. This is no way to lose my cherry, I thought to myself and politely made my excuses. She was practically asleep by then anyway. So instead we cuddled, and I held my breath.

When it came to my degree, the first year at Uni wasn't quite what I had hoped for. I found myself a bit disengaged with the core group of students that I studied alongside, and, as was often the way, placed myself on the periphery of what was going on. We seemed to be primarily focusing on lots of backstage activity: building sets, rigging lights, painting... things, and some god-awful event called Community Celebration, which involved making huge papier-mâché heads and parading them around town. Not my cup of tea. One area I was interested in though was Sound Design. The First Year students often acted as the lighting and sound operators for the Fourth Year students who were directing their final-year plays. Being a DJ, I had a good sense of timing and I enjoyed sourcing the music and sound effects.

When it came to acting, there were numerous opportunities to audition for plays. It wasn't just the final year students putting on productions — plays were being performed all the time. I auditioned for a fair few, but didn't get cast in any of them. "Ah well, there's still three more years to go," I mused stoically.

Despite not bonding that closely with the majority of my fellow drama students, I still had a strong group of friends who were doing all manner of different subjects. None of us were normal. We shunned the typical student activities of hanging around the Uni bar and going into town to dance to cheesy pop tosh in favour of getting stoned and going clubbing. Or we made our own entertainment. I remember trying to organise a one-off event in a room in Darwin College, playing the best in house, techno, and old-school rave. Twelve people showed up.

It was towards the end of my first year that I started to fall in love with a girl called Anthe. Anthe was Greek, beautiful, and incredibly stylish. She was doing the same drama course as me, and was adept at building sets and lighting design — all the things I was useless at. She was a great artist and model maker. She kept intricate diaries. And best of all, she got my sense of humour. We would spend long nights together talking about film and music, and gossiping about all the other students on the course, blissfully unaware that we were probably the subject of gossip ourselves. And, as the nights grew longer, I would stay over — sleeping in the same single bed, but always fully clothed.

I fancied Anthe. Lots. But I was terrible at making the first move. I was mortally afraid that those on the receiving end of my advances would recoil in abject horror, scream for help, and immediately call the police. Yet everyone else I knew had the confidence to do this — why couldn't I?[50]

It was now the start of our Second Year. As we lay in bed together, again fully clothed, somehow our friendly cuddles became more intimate, and a peck on the cheek became a long, loving kiss. We looked deep into each other's eyes, and slowly started to undress. This was it. This was the moment I had been waiting for. I was going to have sex! I was going to be a man!

It was all over in about eight seconds. By the time I had made my way to heaven and back, the lights were on and Anthe was propped up in bed smoking a fag. I felt awful. It was like waiting twenty years for a trip to the moon only to realise you were actually getting a bus to the end of the road. I lay there, forlorn. Anthe stroked my hair sympathetically. I had visions of it never happening. An hour later we tried again, and this time I lasted eight minutes. The Eagle had landed.

* * *

---

50   My editor wants to know why I couldn't too. I think it's because University felt like 'the next level'. This wasn't the experimental times of being sixteen at school, this was an adult playground — and I would inevitably have to work with those around me.

Recent events had made me very, very happy. I was — at last — in a relationship. I'd always vowed never to 'give myself away' too easily, and I was pleased that I had held out for the right person. So it was particularly interesting when, a few weeks later, a friend who was seriously into his spiritualism suggested that we go to an aura reading. I was always slightly cynical about things like this, but as there were a few of us going it seemed daft to miss the opportunity.

We arrived at the bookshop to find a packed room. A few empty chairs were dotted around the place, so instead of sitting together, we broke off, the group somewhat fractured. It needn't have mattered — the person doing the aura reading chose almost all of our group, completely at random.[51] Having seen three of four of my friends (and being pretty accurate with their character breakdowns), she had time for one more person. I put my hand up and, low and behold, she chose me.

I made my way to the front of the room, a cheeky grin slapped across my face. Would she accurately read my aura? I stood there and looked around the room, catching Anthe's eye, who was probably just as intrigued as I was.

And then she began.

She asked me to stand still against a white background so she could see the aura being emitted from my body. I looked around the room again as she focused on my chakras, unsure if this was hokum or a genuine character reading. She fixed her gaze on my body, an intensity evident in her face as she interpreted the colour field. And then she was back. It was time for her assessment.

"I can tell that you're in a very good place right now. It

51   Or was it?

looks like you're incredibly happy. Your chakras — quite rarely — are perfectly in line with each other. The Crown chakra is glowing like wildfire. The purple emitting from it is incredibly rich!"

"What does that mean?" I asked, somewhat nervously.

"It means that you are in touch with Divinity!"

And audible gasp went up around the room. I looked at my friends, and could see a mixture of stifled guffaws and disbelief. Someone put their head in their hands.

As we left the bookshop, I couldn't help but remind my friends about what we'd just experienced.

"Did you hear that? She said I was 'in touch with Divinity'. Does that mean you have to worship me now?"

Groans went up around the group.

"Of all the people she could have said that to, it had to be you," someone observed.

I knew I was happy but 'in touch with Divinity'? How I got my head into the car as we made our way home I'll never know.

11. HELLO CREATIVITY

AT THE END OF THE FIRST YEAR WE ALL MOVED OUT OF THE halls of residence and into our own houses. There was the traditional squabble over who wanted to live with who. Anthe was living in a house in the centre of Canterbury with her Greek friend Costas, a man so tall he had to duck under doorways. I was living in a house a bit further out with a few friends. Location didn't really seem to matter — we always got together, either to go out and get pissed, or stay indoors, get stoned, and play on the PlayStation. *Tekken* was the biggest thing of the moment and whilst I enjoyed playing it I was usually pretty hopeless, often throwing the controller down in annoyance and instead focusing my attention on the decks.

Whilst all this was going on, I was still meant to be doing a degree. First Year over, we were now studying new subjects: American Drama (amazing), Farce (brilliant), and Contemporary Performance (hmmm). Both American Drama and Farce were fantastic. It was the first time I had read *Who's Afraid of Virginia Woolf?* and *The American Dream* — both by Edward Albee. These plays had a massive effect on me: dark subject matter, fractured relationships, bubbling undertones of tension, and incredible wordplay. This was mature, tense theatre, and I indulged myself in as much of it as I could.

Farce was great fun too, albeit taught by a man that made the prospect of watching paint dry feel like a holiday. We studied early farce such as *Box and Cox* and looked at how farce still permeates today's theatre and film. One of our assignments was to write a play. This was more like it! For the first time in my degree I felt like I was being creatively stretched. I dabbled with a few ideas and finally came up with *Hook, Line and Sinker* (or *A Fishy Tale*), a play set in a fish and chip shop. George, the hopeless owner, employs a new girl to run his shop whilst he's off gallivanting about with the new woman in his life. Only, little does he know what Angel has in store for him. It scored me a mark of over 80%. I was amazed, considering how filthy it is in places (plaices?). If you've got a strong stomach, why not have a read. You'll probably never buy fish and chips again.[52]

The other area of the course I had to endure was Contemporary Performance. It didn't really do it for me. Don't get me wrong, I tried my hardest, but I found it difficult. I'm all for expressionism in whatever art form you choose, but the logical part of my brain yearned for structure, character, dialogue. I just couldn't connect with this more abstract way of working. Plus, there was lots of yoga which I was absolutely terrible at, especially when I would turn up to lessons in jeans

---

52   → Not sure that should be the tagline. Still makes me laugh. And written in Comic Sans, for added humour.

sporting a massive hole in the crotch, and would spend more time making sure my appendages didn't fall out than following the instructions of the tutor.

Undeterred by my abject failure at promoting at the end of the First Year, I found myself DJing once a week in a small bar in Canterbury. During 1996, drum and bass had slowly started to emerge as the most cutting edge sound in music. Where jungle had been full of dark, dissonant basslines, ragga vocals and gunshot samples, drum and bass indulged itself in more mature textures and sounds, challenging the listener by combining musicality with complex, chopped-up rhythms. Metalheadz's *Platinum Breakz Volume 1* was the first release where I heard the true scope of drum and bass in all its glory, featuring heavyweight steppers like Doc Scott's 'Unofficial Ghost', the gloriously jazz-infused 'The Flute Tune' by Hidden Agenda, and of course the monstrously frightening 'Armoured D' by Dillinja — a tune that would shape my musical horizons for the next few years.[53]

The bar I was DJing in was run by a guy called Mark and, liking what he'd heard, asked me to play in what is probably the most unique venue I've ever encountered: a disused Russian submarine.

Yup, you read that right: a disused Russian submarine. I couldn't quite believe it either. On the night of the event, we made our way to Folkestone to be greeted by this monstrous vessel from the past. I turned up with a group of friends and a bag of records. The challenge of climbing through the different tunnels and holes to get to our room was enough of an ordeal for me, so I dread to think what it must have been like for

---

53 → I strongly urge you to check out this playlist. Even if you don't think you like drum and bass, I promise you one of these tunes will grab you.

those who had decided to drop acid a couple of hours before.[54] My set lasted for three glorious hours and I didn't put a foot wrong, even though water dripped on my records from the pipes above. The space was industrial and oppressive. I was surrounded by dials, knobs, and other bizarre instruments. It was without doubt one of the most unique events I have ever played, and still is to this day. Like being back at school, I was entertaining an audience and although I wasn't making them laugh, I was making them dance. I loved every second of it.[55]

That wasn't the only event Mark asked me to play at. A few weeks later he organised a huge party just on the outskirts of Canterbury. It was in an abandoned farmhouse, a perfect location as the only thing nearby was a motorway and some fields. I invited Alix up who was now old enough to spend the weekend away, and we had grown closer over the past few years. I went to visit the farmhouse during the day — just to get my bearings and scope out the place. I was told I had one of the main slots: 3am till 4am. Brilliant.

What followed was pure calamity. We arrived at the farm at midnight only to find the place swarming with police. Not being one for confrontation, we decided to leave pretty damn quick, turning around to get back in our taxi only to see it driving off into the distance. We were now stuck in the countryside, negotiating darkened country roads as we aimlessly tried to make our way back to civilisation — all the while weighed down by a stupidly heavy box of records. Half an hour later, the soft glow of a taxi sign emerged and we manically flagged it down.

54 → Imagine being faced with this.

55 → The grin says it all.

Back in Canterbury we decided to have our own little party. At 4am my phone rang.

"Dan? Where are you? What happened?!" It was Mark.

"Mate, are you okay? We got to the farmhouse and the place was swarming with cops! We thought the event had been raided so we turned round and left. Are you alright?!"

He laughed.

"Oh Dan, they were only here to check everything was okay! They must have left after about ten minutes. You should have hung around — the party was amazing!"

I hung up the phone, pissed off at my lack of courage and ambition. I never heard from Mark again.

Despite that monumental cock-up, I was still getting quite a few DJ gigs and it was at the end of my Second Year that I was asked if I wanted to be resident DJ at the new University venue called — inventively — The Venue. This was a great opportunity, and I can't imagine many universities around the country having their own dedicated club. We were one of the few drum and bass nights on in Canterbury during '97–99 and I got to DJ every month under the name of Examiner 5 — supporting DJs such as Goldie, Randall, Matrix, Mickey Finn, Jumping Jack Frost, and more. I was paid £150 every time I played. I felt like a superstar.[56]

Whenever an MC asked me what my DJ name was, they would always laugh at the response. Coming up with a DJ name is hard. I had tried to conjure one up before, but everything sounded rubbish. Unsurprisingly, it was biscuits that came to the rescue. During my final year at school and whilst at Uni, I pretty much became addicted to chocolate HobNobs (I still

---

56 ♪ One of my sets recorded live at The Venue. Excuse the drunk that grabs the mic half way through.

am). They ran a competition in conjunction with Vic Reeves where you had to complete a hilarious sentence in order to win a prize. I entered the competition and a few weeks later a t-shirt with a whacky Vic Reeves splashed across the front landed on my doormat. I tried the t-shirt on and it fitted fine so I did what everyone does once they're happy with the fit, and removed all the stickers from the inside. One of the stickers said 'Examiner 5', and a name was born.[57]

I had also taken up producing music again. Software had developed massively, and I was now working with the far-improved music programme: FastTracker. It was very much like Octamed, but looked better and was easier to use. A friend of mine also had a drum machine and a synth module which he never played with, so I nabbed them off him and, using my limited experience, worked out how to incorporate them into my music. I used it to write one of my first ever drum and bass tunes called 'The Style' which took a sample from a film called *Tales of Ordinary Madness* — a film Anthe and I loved. When I played it at The Venue and the crowd went nuts, I knew this was what I wanted to do.[58]

In fact, sound was becoming a bigger and bigger part of my life. I was often asked to help with the sound for the plays being produced: sourcing the music, editing it appropriately, recording voiceovers, finding the right sound effects, and operating the desk during the performance. We used a mixture of CDs and even BBC Sound FX records, plus something new

---

57   This wasn't my only entry into a 'hilarious sentence' competition. When I was a kid, I entered a competition to win a VHS video of your favourite BBC programme. All you had to do was complete the following sentence: *'The BBC and Kelloggs are great because...'* I answered '...because they both make excellent serials/cereals!' How could I lose? I chose Blackadder The Third. Not bad for a nine-year-old.

58   ♫ From tiny acorns...

called a 'Mini Disc', which I loved to play with. So much so, in fact, that I (naughtily) took credit out with Dixons to get my own recorder. Sound plays such a fundamental role in theatre: fade the music in at the wrong point and everything is ruined, trigger the gunshot two seconds late and the impact is lost. I thrived on the weight of responsibility and I liked the fact that almost all the directors studying the degree asked me to be their sound designer.

As the Second Year came to an end, it was time to consider my Third Year options. I had requested specialising in Sound Design as a module, and I was pretty confident I would get this. The biggie though was Scriptwriting, and I was desperate to get on the course. I wanted to hone my skills at writing sketches and plays, to take all these ideas I had buzzing around in my head and convert them into complete works of art. I knew I had the talent, but did I have the commitment? Had I shown myself off in a good enough light during my Second Year to get the choice I wanted? Surely I had — script writing was my destiny!

Actually, it wasn't. I didn't get on the course. My tutor told me that I had "messed about" a bit too much during my first two years, and it was felt that I hadn't shown enough dedication to my other subjects. So that resulted in me having to go with my second choice.

"I can't even remember what I ticked I was so convinced I was going to get Scriptwriting. Remind me, what did I put down again?"

My tutor looked at his notes and then looked up at me.

"Gender Theory."

12. FRUIT

To say I was chuffed to be studying Gender Theory would be a massive lie. I appealed and begged to be let onto the Scriptwriting course, but they were having none of it. So I resigned myself to studying a subject I knew nothing about and had absolutely no interest in. Hoo-bloody-ray.

On the first day of the course, I walked into the classroom to be greeted by twelve girls and a lesbian feminist tutor. Memories of Clifton High came flooding back, but this was as far removed as you could get. I felt so out of my depth it wasn't funny, but I was determined to make the most of it. The tutor introduced herself and spoke about her work in the theatre. She was opinionated and feisty and I immediately took a liking to her. We went around the room and introduced ourselves.

"And why did you want to study Gender Theory, Dan?"

"To be honest, I didn't. I wanted to do Scriptwriting."

"Okay. So what're your thoughts about gender in theatre and art today?"

I paused and contemplated this for a moment. "I'm just worried about the Spice Girls and how they're trying to take over the world," I blurted out naively.

She rolled her eyes. Clearly my concern that we were to be worried about the Spice Girls as a radical feminist movement was the most ludicrous thing she'd ever heard. I could tell this was going to be fun.

To be fair, the course was actually pretty enjoyable. We studied the role of men and women in the visual arts: exploring the Oedipus complex, particularly Freud's take on it, in films such as *Black Widow*. We also explored what a woman is expected to be in the film *M. Butterfly* (*"Why, in the Peking Opera, are women's roles played by men?... Because only a man knows how a woman is supposed to act."*)

As part of the course, we were required to put on a show. It was entirely up to us what the content and context would be, so after some discussion, we came up with the idea of exploring the world of cross-dressing. During the performance, all the girls would transform into men and all the men (i.e. me) would become women.

However, people changing gender wasn't quite enough to make for an engaging night's theatre, so it was agreed that all of us would perform a short group piece or a monologue too. This got my creative juices flowing. Sadly, up to that point, I had not been cast in any of the plays produced thus far, and not for lack of trying either. I had auditioned for everything but, be it my looks or my talent or the fact that I didn't 'fit in', I was yet to be given a role. But now I found myself with a chance to perform to an audience, and I had total creative control.

Curtain up. The evening's entertainment starts off with performances from a few of the girls, the rest of us looking pretty inconspicuous. Then, as the evening progresses, we start to change our clothing into that of the opposite sex. The ladies draw moustaches on their top lips, don trousers and braces, and thrust their loins out in mock masculinity. I haven't started to change yet — it's my performance piece up next. Wearing just a t-shirt and boxer shorts I place myself in the corner of the room, waiting for the audience to notice me. Voices fall silent. The lights come up and I slowly lift my head and take a deep breath.

Silence.

I gently start to run my hands all over my body. Making direct reference to the Bill Hicks sketch, I observe that women are purely sexual objects in advertising and that adverts are, in essence, pornography.

"Here's the advert they want to make. A camera is focused on a beautiful woman — she's naked. Camera pulls back — she's fully naked, legs spread, and two fingers touching her pussy. And all it says is, 'Drink Coke'."

The crowd laugh. Then silence. I stare back at them. More silence. The room feels nervous.

"Now, let's imagine a different world. Let's imagine it's a man in that advert. A camera is focused on a beautiful male. He's naked (I take my t-shirt off). The camera pulls back — he's fully naked (I drop my shorts), legs spread, and two fingers touching himself (I turn around, bend over and splay myself.) And all it says is, 'Drink Coke'."

Possibly not the nicest image you could imagine, but I was

trying to make a point about the role of men in advertising too. Who knows if it came across, but at least the room didn't fall deathly silent, and I wasn't kicked off the course. I asked the lighting operator to fade to black as soon as I bent over and mercifully he did, otherwise I can imagine there being a lot of scarred people that night. And they probably never drank Coke again. Actually, mission accomplished.

After that, all I had to do was slowly transform myself into a woman. Having just splayed my buttocks to a room full of people, I felt I was deserving of a glass of wine. Or two. Or four. By the end of the night I was in full drag, standing on a speaker and belting out 'Dancing Queen'.

"Are you a transvestite?!" Anthe asked as we walked home, her lip beginning to tremble.

"Of course not! I was acting!"

The tears suggested she thought otherwise. I could understand the shock. I suppose seeing your partner's private bits on stage followed by a full gender transformation may make you question their sanity. But it really was just a performance. Honest, Mum!

* * *

Gender transformations aside, my Third Year was going pretty well. I was still resident DJ at The Venue, I was meeting more and more of my drum and bass heroes, and I was still writing music — each track more developed and polished than the last. The only downside was, it was time to find a job.

Dad had supported me financially all the way through my First and Second Years, giving me an allowance every week. And even though I had decided to take out a Student Loan in my Third and Fourth Year (I didn't really need to but hell, it was there for the taking), Dad still wanted me to get some work — not just so I had more money in my pocket but so I could appreciate the value of earning it. I begrudgingly understood and started looking for employment.

During my final couple of years at Uni I found myself undertaking a myriad of jobs. For a couple of weeks I worked in a fruit-packing factory, picking and sorting rotten fruit. My favourite part was when they tipped a huge vat of oranges into a container for sorting. I particularly enjoyed the moment when the rotten oranges, now practically dust, exploded in my face. I decided not to hang around much after that. I also went to work in a warehouse that designed and fitted window frames. By the end of my first day I'd smashed two panes of glass, and hit someone on the head as I carried a frame out to the lorry. They didn't ask me back.

I finally found myself a job when a friend studying on the drama course told me there was a vacancy going in a local restaurant called Ricemans — part of the biggest department store on Canterbury High Street. It was a bit of an institution, reminiscent of the 1950's and 1960's stores of old. And it felt like the clientele hadn't changed much either. Swathes of elderly women would congregate from 9am onwards for tea and cake. My application was successful and I started work there two days a week, first on washing up duty, and then after a couple of months I was promoted to clearing the tables. I was never asked to serve the customers. Life can be cruel.

What made the job more bearable than most was the two chefs that worked there: Phil and Bob. They were hilarious. They would constantly take the piss out of the staff, but weren't afraid to have the piss taken out of themselves, and in fact positively encouraged it. It didn't take long until going into work actually became something to look forward to.

It was one summer's day that Phil called me into the kitchen and pulled me to one side.

"Dan, you can get hold of that Internet thing can't you?"

I knew what he meant.

"Yeah, I can get access to the Internet. Why?"

Bob came over to join us.

"Do us a favour. I want you to find the most disgusting picture you can. No death or anything illegal, just something disgusting. Can you do that?"

I looked at them quizzically and nodded my head in macabre delight.

I turned up the next day with a piece of folded-up paper tucked very securely into my back pocket. I wasn't proud of what I was doing, but I was secretly laughing inside. I checked in, made my way up to the kitchens, and headed over to Phil and Bob.

"Have you got it?" they asked, like kids waiting for sweets.

I nodded my head, pulled out the piece of paper and handed it to them. They slowly unfolded it and immediately burst out laughing.

"Hey, Laura! Come and have a look at this!" Laura, the lovely young kitchen assistant, innocently walked over only to have the picture thrust in to her face. She instantly recoiled, but then looked again, mouth hanging in disbelief.

For the next hour they called almost every waitress into the kitchen to show them the picture I had found. I was working on the washing up and all I could hear were howls of laughter and shrieks of "that's disgusting!" And it was. Have a look for yourself.[59]

It was nearing the end of my shift on what had been one of the funniest days of my life. And it was about to get better. As I was clearing away the last few tables, Laura came out to the restaurant and said, "Bob and Phil want to see you. Now." Had I done something wrong? I made my way into the kitchens to be greeted by a scene I will never forget: Bob laid on the floor, his mouth wide open while Phil crouched over his face, a piece of rolled-up pastry, covered in gravy granules, dangled from between his legs. I almost died.

Work is normally rubbish — wherever you are — but when your colleagues are prepared to re-enact someone pooing into someone else's mouth, you know you've found somewhere special.

---

59   Only kidding!

13. BLIND AND DUMB

I F EVER THERE WAS A PART IN A PLAY THAT WAS TAILOR-MADE for me, it was that of Tiresias the Blind Prophet.

Whilst I was undeniably grateful for the opportunity to finally appear on stage, the actual star of the show was the sound. I seem to recall that my appearing in the play was the pay-off for agreeing to do the soundtrack. The things final-year directors will do to get the best grades.

The part of Tiresias may have been small, but the soundtrack was huge. *Oedipus Rex* (written by Ted Hughes) is set in a wasteland — a harsh and desolate terrain where our protagonist would find out his terrible past. When asked to come up with an appropriate soundscape, it was obvious to me that drum and bass would be the only apt genre to accompany this barren playground. Drum and bass was going through a pretty industrial phase and Dom and Roland were at the cutting edge. Their track 'Quadrant 6' set the scene with its ethereal horns and razor-sharp synth stabs. To increase dramatic effect, we recorded the Riddle of Oedipus over the top of it, the final word echoing off as the drums came crashing in. It worked like a charm.

The rest of the play was filled with jarring sound effects — one of which was a huge needle-scratch taken from Dillinja's 'Unexplored Terrain'. The play ended on an Optical track called 'The Shining': a beautifully haunting tune that morphs into dark, twitchy synth sounds. It somehow seemed to encapsulate the play perfectly. It wasn't all drum and bass though. I worked with a lovely American girl called Jana who played the part of Oedipus' wife and (SPOILER ALERT!!) mother who recorded a speech about Icarus flying too close to the sun. I wrote and produced the backing music and effects and it was a soundscape I was really proud of.[60]

When it came to reviewing my work on *Oedipus*, my tutors commented that they had heard nothing like it before — in a good way I hasten to add. I was beaming. I knew I had redeemed myself after a less-than-perfect two years, and it no doubt helped me secure my final year specialism.

We had three options in the final year: Set Design, Radio Drama, and Directing. My immediate instinct was to do Radio Drama — primarily because I loved sound and not because I was particularly interested in the medium. Radio had never really done it for me, although I fully appreciate the skill behind producing a radio show. I was, I realised, a visual man. Ironic considering I only had one eye. I 'ummed' and 'ahhed' about what to do. Directing hadn't even crossed my mind as an option, but the opportunity to be in charge of

60   ♫

a production — to work with actors, to choose my own plays — suddenly became a shining light at the end of a four-year degree tunnel that had afforded me very little in the way of 'being a star'. I was a performer after all, and perhaps this was my opportunity to shine.

I was accepted.

We were tutored by a brash American called Alan Pearlman — a powerhouse of a man who was feared and revered in equal measure. I loved working with Alan. I wasn't afraid. Yes, he challenged, but that's exactly what I expected — I would have been disappointed if he hadn't. Our first task was to direct a fifteen-minute play for the end of term one. Finding plays that short is often quite difficult, and I looked long and hard but couldn't find anything I wanted to do. And then it hit me — Doomsday! That play I had done about the death of Superman for my GCSE Drama would be perfect. It was about fifteen minutes long which was ideal and, because I'd written it, I could tweak some of the writing that was perhaps a little bit immature, now that I was reading it with a more developed creative mind. I dug up the old script, blew off the (virtual) cobwebs, made my amendments and set to work on producing the greatest play UKC had ever seen.

Sadly, that wasn't quite how it turned out. It had some good features (the use of masks to heighten dramatic effect worked well), and choosing 'It's the End of the World as We Know It' by R.E.M. as the outro music was inspired, but overall it didn't really meet the mark. Perhaps that's the trouble with working on your own writing: I was too close to the material.

Short plays were fine but I wanted to get my teeth into something a bit meatier: a play with some real depth and development. Instead of fifteen minutes, our choice of play could now be an hour long. Finding the right script was probably the hardest part. I trawled through the University library, eager to discover something that didn't have a large cast, and was set in one location. I finally found what I was looking for, and it was Harold Pinter's *The Dumb Waiter*.

I had always been a massive Pinter fan. I'd studied *The Homecoming* in previous years and was in love with his menacing language, his use of... pauses, and the idea that what is left unsaid is often far more powerful. *The Dumb Waiter* starts off slow and ends in a real cliffhanger. This was really going to test my skills at keeping the audience entertained.

For the first time we had the chance to audition our actors. Once done, the directors would meet and talk about who they wanted before fighting each other to the death in a pit of mud and alligators. I jest, but there was definite competition for the better actors. I knew exactly who I wanted and was determined to get them.

The Dumb Waiter is a play about two hitmen, Gus and Ben, sent to carry out a job that they know nothing about. They wait in a dingy basement for their victim to arrive. Gus, the junior hitman, is a pain. He talks about tying his shoes. He plays with a box of matches. He questions and fiddles. And by doing so he annoys the surly Ben. Ben just lies there, reading his newspaper, trying to shut Gus up. He's waiting for the job, Gus is questioning everything. The tension is palpable.

In casting these roles it was vital to get a real relationship between the two characters. Casting Ben was reasonably easy. I requested an actor called Barry Forward who had done some performances at UKC before, but wasn't, what you might call, a 'star' actor. This was perfect forme. Barry was a rugby player with a dark sense of humour — ideal for themenacing, brooding Ben.

Gus was harder to cast. I needed an actor that would fill the stage and play to the comedic element of the role without hamming it up. I managed to cast Joe Leeder who was usually highly sought-after. When I said I wanted him to play the part, eyebrows were raised.

"Joe's a very lively actor — are you sure he can tone it down for this role?" That was exactly the type of challenge I wanted.

Once casting had taken place, we met with our actors to do read-throughs of the scripts. Well, that was the usual process: meet, read, act. I wanted to try something different.

I arranged our first rehearsal with Barry and Joe and, as predicted, they expected a read-through. They were surprised when I didn't give them a script. Instead, we spent the session talking about them, their expectations, and how they'd worked on previous plays. Then over the next few weeks we spent every session purely focusing on building character. I would feed them nuggets of information about how they might want to behave in a certain situation, or ask them to improvise about their past and their upbringing. Not all of it would work but when we hit something right it was pretty special.[61]

In one rehearsal I asked one of the actors to leave the room so I could focus on working just with the other one. Once alone, I would get them into character and push them to a real level of annoyance (for Ben) or a level of subjugation (for Gus) and — when I felt they were at a peak — I would give them a command.

---

61 I had also been studying Mike Leigh for some time now, so this method of using improvisation to develop character was one that I really wanted to explore.

"Go down to the bar and ask for a glass of water."

Not once did they look at me as if to say, "What are you talking about?" — they just did it, and it worked brilliantly. That isn't to say the bar staff weren't a little shocked, but it was worth the potential embarrassment as it demonstrated to me that the actors were now fully in character, and trusted me when I placed them in certain situations. We were now ready to look at the script.

* * *

The night of the first performance. Mum, Dad, and Alix had travelled up. Friends were in the audience. I was confident but nervous — my play was second in the bill. The lights dimmed. On first was a play about modern sexuality that started with a very striking image of a girl sat naked in a bathtub. This proved to be a real eye-opener for the retired ex-policeman who had driven my family up from Weston — especially as he was seated in the front row, slap bang in front of her naked breasts. He didn't know where to look. My dad sat next to him, barely able to contain his laughter.

The play ended. Interval time. I made my apologies and prepped my actors, getting them into character. It's a bit like preparing boxers before they go into the ring. My concerns were not about them, but more about the technical aspects of the play: especially the dumb waiter itself.

I retook my seat and nervously looked around at the audience now filtering back in. The Ink Spots song 'I Don't Want To Set The World On Fire' played quietly in the background, a subtle precursor to the night's proceedings:

I've lost all ambition for worldly acclaim / I just want to be the one you love [62]

The audience were all seated. The stage manager looked up to the lighting booth, spoke into her microphone, and the lights slowly began to dim. Mum put her hand out and held onto mine.

Lights up and we see Barry and Joe — or Gus and Ben as they were for the next hour — positioned on stage: Ben reading his paper, and Gus tying his shoelaces.

Watching a play as a director is so different to watching a play as a member of the audience. I was watching intently but also taking notes, observing moments that could have been tighter, spotting lighting changes or sound effects that should have been smoother, and, most of all, paying attention to the pesky dumb waiter that had been the biggest complication in the whole production. I reminded myself that this was only the first night — that there would always be things to tweak. And as the play ended to the sound of Henry Hall's 'The Teddy Bear's Picnic' (I edited the track so the first few notes were repeated three or four times for extra menace, building in volume each time), the audience applauded and Alan beckoned me over. [63]

We both agreed that it was a good first night but that there was room for improvement. I was encouraged by his feedback and by the fact that we were thinking along the same lines. I met with Barry, Joe, and the rest of the crew, congratulated them on a great first show, and gave each member their

---

62   → Maybe it's me, but I've always thought this song has a subtle menace about it.

63   → This one *definitely* has menace.

feedback. Tomorrow was the final performance, and time for us to really nail it.

That final performance was as perfect as I could ever have wished for. The tension between Ben and Gus was electric, all the technical elements worked like clockwork, and there was even a gasp at the final reveal. I felt a huge sense of achievement as the lights went down and the audience broke out in applause. I remember Alan leaving the theatre, patting me on the shoulder and muttering, "Very good. Very, very good." I guess my methods must have paid off — I was awarded the highest-marked play for the year. The drama department nomad was now the star pupil.[64]

The second term was over. After years of being in the drama wilderness, I finally felt like I was King of the Jungle — made more so by the compliments I received for *The Dumb Waiter* from my tutors and peers alike. It was now time to embrace the third and final production — and this was the big one.

---

64   → A few pictures from the production. I'm still so proud of what we did.

14. DEMONS / ANGELS

ONE GREAT THING ABOUT HAVING A GIRLFRIEND FROM Greece was that she came from Greece. And that meant free holidays.

After *The Dumb Waiter*, we decided to go and visit Anthe's mum for a week. Greece was amazing. I had been a couple of times before and had seen beautiful little islands and eaten fresh calamari. I'd experienced Athens on New Year's Eve. It really was a special place. This holiday though was a chance to chill and relax. We stayed with Anthe's mum in the centre of Athens, a fantastic little apartment full of books and culture.

One evening her mum came and sat next to me.

"I want you to have this," she said, and presented me with a ring. I was shocked. I took it from her and could immediately feel the weight. I lifted it to my eyes to see an ancient coin set into the face. I felt honoured. I hugged her and slipped the ring on to my wedding ring finger — NOT as a sign of my intentions, I quickly pointed out, but because that was the only finger it fitted. I've always had big fingers and had never worn a ring before. This one fitted just right.[65]

A couple of weeks later we were back in Canterbury having a nice, quiet lie-in when there was a knock at the door. Anthe went downstairs to answer it and then came running back up.

"Dan? It's the police!"

"What?"

I threw on some clothes and made my way downstairs.

"Are you Mr Daniel Jeffries?"

"Yes?"

"And do you have a thousand pounds with you today?"

"No, of course not! Why? What's this all about?!"

"We're here to arrest you for non-payment of TV License fines. You'll need to accompany us to the station. We'll let you get dressed first."

I ran back upstairs, chucked on some clothes and kissed Anthe goodbye. I could feel myself shaking. And then I was out of the door, and straight into the police car. I looked at Anthe out of the window. She didn't look too impressed.

Don't worry, dear reader, this was not the moment when I suddenly entered the world of violent crime, thus giving me ammunition to pen my memoirs and to 'sort aat a few bleedin' wronguns!' Far from it in fact. How I came to be arrested that morning goes back a whole eighteen months.

When we were living at our previous property in the Second Year, way before Anthe and I got together, we had a knock at the door one evening. It was the TV License

---

65   → As you can see here, whilst doing my famous 'Churchill' pose.

inspectors. Being poor, lowly students we hadn't bothered to sort out a TV License and, quite simply, we had been rumbled. The unfortunate person who answered the door (not me) had his name put down as the occupier of the property and the person responsible for organising a TV License ASAP. A few months later we moved out of that house, and it just never happened.

Fast forward a year and a half, and we were now in our new property — TV License intact. During my Second Year and into the Third Year, one of my housemates had become 'friends' with a local lad named Ryan. Ryan was a little bit 'waaaay', a little bit 'wooo'. He could get you anything you wanted, and usually did so without you asking. He was also homeless and had a pretty shit life, and — I can't deny — I felt sorry for him, and now and again let him stay over in the house. What I didn't realise was that he was harbouring stolen goods and ferrying nicked bikes round the back of our house, and flogging them off to others. What I also didn't realise was that the police had been watching our house. Clearly they'd been told that there was an outstanding fine for a TV License somehow connected to my name, and thus they turned up one morning to see if they could get their money back.

I sat quietly in the back of the police car. This was a first for me. As we got to the station, I was escorted towards the cells. To be fair, the police officers told the officer on duty that I had been very well behaved and was no trouble at all. Of course I wasn't. I was hardly going to kick off over a TV License fine, was I?! I can just imagine it now: me running down Canterbury High Street, pants round my ankles, screaming, "YOU'LL NEVER TAKE ME ALIVE YOU FUCKERS!" It just wasn't my style. I was placed in a cell and told that someone would come to see me in an hour or so.

Three hours later and I heard the latch on the cell door slide back. Freedom at last!

"We're serving lunch. Do you want lasagne or a sandwich?"

Oh. Hating pre-packed sandwiches, I opted for lasagne. Ten minutes later the door opened again and I was handed a plastic bowl with some food in it. Much to my amusement I was given a plastic spoon to eat it with. The idea that I might try and escape through the walls, or slit my wrists with a plastic knife and fork made me chuckle.

"When will I see the Judge?" I asked, tentatively.

"After lunch. Do you want someone to represent you? If so, it won't be till later this afternoon."

I thought about this for a moment and then decided against it. If I needed a lawyer to advise me on what to say about why I hadn't paid for a TV License then there was very little hope for me for the future. A couple of hours later the latch slid back again and I was taken to Court. I stood in the dock, the room empty except for the Judge and a police officer.

"Daniel Jeffries, you are here for non-payment of TV License fines. What do you have to say to the charge?"

"Well Your Honour, I wasn't aware that there was a charge outstanding. I hadn't signed the document to say that I would pay, though I do acknowledge that I lived in the premises at the time."

"And if you had known that there was a fine outstanding, would you have paid it?"

"Of course, Your Honour!" I lied.

"Very well then. Fine reduced to £350. Case dismissed."

And with that I was lead out to freedom. I paid off the fine over the course of the next two years — a grand total of £14 per month. As I walked down Canterbury High Street, I bumped into a friend of mine and asked him if he had a cigarette. I lit up, my hands a-tremble with nerves and hunger.

* * *

My own little drama over, it was time to get started on my third and final production.

Term three's play was to be performed at the Gulbenkian, UKCs very own commercial theatre. I'd watched plays here over the past three years, and now it was my turn to produce something for this 340-capacity venue. Having directed a two-hander for term two, I now wanted to direct something on a much bigger scale. But finding the right play was even harder than finding *The Dumb Waiter*. Everything I wanted to do was either too long, too complicated, or just didn't interest me.

The library had now become my second home: there every day, desperate to find the perfect play. Time was running out, and I was on the verge of resigning myself to 'the B-list': plays I had put to one side in case of an emergency. Having almost given up hope, I picked up *Angel City, Curse of the Starving Classes and Other Plays* by Sam Shepard and read the back cover. I'd heard of Sam Shepard (I had done the sound design for a production of *True West* the year before which involved recording cars skidding down a road — it was great), so maybe something would jump out at me in the *Other Plays* section.

I turned the first page and saw *Angel City* in huge letters. The name *Angel City* didn't sound that appealing but, once I'd read a couple of pages, I knew this was the play I wanted to direct. I quickly scanned through the script to make sure there were no humongous stumbling blocks. Actors? Six. That's okay. Length? About an hour. Good. Acts? Two.

Arse.

This was going to be a difficult one to get past Alan. One-act plays were considered best because they didn't require an interval. This one did and there was no getting around it. I read through the rest of the play and was utterly hooked right up to the final dramatic tableau. Any play that has people turning into monsters was fine by me. But it wasn't so fine with Alan.

"It's got two acts!" he exclaimed.

I didn't care. I'd get round it. The play was finally agreed — though there was a constant air of caution from Alan and the others.

"It's just weird for the sake of it," said a fellow student. Clearly they had never taken acid.

Diana Spinrad of the Chicago Reader does a great job of trying to sum up what the play is about:

> *"Angel City is quintessential early Sam Shepard - which means it's virtually impossible to explain rationally."*

This was just what I was after: a challenge, a puzzle, something visually stimulating and cerebrally exhilarating. And not only did I have the challenge of directing a play with two acts and an interval, I also had to find a set of timpani drums and a saxophonist. I was loving this play more and more.

As with *The Dumb Waiter*, I worked on character development with the actors for a few weeks before looking at the script. Joe, who had played Gus the term before, was cast as Wheeler, the brash, erratic movie mogul needing a miracle.

This was much more up his street — brash and erratic was what he did best. I also cast a wonderfully talented girl called Gemma in the role of Miss Scoones, the secretary that falls into a trance halfway through Act Two and a powerhouse of a man called Ben who played the role of Timpani, and beat those drums with verve and gusto. Paul played Rabbit, the mysterious soothsayer — summoned to conjure up a miracle. I had even found a live saxophonist. And then there was Hassan. He was to play the part of Lanx, Wheeler's sidekick.

However, as we moved deeper into rehearsals, it was becoming clear that Hassan was not as committed to the production as I would have hoped. He was missing rehearsals and after an honest and open chat it was apparent that he wasn't going to be able to play the role. CRISIS!!! you might think, but, as one of our tutors used to say, "There's no such thing as a problem, merely a solution opportunity." And this was the mother of all solution opportunities.

I decided to play the part myself.

"Oh yes Dan! Did you *really?*" I hear you cry. It's important to stress that this was purely a decision based on practicality. We were nearing the end of the year, and everyone was up to their eyeballs in work — finding a new actor to take on the role would be nigh on impossible. Plus, I knew the play better than anyone else. The fact that this was my one and only opportunity to finally get a leading role on stage bore no relevance in the decision making process whatsoever.

Preparation for *Angel City* was far more intricate than *The Dumb Waiter*. Whilst *The Dumb Waiter* had the perils of a live pulley system, *Angel City* had its own different set of complications: scene changes, timpanis, monster costumes, a huge floating cinema screen, green ooze, weirdness, and more. And, of course, the dreaded interval.

The purpose of the interval was to give the actors time to change their costumes, and for Wheeler to morph into a monster. I understood the concerns surrounding the interval: we didn't want the audience to become restless, thinking this was their chance to nip out for a quick fag or top up their wine, so I had to come up with some form of entertainment during those 5-10 minutes. I had been listening to an album called *Let Us Replay* by Coldcut, and in a moment of inspiration it struck me that the final track of the album — 'The Tale of Miss Virginia Epitome' — would be an absolutely perfect intermission. It had a sluggish, bluesy feel to it and lyrics that couldn't fail to catch your attention. The singer's called Selena Saliva. Need I say more?[66]

It went down a storm. We could hear people laughing over the Tannoy backstage. The audience were gripped (who wouldn't be after *that* opening line?) and, to top it all off, we were able to get the saxophonist on stage to jam along to the last section of the song.

For me, *Angel City* was a total success even if it didn't get as high a mark as *The Dumb Waiter*.[67] Alan thought it had 'issues' and I had to agree: directing and acting in the same production was never going to be easy, and something inevitably had to give. But I had taken a difficult, obscure play with big themes and a bizarre structure and turned it into a live spectacle with monsters and saxophones and dripping green ooze. And I did all this whilst my flat burned down.

Yup — for halfway through that production, the flat I was

66 → Amazing music, amazing drumming — very wrong lyrics.

67 → A few pictures from the dress rehearsal, hence why the cinema screen is bare. That final image is one of my favourite creative moments ever.

living in caught fire.

Myself and six friends lived in possibly the best student accommodation in Canterbury. It was huge, had original wooden beams, and barely a neighbour in sight. We used to have house parties that would last for two days. Unbelievably, we once received a box of chocolates from a neighbour thanking us for not making too much noise! The downside was that we lived above a kebab shop, which brought its own set of challenges. One evening I was sitting in the lounge when someone burst in and said, "There's shit-loads of smoke in the kitchen!" I ran to have a look and could see the smoke billowing out, an orange glow throbbing menacingly in the corner. Josh, who was in the bath, jumped out, wrapped himself in a towel, and, along with the rest of us, legged it downstairs. We stood outside in the freezing cold and watched our flat slowly disintegrate. Firemen ran in and out in an attempt to dampen the flames, doing the same in the kebab shop below. What we didn't realise was that the flue from the kebab shop extended into our kitchen, so once that went up we had no chance.

We were gutted. And so was the flat. It was declared uninhabitable and we were moved from one of the nicest properties in town to a horrible little student house miles from Uni. That sounds so ungrateful but it really was a huge upheaval. Everything stank of smoke, including my records. I was amazed that they hadn't melted in the heat. I hugged them as if they were my children.

A few days later, I was hugging those records again. The University had kindly offered us some storage space for our worldly possessions whilst we sorted ourselves out. A student rep came and picked us up in a minibus, and we loaded it up and made our way to one of the halls. As we were driving up that steep hill to the Uni we reached some temporary traffic lights, and the driver stepped on the brakes a bit too hard. Suddenly, the back doors of the minibus flew open and I started to slide down the seat towards them! I stuck my foot out to stop one of my boxes of records flying out the back, which in turn steadied my balance and position. I reached out, grabbed the handle, and slammed the door shut. The look of horror on the face of the driver behind us is something I'll never forget.

Now that *Angel City* was over, all that remained was my final *viva voce* (a verbal 'exam' to critique the productions), and a dissertation on the work of Mike Leigh. I came away with a 2:2 which — considering how much I'd arsed about in the first couple of years — I was pretty pleased with. I wasn't overly worried about my final grade — getting a degree was enough for me, and I was the first in the family to do so. For me, it was all about the experiences: DJing on a disused Russian submarine, being a resident DJ, composing sound scores, recording sound effects, directing three plays (and getting the highest grade of the year — I was proud of that) and, of course, my time with Anthe.

Graduation day arrived and it was held at the prestigious Canterbury Cathedral.[68] Dad, having bad eyesight, had managed to secure himself seats right at the front of the proceedings. I often think occasions such as these are more for the family. Yes, it's nice to be recognised, but I'd already received that in the applause I had got for the plays I'd directed. I'd like to think that's a typical 'artists' view on it all: the roar of the crowd will always outweigh the awards received, and

---

68   → A proud moment. Though maybe not so proud of that tie.

hopefully that doesn't make me sound too wanky.

After the ceremony, there was an event for all the graduates and VIPs up at the University, a last chance to say goodbye to fellow students and tutors. I declined. Sometimes — stupidly — I go by the old adage of 'I don't want to be part of a club that wants me as a member', so instead my family and I went for a massive Chinese meal at one of the most exclusive restaurants in Canterbury. It was brilliant. Family warmth felt far more important than faux-goodbyes and adieus though, in hindsight, I do regret missing out on that final soiree. I hadn't realised until the day of the ceremony that Brenda Blethyn was to be awarded a Doctor of Letters. I had written about her when completing my dissertation on Mike Leigh, watching her mesmerizing performance in *Grown Ups.* What an opportunity to talk to her about her work. What an opportunity missed! It could have been such a special moment — something I could have treasured forever. But now it's gone, never to be returned, lost in the annals of time.

Ah well. At least the spring rolls were good.

Well, that's it!

That's the story of my life.

Who'd have thought I'd end it by talking about spring rolls?

Ah, of course not. I'm only kidding. As the song goes, "... we've only just begunnnnn!"

You may, however, be thinking to yourself, "Dan, you're a liar. I bought this book on the basis that I would immerse myself in a tale about the terrible fate that befell you, or how you contracted some incurable tropical illness that caused your ears to grow to the size of cars, but all you've done is talk about school and girls and being brilliant.[69]

I WANT MY TRAGEDY!"

And you'd be right. But really, if I had started talking about all the weird and wonderful experiences that I'm about to share with you on page 2, wouldn't you have felt *more* cheated?

So I solemnly swear — on my life, whilst doing the Scout's Honour — that the rest of the book will give you those moments that caused you to spend your hard-earned cash in the first place. However, in the meantime, you may also fancy a little break. Why not go back and read *Doomsday* or the hilarious farce *Hook, Line and Sinker?*

Or you could listen to some of the music I wrote when I was younger.

Or you could just read the rest of the book.

Or I could just shut up.

---

69   You may not have thought that bit.

15. WHEN THE CHIPS ARE DOWN...

C ANTERBURY WAS LOVELY BUT I COULDN'T LIVE THERE ANY more.

I always knew that I was going to move back to Bristol after university. There was little opportunity to broaden my horizons in Canterbury when it came to directing or writing or DJing — in fact, anything to do with the arts. I'd said farewell to Ricemans during my final year (the plays were just taking up too much time) but now university was over, and it was time to find some summer work before moving back to Bristol. I tried bar work but I was absolutely hopeless (I think I managed half an hour before they politely asked me to leave), so I settled on working as a cashier at a petrol station.[70]

It was the weirdest petrol station I had ever worked in,

70   Apropos of nothing, opposite the fish and chip shop that was the inspiration for *Hook, Line and Sinker*.

not that I had worked in many. I'd arrive at 6am to find my colleague — a rather large man — already there, chirpy as anything, and sweating his nuts off. I soon realised that the chirpiness and sweating were a direct result of a diet of speed, fed to him by his missus first thing in the morning "like sugar on my cornflakes" he casually informed me. Add to that a mad South African with an immense distrust of the world, and the responsibility of trying to stop the whole of the Medway area from stealing crisps and petrol, and you had a job that was — you might say — 'challenging'.

Selling petrol to the people of Canterbury was probably as close as I was going to get to being near a car. I had tried driving lessons when I was seventeen, during a summer holiday in Weston. Considering how poor my eyesight was even back then, I didn't do that badly. There were two noticeable issues however:

1. I couldn't reverse around corners (close your left eye and give it a go. Actually, don't.)

2. I had no idea of the distance between my car and cars to the left of me, to the extent that my driving instructor had to keep nudging the steering wheel to avoid a scraping.

In light of this, accepting a film role that involved driving a car was perhaps a little foolish.

That summer, a film student was looking for an actor to help with one of his projects. I can't remember what the part was or what I had to do, but it did involve going to the woods (yes, I realise how bad that sounds) and some filming in his car. Seeing as I hadn't had many roles and hot off the success of *Angel City*, I overlooked this minor requirement, and told him I was good for the role. Once we had finished filming he asked if I could drive.

"Err... no, not really. I thought you meant just shots of me sat in the car. Is that going to be a problem?"

"Well, I was hoping I could film you driving back up to the University."

"Oh, okay. I had a few lessons some years ago but I haven't driven in ages. I haven't got a license either."

"You'll be fine. It's dead easy."

I looked at him, looked at the car, took a deep breath, and made my way to the driver's seat. It's amazing the power you get from sitting on that side of the car, especially when you're not used to it. I gripped the wheel, pressed a pedal (I had some idea of which was which), and turned the ignition. The car roared into life and I put my foot on the accelerator, revving it gently. Piece of piss, I thought and raised my courage level, revving it some more. I looked over at the director and he looked back at me, camera in hand.

"Ready?"

"Ready."

"ACTION!"

With that I revved the car one last time and suddenly realised we weren't moving. Ahhh of course — the handbrake! I lifted it up just as I my foot pressed down on the accelerator and shot forward, smacking into a car parked in front of me. I gripped the wheel, desperate to take control, particularly as we were hurtling towards a solid brick wall.

"SLAM ON THE FUCKING BREAKS!!" he screamed.

I duly acknowledged, thinking this was the best piece of

directing he had given all day. The car came to a screeching halt, my heart pumping so hard I could feel it in my ears. We sat there in silence. I had missed the wall by inches.

At the bottom of the road, one by one, men started to appear from the pub, looking over to see what all the noise was about. I turned to the Director.

"I think we should go."

We quickly got out of the car, swapped seats, and he calmly pulled away. Pairs of eyes followed us as we reached the bottom of the road. We turned left and were gone.

Once safe, we burst into laughter. I apologised profusely but quickly reminded him that I had said I couldn't drive. He was fine with it and realised it probably wasn't the best directorial decision he had ever made. He dropped me off, thanked me for my time, and we never saw each other again.

After that I realised my dreams of racing Formula 1 cars was unlikely, and set off for Bristol to pursue a more realistic goal: a life in the theatre. There was one more thing to sort out before I left though, and that was me and Anthe.

Before leaving for Bristol, I met her at the airport and I could sense that something was wrong.

We sat and spoke honestly about how we were feeling. She no longer wanted a relationship and, as sad as it was, I knew it was the right thing to do. Anthe was going to be with a new group of people, studying for a new qualification — a whole new life ahead of her. What did I have planned? Nothing. No job, no dreams, save for a wishy-washy desire to be a writer: nothing. I resigned myself to the fact it was over but for some reason — and I always find this hard to rationalise — I didn't want to fight for her love. It's not that I didn't want her or care for her, but if the other person isn't happy, why prolong the agony? It would only get worse.

Whilst Anthe was living the dream, I was living the nightmare. I had moved back to Bristol, certain I could get a job as a writer with the BBC, or full-time work as a DJ. Utterly ludicrous of course and maybe that's the security blanket getting a degree gives you. That blanket was now fully soaked in piss, and I needed to give it a thorough wash.

And so the hunt for an income began. There were only two things that I promised not to allow myself to do: work in a call centre, and go on benefits. Not that I'm against the concept of welfare in any way, but I had the fear that, if I did, I wouldn't bother looking for work again. Nobody likes working, but sitting at home every day in front of *Trisha* was far less appealing. So I registered with a few employment agencies and would call them every day, eager to see if any new jobs had become available.

Whilst looking through the Bristol Evening Post an advert caught my eye.

'Grosvenor Casino are looking for new Croupiers to work in our venue. Call us for more information.'

Oooohl! A job in a casino! Now *that* sounded cool. I started to imagine the glitz and glamour of casino life: Robert de Niro standing at the back of the room, watching over high stakes gamblers and their gorgeous girlfriends as they won or lost a fortune on the flip of a card. This was going to be amazing.

Nothing could have been further from the truth.

I got on the phone and spoke to a manager and was told I could start training on Monday. Brilliant! Work at last. I was chuffed to bits.

As I arrived at the casino the next morning, a beautiful girl walked in at the same time as me. "Are you here for the training?" I asked. She said she was. This was getting better and better. It was weird being inside a building with no natural light at 9am, but the smell of the cards, the whirring of the machines, and the heavy air of money made it quite enticing.

And then we met Simon, the guru who would be turning us into world-class croupiers. Simon was rude, crude, and completely irresponsible, and we immediately hit it off. It transpired that we were both particularly huge fans of *Viz* and their newly published *Profanisaurus*: a dictionary dedicated to crudeness, rudeness, and swear words. We were like kids in a very dirty sweet shop.[71]

It wasn't all schoolboy humour though. There was a job to do, and it wasn't easy. Being a croupier involved working the roulette table, the poker table and the blackjack table. Maths was a huge factor. What's 35 x 12? Too slow. You couldn't work out the sums — you had to *know* them. Stacking chips was also a key skill, but my fingers were so big that I just couldn't do it properly, and the stack of twenty chips would often end up crumbling under my touch. Simon reassuringly referred to me as 'Bowyer Boy', i.e. I had fingers like sausages. I laughed, but I knew it was going to be a problem.

I was much more comfortable dealing blackjack and poker. They involved cards and only a few chips. Plus you were *playing* the game too — not that you could yell, "YES! In your face!" if you beat your opponent. The maths was easier and it was far less frantic. With roulette, people could

---

71   For example: bum cigar n. In after dinner conversation, a stool. 'Well, if you'll excuse me, I think I'll nip upstairs and light a *bum cigar.*'

chuck their chips pretty much wherever they wanted, and you needed eyes in the back of your head to see what people were doing. An abundance of eyes was something I didn't have.

Six weeks of training passed and we were ready to be unleashed onto the public. Having already cut our teeth during lunchtime sessions when it was reasonably quiet (this was before casinos were granted twenty-four hour gambling licenses) we were now ready for some night-time action. It was at this stage that being a croupier started to lose its dreamy glow. My hours were either lunchtime until 8pm, or 8pm until 4am. I really struggled with sleeping during the day — not conducive for an active brain trying to calculate maths. There were no clocks in the building either and no windows (the casino doesn't want you to have any sense of the passing of time). You couldn't go outside to get some fresh air. Food was provided but it wasn't the best. This was not a healthy way to live.

It all came to a head when, one Saturday night, I was running the roulette table. It was absolutely heaving. My table must have had eight or more players — all of them throwing down large stacks of chips and wads of money — and it was my job to make sure their bets were accurate before the game could begin.

I placed the ball on the roulette wheel and went to spin it, but misfired. I often did this. Every other croupier I knew had the delicate touch to spin it just right — when I did it, it was like watching an elephant pick a daisy. I tried again and this time managed to get the ball to spin — giving me time to review the table. I checked that stacks were placed where they should be whilst handling requests for money bets as they came in thick and fast. Out of the corner of my eye I noticed one number seemed to be particularly loaded: piled high with six different coloured chips. Please Lord, I thought to myself, don't let it land on this one. I waved my hands across the table and declared, "No more bets!" and turned to the wheel to see where it would land. As the ball started to slow down I looked back at the table, eyeing up that number with all the venom I could muster, convinced that if I glared at it long enough the ball would land somewhere else.

And what do you know — it landed on it.

Huge cheers around the table as my shoulders visibly sank. I cleared away the losing colour in two big sweeps (one of the benefits of having big hands), and took a deep breath. As I had been taught so many times before, all I had to do was arrange the stacks so I could calculate what needed to be paid out. Easy. With that in mind, I lifted the first pile of chips only to knock the entire stack over, scattering them across the table. Cries of despair shot up around the table. I looked for the Pit Boss who was already on her way over, and within seconds she had surveyed the damage and rectified the situation, promptly paying out the correct amounts to the right people. She apologised and explained that I was new. I thanked her, avoided the glaring eyes bearing down on me and announced that it was "time to place your bets!"

I knew from that moment on I wouldn't be coming back. Not that I was embarrassed or despondent or worried, but because I was a hopeless croupier. That and the god-awful hours. And the horrible food. And the lack of daylight. And seeing people turn up as soon as the doors opened having slept in their car all night. And all for under £9k a year.

This was not the dream I was after. It was time to find a new one.

16. THE TEMP FROM HELL

ZXCVBNM   ZXCVBNM   ZXCVBNM
ZXCVBNM   ZXCVBNM   ZXCVBNM
ZXCVBNM   ZXCVBNM   ZXCVBNM
ZXCVBNM   ZXCVBNM   ZXCVBNM
ZXCVBNM   ZXCVBNM   ZXCVBNM
ZXCVBNM   ZXCVBNM   ZXCVBNM
ZXCVBNM   ZXCVBNM   ZXCVBNM
ZXCVBNM   ZXCVBNM   ZXCVBNM
ZXCVBNM   ZXCVBNM   ZXCVBNM
ZXCVBNM   ZXCVBNM   ZXCVBNM
ZXCVBNM   ZXCVBNM   ZXCVBNM
ZXCVBNM   ZXCVBNM   ZXCVBNM
ZXCVBNM   ZXCVBNM   ZXCVBNM
ZXCVBNM   ZXCVBNM   ZXCVBNM

Now that I was unemployed, my obscure obsession with the QWERTY keyboard was going to have to help me generate some income. Having realigned my sleeping patterns (how nice NOT to have to come home from work at 5am), I set about the merry task of trying to find myself a job.

Bristol was — and still is — flooded with recruitment agencies. So I wrote up my CV, donned my best attire, and visited as many of them as I could. Some of them specialised in warehouse and industrial, and I always used to chuckle at the prospect of me driving a 7.5 tonne HGV through the streets of Britain whilst my driver's mate would subtly nudge the steering wheel.

So rather than being asked to show my driving skills, the agencies would test me on my admin skills.

"Have you ever done copy typing?"

"Nope."

"Audio typing?"

"Nope."

"Do you know what your typing speeds are?"

"Nope."

I was clearly hot property.

The first thing they would get me to do was type. I'd sit down with a script to the right of me, and would be given a minute to bash out as much as I could. I stretched my fingers, cracked my knuckles, and summoned the QWERTY spirits to aid me in my quest. Much to my surprise I was typing at around 80-90 words per minute. I tried audio typing and was getting pretty much the same speed. Oooh, I thought, something I'm good at! Typing at this speed meant I was in the higher hourly-pay bracket too, so the world really was looking rosy.

For the next few months I was a little admin strumpet — moved from pillar to post to satisfy the needs of the suits. I worked for banks, insurance companies, solicitors, courts, hospitals, surveyors, probation services, and even — ironically — a recruitment agency. Work was never guaranteed though, and I was just as likely not to hear a thing on a Friday afternoon as I was to receive a flood of offers. It wasn't a great way to live.

It even almost got me arrested.

At the end of another slow week I received a call from an agency.

"We've got you some work, and it could be a permanent position!"

"Fantastic. Where is it?"

"Horfield Prison."

Not the answer I was expecting.

Monday morning, and I got on the bus and made my way to the prison. I climbed the steps to the top deck and sat down. As I looked out of the window, I started to notice a familiar smell: weed. I turned my head and saw someone sat at the back of the bus smoking a huge reefer out the window. Great, I thought. Just what I needed.

I got to the prison gates and rang the bell. An intercom buzzed.

"Yes?"

"Hi. I'm here for the admin job."

"Show your ID, please."

"Err… what ID?"

Thankfully, the agency had completely forgotten to tell me that I would need to bring ID with me in order to gain entry.[72] Cue twenty minutes of phone calls between the prison and the agency as they determined whether I really was the admin boy they had hired, and not someone trying to smuggle in ropes, fags, and an assortment of chisels.

Finally, a guard met me at the entrance.

"I'll walk you to your office."

I'd never been in a prison before. It was huge. And surprisingly quiet. As we walked across the yard, that silence was shattered when three huge Alsatians started barking like mad — at me! I looked at the guard, and he looked at me.

"Do you have anything on you you shouldn't have?"

"No," I whimpered.

"Do you smoke drugs?"

And suddenly my mind raced back to the bus, the top deck, and that weed-smoking commuter. Unbelievable. I must have stunk of it. I couldn't deny I may have had a spliff in the previous thirty days too — the smell no doubt lingering on my clothes. I explained that someone was on the bus smoking weed, hence why the dogs were probably going mad. He looked at me suspiciously. This was not going well.

I edged my way slowly past the salivating hounds and followed the guard to my office. To get there, I had to walk through a corridor with cells on either side. Men looked at me. Not like that, but still, they looked. I was so out of my comfort zone. We finally made it to the office where the guard instructed me to wait for the office manager. I duly obliged. I looked out of the window, and saw that my view was a huge pile of rocks.

Yet again, this was not the dream I was after.

---

72   It seems kind of obvious now.

Before I had even typed a word I knew that I wouldn't be coming back. If I'm being honest, I used to mess recruitment agencies around something rotten. I'd swear on my life that I was after a full-time job, and that I was prepared to do *anything* to get it but the reality was: if I didn't like it, I wouldn't do it. I wasn't prepared to sell eleven years of school and university down the river to be stuck in a job where my view was a pile of rocks. And because I didn't 'play the game', I ended up getting a bit of a name for myself — agencies stopped calling quite so often, work started to dry up, money was running out. I needed to do something, and fast.

* * *

By sheer chance, I happened to bump into my old drama teacher from QEH. We spoke about how the school was doing and what productions had been on, and that I was - sob sob sob - out of work with nothing to do.

"The theatre's free over the summer," he said. "Why don't you put on some workshops?"

What a brilliant idea. And finally — a use for my degree!

I made up some posters and visited all the schools in Bristol that were reasonably close to the theatre, and asked if they would be good enough to advertise the workshops. They kindly obliged and, slowly but surely, people started to enquire, asking what my experience was and what the workshops would be about. I was dealing with parents here so I had to be professional.

A couple of weeks later and the first day had arrived. I made my way to the theatre, slightly nervous about who might turn up. What if I had hundreds and I couldn't cope? Or, even worse, no one? What if the parents thought I was a sham or a charlatan or — heaven forbid — a paedo? Thankfully, the Lord decided to make the workshops as simple as possible by deploying twelve teenage girls into my care. Yes: twelve teenage girls. Not one boy. And, as you would expect, their parents had some questions.

If I wanted to do this today I wouldn't have a hope without the correct paperwork and qualifications, and rightly so. I had nothing — except common sense, theatre experience, and, I hoped, a trustworthy aura about me. I spoke to all the parents and endeavoured to put their minds at rest. Minds rested, I made my way into the theatre and introduced myself to the group. Then I found out a little more about them. And for the next two weeks we spent every day reading scripts, improvising ideas, and acting out scenes and sketches. The whole experience was hugely enjoyable. And even though I was twenty-three and they were fifteen, there was a definite bond between us. Except when it came to music — they hated mine and I hated theirs, and I was all the happier for that.

Our two weeks together had come to an end and, with dramatically damp eyes, we said our goodbyes. We all vowed to stay in touch via MSN Messenger, but, as expected, that didn't really happen, except for the odd "Hello" or "How you doing?" or "Are you still listening to that shit music?" It would be over a year until I would bump into one of them again — an encounter that would completely change my life.

* * *

Unemployed. Again. The money from the workshops had helped, but the reality of finding another job was fast approaching. It was time to trawl the recruitment agencies once more to see what was out there. I was by now on first name terms with most of them — a familiarity which had its plus and minus points. At some stage, you're going to have a 'bad' job. I had, for example, completely sacked off a job in Avonmouth that started at 11pm — even though I had sworn on my life that I would be there. That doesn't tend to go down too well. But then other agencies loved employing me because the speed and accuracy of my work meant that I could get through jobs quickly.

One of the more interesting typing jobs I had was for Hewlett Packard. HP had been doing research into digital photography and the power of the physical picture. They had worked with a focus group and recorded long discussions about the memories that photos can conjure, especially the powerful emotions that physically touching a photograph can produce. What HP had developed was some prototypes whereby your photograph 'interacted' with you. So, for example, taking a picture that also recorded ten seconds of sound, to 'capture the moment'. This was groundbreaking study back in 2000, yet go to the App store today and you'll find dozens of products doing similar things and more. And my role in all of this was to type up the focus group discussions, word for word.

This was a really difficult but fascinating assignment. When you're audio typing, you usually have a foot pedal that controls the tape: allowing you to rewind it when necessary just in case you missed a word. I had none of that, because the entire discussion had been recorded on video. Instead, I had to manually press the rewind button every time I wanted to hear something again. People spoke over each other, so trying to decipher what was being said was hard work. However, being the typing *wunderkind* that I am, I managed to complete the job in a week — not bad when I had been allocated two. I made sure I got paid for the second week and I was off, back on the hunt for my next slice of employment.

Trawling through the weekly paper I noticed an advert from the BBC — something that doesn't crop up very often. I read it open-mouthed: this was the job for me! They were looking for people to work on a new exhibition called Future World, designed to raise awareness about Digital TV (a relatively new concept back in 2000) and, most of all, encourage those who had never used a computer or the Internet to come and see what all the fuss was about. Wow. At last, a job that I actually *wanted* to do!

Job applied for, I still had to earn money. The phone was dead and I was struggling. Badly. But a week after sending off my application form, a letter came through the post asking me to go for an interview at BBC Bristol. HURRAH! I was so excited. I knew this was mine. And, in an utterly ridiculous moment of self-belief, I contacted all the agencies I could think of one more time to try and get some work — even if it was just for a week because I knew that — in a month's time — I'd have a new job and it would be amazing.

Luckily enough, one of the agencies did have some work for me: general admin duties at an office in Central Bristol.

"Now, they're really looking for someone to take this role on a permanent basis. Are you sure you can commit to this, Dan?"

"Yes of course! I've realised that permanent work is really what I want to do," I lied.

The job was the usual day-to-day admin work:

photocopying, filing and... err... that was about it. I was, in all honesty, piss-bored. The only additional task they gave me was to write out some cheques. The senior administrator showed me the spreadsheet and told me what to do. Now, being a bit naive and not very business savvy, I asked, "Do you want me to sign them too?" She looked at me like I was brain-dead.

"Why, are you a Managing Director now?"

There's nothing I love more than being treated like an idiot, so from that point on I was dead to the job. And, as it has so often been pointed out, the Devil makes work for idle hands — so whilst they gave me nothing to work on I would browse the Internet, or write down an idea or two for a script, or have online chat sex.

Yeah, not the wisest thing to do in an office environment. I had been, for a while, in what you might call an 'online relationship' with a lady on the other side of the world. It's a very bizarre thing to try and explain because you never meet, you rarely talk, and it's purely the power of words that brings you together. Remember — this was in the days of dial-up modems, so the concept of webcam chatting was unheard of, primarily because it cost a fortune. So yeah, we used to joke and laugh and, now and again, talk dirty. And I could think of no better place to do it in than the most boring office in Bristol.

A week into the job and it was time for my interview at the BBC. There was no way I was going to tell the agency that I had an interview for another job, so I told them that I had a hospital appointment at lunchtime and that I was going to be off for the rest of the day — one of the few benefits of having weird and complicated medical conditions. I made my way over to the BBC on Whiteladies Road, a building I had seen so many times but never been in. I was nervous, excited, apprehensive, and confident. I was all of these things and none of these things, and all at the same time.

The interview went really well. They asked me about my experience of using the Internet, so I spoke about all the great websites that were out there (I decided not to talk about chat sex), the BBC's use of the Web, the very popular EastEnders website, and how, these days, you would see websites at the bottom of the screen to encourage people to engage more. They liked that. They also asked me about Bristol's role in the BBC's creative output, so I spoke about how BBC Bristol were responsible for gems such as Casualty, the raft of daytime antiques-based shows, and other hits such as Wallace and Gromit. I also pointed out that BBC Bristol was the home of the famous Natural History department and that it was renowned the world over for making exemplary wildlife documentaries. They *really* liked that. They asked me if I would be available to do some training in London and could I commit to this for a few months? I said I absolutely could. We shook hands and, as you would expect, they said they'd let me know.

I walked home with a spring in my step. That had gone so much better than expected, even if I had turned up drenched in sweat (suits, nerves, and a long walk can do that to a man). I also had the afternoon off — what with work thinking I was at the hospital all day. I was in a good mood.

I got home, walked into the lounge, and could see the answering machine was flashing.

Two messages.

BEEEP

"Hi Dan, this is Sarah from the recruitment agency. We've had a call from the office you're currently at and… they don't want you back. They feel that you're not getting on too well and… erm… they've also looked through your Internet history and found some inappropriate activity. So please don't go back. And we would like to see you in the morning to discuss your future here with us."

Shit. Shit shit shit.

BEEEP

"Hi Dan, it's Jane from the BBC. I am delighted to inform you that your interview was a success, and we would love you to come and work at the Future World exhibition in Bristol, starting next week. Please call me back to discuss further."

YES! IN YOUR FACE, RECRUITMENT AGENCY!!

I called my parents and told them the great news. I think my dad was particularly pleased that I had found some steady work at last, as it would no doubt ease the ever-growing hole in his bank balance. After taking a deep breath, I called the recruitment agency back.

"Dan, your behaviour was disgraceful."

"Well, I'm sorry, but they treated me like an idiot when all I did was ask a simple question about signing a cheque."

"But that doesn't mean you can go and send dirty emails!"

"Well, if they actually gave me some work to do then maybe I wouldn't!"

"Regardless, Dan, this is very unprofessional and we'll no longer be able to offer you work."

"Aww, really? That's a shame. Good job I've just been offered work with the BBC. Bye Bye!"

And with that I put down the phone, looked to the sky, and dreamt of a career with Mr Blobby.

17. LORD OF THE RING

WORKING FOR FUTURE WORLD WAS GREAT. HERE I WAS — having spent months lost in the wilderness of audio typing and filing — now submerged in interesting people, media, and technology.

'The Beeb' sent us off to London for the initial training, and it was clear from the off that I was pretty *au fait* with using the Net while for some it was still new terrain. That's not to put them down, but the Internet wasn't as big a part of life in 2000 as it is today, and I guess I had been lucky to have had an amazing setup when I was at University four years before. I actually had to learn to take a bit of a back seat: something I found challenging at first, but soon realised that you could get just as much joy from watching people learn.

Bristol was the last city of the Future World tour and it was held in an exhibition centre next to Temple Meads railway station. The space was filled with dozens of computers all connected to the Internet. There was an exhibition about *Walking with Dinosaurs,* a media room where you could have a go at reading the News, a virtual Peter Snow talking about digital TV, and twice-daily presentations on the global impact of the BBC — featuring clips from flagship shows such as *Fawlty Towers* and *Only Fools and Horses.*

As much as I loved working there, hearing "Basil!" and "Keep it nice and cool, Trig, nice and cool" every day became a little tiring, but I soldiered on. I was there to help people learn how to use the Internet: from creating an email account to learning how to search online — even down to incredibly simple tasks like how to click a computer mouse. We take all these things for granted these days — even concocting the term 'Digital Native'.[73] But for a senior citizen, new technologies can be frightening. It's like your Nan trying to understand Teletext thirty years ago. We were there to help, and those 'silver surfers' that did pop in generally spent their time looking up family histories and researching into areas that interested them — they weren't sticking up pictures of LOL CATZ or memes of Miley Cyrus twerking.[74]

Whilst the exhibition was organised and managed by the BBC, there was considerable input from British Telecom who provided the technical infrastructure. One of the highlights of the event was a booth that created an avatar (a digital version of yourself). The machine would take pictures of you from four different angles and create a 3D image. Once created, it could put you in any situation: for example, you could

---

73   In other words, someone who was born after the technology revolution and, having experienced it from an early age, is more than comfortable using it. Babies with iPads, for example.

74   If you don't know what any of that means — kudos to you.

have your emails read to you by the person that sent them. Futuristic stuff. For this exhibition, your avatar could ride a skateboard.

Interesting, I thought. I wonder what it can *really* do?

So one night, after the exhibition had closed, I decided to push the machine to its limits. I took off all my clothes, jumped in the machine, and waited as I listened to the giggles of my colleagues. The results were horrendous. Mercifully, you couldn't see everything, but what you could see was a white mass riding around a skate park like a blancmange on wheels. Due to a technical error, my avatar was horribly distorted and it gave my 3D self a bum shaped like the Elephant Man's head. It was truly awful but utterly hilarious and the team were in fits. I got to keep a copy of it which, luckily for you, I've lost. However, the guys at BT asked if they could keep it 'for research purposes'. God knows where that might have ended up.

* * *

Working at Future World was perhaps the first indication that something wasn't quite right. It was another normal day and the exhibition hall was reasonably quiet. I was standing talking to a couple of work colleagues when all of a sudden my vision started to go fuzzy. It's really hard to explain — I wasn't losing my sight (remember, only one eye here!), but everything just went blurred, sparkly, distorted. It was like my eye had turned into a kaleidoscope. Not like those weird little microbe parties you get — this was different. The edges of my vision had become fractured, and there were sharp lines going right across the centre of my sight. I also had a blind spot: I could look but I couldn't see. I had no idea what was going on and started to become a little concerned. I sat down and held my eye — all the while feeling this terrible headache coming on. Thirty minutes later it had passed, but I had no idea what had happened. It would be years later that I would discover this was called a *retinal migraine*. It's not uncommon and some people have tried to capture what it's like to experience it.[75] I took the afternoon off, somewhat worried about this odd occurrence. The headache and nausea soon passed, and I returned to work the next day.

Being a BBC event, the Beeb themselves were naturally very interested in what we were doing and, a couple of days later, we were told that Radio Bristol would be transmitting their entire breakfast show from the exhibition. How exciting! Some of the group were nervous — I couldn't wait. And this was not my first encounter with Radio Bristol either.

When I was a kid, I used to listen to the late night phone-ins on my Walkman. Every night they would run a competition where they'd play a couple of notes from a song and you had to guess what it was. One night I was listening in and, upon hearing the two notes, I shot up in bed — I knew what it was! I dashed downstairs (I know, I should have been asleep) and yelled, "Mum! I know what it is!" She had no idea what I was talking about but I picked up the phone, called the number, and got straight through.[76]

"Radio Bristol, what's your answer?"

"Hi! It's 'You Ain't Seen Nothing Yet'!"

"Well done! And who's it by?"

---

75 → It really is just like this.

76 ♫ Want to have a guess before you read the answer?

"Oh. What? I have no idea! Hold on a minute!"

I wasn't expecting them to ask me who sang the bloody thing! I ran to the garage, climbed into the car, and frantically pulled out every cassette cover from the glovebox. Minutes later I found it, ran back in, and picked up the phone.

"Hello? Are you there? The band is Bachman Turner Overdrive."

"That's right! Hold on, we'll put you through now."

Oh my goodness, oh my goodness! I was going to be famous! I got through to the radio host, the late Roger Bennett, and we chatted a bit about what I did (school) and no doubt he quipped about me being up late. He asked me what the song was and who it was by and I told him. Cue the sound of applause and a trumpet fanfare as he congratulated me on my answer. And then it was time to find out my prize. And what did I win? After all that running around and ransacking the car, what did I win? A sachet of coffee. Yup, a sachet of sodding coffee. I didn't even drink the stuff!

Despite my disdain for the much-loved bean, it probably would've come in handy the morning Radio Bristol arrived. We all got there super-early and within minutes of opening, the venue was full. John Turner, the host of the show, was milling about, interviewing people about their experiences of the exhibition and about using this new thing called 'the World Wide Web'. It wasn't long before the exhibition co-ordinator got us all together.

"Who wants to be interviewed about the exhibition?" she asked.

It was one of those moments when everyone seemed to take a step back and I found myself the one left at the front. I looked around, saw no one was particularly interested, and

— not being one to shy away from the limelight — offered my services. I made my way over to the stage, took my seat, and shook John's hand. I can't remember if this was before or after my naked avatar experience, but I made a mental note not to talk about it. I cleared my throat and called upon the Gods of Confidence for an inspirational radio interview. They must have been listening because it went really well. I was quick-witted and confident and I loved the verbal sparring match we had going on. I just hope David Gray never gets to listen to it. [77]

When I wasn't being interviewed on breakfast radio or stripping off naked for skateboarding avatars, most of my time was spent walking around the exhibition helping out young and old alike. I remember Mum and Dad came to see what I was doing, and trying to get Dad to use a mouse was harder than you may have thought. It's funny to consider that he now has his own laptop and is a dab hand at finding his favourite songs on YouTube and Spotify, even when it's two in the morning.

If it wasn't particularly busy, I would listen to music online or see how my own tunes were doing. I was, by this stage, writing a fair bit of drum and bass on a software package called Reason. I'd become pretty proficient at using it and would put my tracks on a website run by BT called *GetOutThere*. My music was often reviewed and got some great feedback: particularly one track called *Sicilian Beat*.[78] This was well before the days of YouTube, Soundcloud, and other forms of

---

77 ♫ Points to note: a) I sound so young, b) my voice is so much more high-pitched and, c) I occasionally sound like a numpty.

78 ♫ Some of my very early drum and bass. A little rough around the edges, but still gives me a tingle.

social media, so mass exposure was not a real consideration here — it was just nice to talk to other musicians and get some constructive criticism. Whilst listening to music, I'd usually chat to friends on MSN Messenger too. Sometimes one of the girls from the drama workshop would pop up and say "hello" and threaten to come down and ransack the place with the rest of their mates. However, on this occasion, it was an old University friend who popped up and engaged me in one of the most bizarre online moments I've had. And I've had a few.

I'd known Daniel since the first year of university. Daniel was, and still is, one of my best friends. He's a few years older than me — something I'll always have over him. He always carries an air of gravitas that I often lack, but is never pompous or arrogant. He's also a really strong actor and, whilst not doing the actual drama degree itself, was often cast in some of the big productions throughout the year. He was good at anything he turned his hand to. He could juggle fire clubs for crying out loud! I hate him.[79]

Whilst I was working at Future World, Daniel was a lowly being like me trying to make his fortune in the world of website design. It was on this fateful day that he sent me a message on MSN, and the conversation went something like this:

"Dan! How are you?"

"I'm very good, Daniel! How are you?"

"How's Future World going?"

"Yeah good, good. How's the website building going?"

"Great! I'm building a website for a body piercing studio."

"Ooooh!" I laughed. "How exciting!"

---

79 I don't really. Not all the time, anyway.

"Indeed it is."

Pause.

"So... ever thought about getting your knob pierced?"

"LOL"

"I can get it done for you for free."

"I'm sure you can but I don't want my knob pierced, thanks."

"Yes, you do."

"No, I don't."

"Yes. You do."

"No! I don't!"

"Great. I'll come and pick you up tomorrow."

And with that he went offline and the conversation was over.

Me, get my knob pierced? What an utterly ridiculous idea, I thought to myself as I walked over to an old lady flapping her arms at me for help. But whilst I was showing her the delights of how to set up an email account, the ludicrous seed that had been planted in my head slowly began to grow.

I haven't done anything whacky for a while, I thought to myself.

"It could get me laid!" I chuckled.

How do I ask work for time off for *this*? I pondered.

"It could get me laid!"

Not surprisingly, that seemed to be the recurring theme. I hadn't been intimate since leaving Canterbury and my loins were starting to twitch. I finished work for the day, went back home, called Daniel, and asked him what time he was going to pick me up.

* * *

Sitting in the car on the way to Bournemouth, I looked at Daniel — not for the first time — and asked him why I was doing this.

"It's something different!" he exclaimed.

This was true.

"And it's all for a good cause. The guy who'll be doing your piercing is a trainee."

WHAT?! I grabbed the car door handle and tried to make my escape — ready to leap to my death on the A32 rather than have my dingle-dangle butchered by an inexperienced piercer. Daniel laughed and assured me that I was in safe hands. Somehow that sounded worse.

An hour later and I was sat in the treatment room, more nervous than I had been at any hospital visit — which is saying something. The piercer walked in covered in blood.[80] He explained that I would be having a 'Prince Albert' — a ring through the helmet. He showed me a picture.[81] Fine, I thought. This is all perfectly normal. We went into a small room, and he asked me to lie down on the bed. I pulled down my trousers and boxer shorts to reveal a willy the size of an acorn. I was clearly very nervous.

He got his instruments ready, sanitised my milkman and proceeded to stick a circular blade inside the urethra which — with a little push — made a hole just below the helmet. It was actually pretty painless. Seconds later I looked down to see a ring and, Bob's yer uncle, I had a Prince Albert.

"Now," he said, "whilst I'm here... fancy a ring in your ball-bag?"

---

80   Not really.

81   → Obviously don't look if you don't want to. It's just a willy though. Not mine, I hasten to add.

I laughed. "Fuck it, why not!" and he proceeded to pierce me in the lower region of my nutsack. I had no plans for this whatsoever, but I was feeling brave and undoubtedly drunk on endorphins. I was also thinking of the great story I had to tell the folks back at Future World. Maybe I could test this out in the 3D avatar machine too! Ring inserted, he announced that it was all over and helped me off the bed. To finish the proceedings he wrapped my bits in a mass of bandages and, best of all, put a surgical glove over the top, to keep it in place. It looked like I had a chicken between my legs.

I left the studio with a bulge in my pants like Errol Flynn on a good day.[82] I had been instructed not to do anything too adventurous, which scuppered my plans to go rock climbing that afternoon. Instead, we traipsed around the shops of Bournemouth, counting down the hours until I could 'unwrap'.

As it happened, I was also going to appear on TV that very same night. A few weeks earlier I had recorded a short piece for *Right to Reply* — a consumer programme that challenged TV makers about their programmes, schedules, and more. Some months before I had emailed them, concerned about the ever-increasing amount of alcohol adverts that were now starting to appear in the ad breaks during soaps, sporting events, and family entertainment. They were interested in pursuing this further, and asked me to come to London to talk to some industry heads. Cool! I travelled up the night before as I was determined to be fresh for the next day. Typically, I barely slept. I couldn't stop thinking about what to ask and when I 'awoke' the next morning I felt lethargic and brain-dead. To make things worse, when I met with Channel 4 they

---

82   Did you know that the phrase 'In like Flynn' is directly related to our Errol? The dirty little monkey.

had changed the agenda. They now wanted me to talk about changes to advertising on ITV — something I knew nothing about. It ended up being a bit of a disaster as I had no questions prepared, didn't really know what I was talking about and, thanks to no sleep, had the mental capacity of a zombie.

However, piercing or not, I was still going to be on television. By the time we got back to Daniel's flat I was absolutely starving, so we ordered a load of Chinese food and I prepared myself for my moment of stardom. I suddenly remembered that, earlier that day, I had gotten my knob pierced. I looked down at my bulge. All day I had been as careful as could be to ensure I didn't knock it or loosen it, but curiosity was starting to get the better of me and I was desperate to see what it looked like.

"Do you mind if I have a quick bath?" I asked Daniel and his girlfriend Jenni, thirty minutes before I would become a household name.

With no immediate resistance from my genial hosts I ran the bath — making sure it wasn't too warm as hot water and freshly-pierced genitals tend not to mix. I carefully got myself undressed, the cockerel between my legs looking up at me. I laughed at how ridiculous all this was. I slowly pulled the surgical glove off, which in turn made a satisfying 'pop'.

I gently lowered myself into the bath. This was the moment of truth.

As I began to slowly unwrap the bandage I could see some spots of blood starting to appear. No real surprise, I thought. I did get a bit of a shock, however, as I started to unwind the last piece of bandage: I could see a blood clot the size of a cricket ball on the end of my knob. I gulped. And suddenly felt very faint. What should I do?! I couldn't just leave it there, dangling like some gory bauble. So, like a kid with a scab, I poked it. Nothing. I tried to prise it off when suddenly it detached itself, causing a plop in the water where it burst upon impact. I was now sat in a bath of my own blood. I felt myself get weaker and weaker and, accepting this grim reality, lay back and closed my eyes.

"DAN! YOU'RE ON THE TELE!!"

sigh

So there I was, sat in a bath of my own blood whilst in the other room I was missing my first national TV appearance and a pile of spare ribs. I slowly pushed myself out of the bath and — recognising the situation I was in — called out for Daniel, asking if he was free for a minute. I thought it was better asking for him than Jenni because I guessed she probably didn't want to see my genitals covered in blood, let alone her bathroom. I dried myself off, wrapped my bits in some new bandages, and made my way back to the lounge.

Daniel cleared his throat.

"I think it might be best if you slept in your own bed tonight."

Two hours later I was back at home.

He was right. The next morning I awoke to find that I had bled so badly it had gone through to the base of the mattress.

Still, at least it was free.

18. OMG

FUTURE WORLD WAS COMING TO AN END. FROM TEACHING the young and old how to use the Internet, to explaining the rise of digital TV, to appearing naked in a 3D avatar machine, my time was up.[83] It culminated in a huge bash in London for all the cities that had hosted a Future World event where I proceeded to drink my body weight in wine (no mean feat I can assure you). I was remarkably okay until the minibus journey home whereupon I spewed numerous times — made all the more interesting by the fact that my dad had sorted out the minibus hire. Our driver was not impressed. A week later we congregated again for our own local meal which was brilliant fun, especially when everyone asked me to show my piercing which I promptly plopped out on the table. My boss was not impressed. Clearly, this was not a good time for

83 → It really was a great team. I somehow look exceptionally studious in this one.

impressing people.

As luck would have it, I managed to find some work as soon as Future World finished, and it was something I had vowed never to do: telesales. Well, that's not quite true. It was working for a well-known ISP (Internet Service Provider) and my job was to set up new accounts for those wanting to join the Net. Whilst the notion of working in customer services had always sent a shiver down my spine, this didn't seem too bad — especially considering I had just spent three months showing people how it all worked. Also, I wasn't selling anything — they were coming to *me*. Plus, I got a pound for every account I set up on top of my hourly pay. I signed up thirty on the first day. This I could do.

It was becoming quite apparent that I had a good face for telephones. I had always felt confident talking on the phone. Maybe this confidence stemmed from the days of nervously calling Red Maids, or long, soppy phone calls with girlfriends during my teens.[84] I'd also proved this to myself when I went through the university clearing process at eighteen, but I was a few years older now and a few years wiser too. Fortunately, even though I had gone from Bristol to Canterbury and back again, I had no discernible accent. My telephone voice was rich and warm. It could sympathise, flirt, inspire. Whether you were eighteen or eighty, I somehow had the skills to communicate in a language you could understand. Working on the phones afforded me a degree of anonymity I was comfortable with. Like I said: a good face for telephones.

One benefit the employees had was the full use of their in-house chat programme — a bit like MSN Messenger or

---

84   "You hang up". "No, you hang up". "No, *you* hang up". Etc.

Facebook chat today. You could login, see who was online, and start conversing.

It was during one dull evening that I started chatting to a girl called Mandy. We'd spoken a couple of times in reality when we bumped into each other in the kitchen but, as was the way with me, I was usually a tad shy when talking to girls. I needed a bit of time to get comfortable, to find my voice. But communicating through chat was a method I was comfortable with. Just like the phones, it afforded me a degree of anonymity and words were now my weapons.

I don't know how it happened, but our chat started to get a little naughty. And then more and more naughty. Until, finally, we were pretty much having full-blown chat-sex at work. My fingers were a blur.[85] I looked up over my computer monitor and her eyes caught mine. We reached our virtual climax and breathed a virtual sigh of relief. I offered her a virtual cigarette.

Mandy typed:

BRB

And I looked up to see her dashing out of the office.

Five minutes later she returned — wicked grin intact.

Sorry. Had to nip to the loo. I needed that. You were amazing!

And I was. At last, I thought to myself, all my years of writing are finally paying off!

11pm and we were finished for the night. We shared the lift down, signed out, and stood outside in the cold. We laughed about the experience — and then we snogged. Properly this time. We arranged to go for a drink the following night.[86]

---

85   From typing, Mum. From typing!

86   Mum and Dad: adult content alert!

The next night couldn't come fast enough. Having been in the sexual wilderness since moving back to Bristol, things were finally starting to look up. I made a mental note to get my genitals pierced more often if this was going to be the outcome! We met at a restaurant in the centre of town, but within an hour we were back home and shagging like rabbits. I thought Christmas had come early — which was a coincidence as it was only a few weeks away. Seriously though, this was amazing for me. It reminded me that:

a) I was attractive to someone
b) I could have sex and
c) I could make someone orgasm.

That was the best bit. I'm not quite sure if my housemates agreed as she screamed the place down but I couldn't have cared less — I was loving every sordid second of it.

This all seemed too good to be true and I quickly found out that it was. She soon told me that she was, in fact, engaged. Oh joy. How should I feel about this? A very large part of me felt sorry for the guy in question but then part of me thought, well, you're clearly not happy in your relationship if you've made this choice so let's carry on making whoopee. But it put a slant on things for me — a slant I soon forgot the next night when she gave me a blowjob in a shop doorway.

It was getting closer to Christmas. I'd already had a years worth of treats in the space of two weeks, and now Mandy wanted to shower me with extra gifts too. What had I done to deserve this?! Whatever it was, I wasn't complaining. That Christmas I was given a new mobile phone and a shirt with *Porn King* emblazoned on the back. The only way I could have felt more special is if she'd bought me a sack load of myrrh.

Christmas came and went and after a traditionally heavy New Year I was now faced with the prospect of having to work on January 2nd. Hallelujah. I was praying that most of the UK would be too tender to want to sign up to a new Internet provider, so I turned up for my shift expecting it to be a quiet day. How wrong I was. No sooner had I walked through the door than I was collared by my manager.

"The New Accounts system isn't working. We want you to work on a different area today."

"Okay. What's that?"

"Stopping people from leaving."

"What?! I've got no experience of that at all, and I've had no training either."

"Well, just do the best you can."

"Are you serious? Surely this is really bad business. If I was thinking of leaving and was put through to someone who didn't know what they were doing, I *definitely* would decide to leave! Putting me in this role is a bad idea. Why don't I go home and when the lines are working again, I'll come back?"

"No. We want you to do this."

"Well I'm not going to do it. It's bad business acumen. Call me when the lines are fixed."

And with that I left, chuffed to bits that — for the first time in my life — I had used the word 'acumen'.

Just as I got home my new mobile phone buzzed in my pocket. It was the recruitment agency.

"Why have you quit?!" a voice screeched at me.

"I haven't quit! The job I was employed to do is temporarily unavailable and I refuse to do something that I have no training in! Why put me in a situation that is likely to annoy their customers even more? Can't you understand that?"

"Well, they don't want you back."

And with that I was out of work.

19. LOVE

IT WAS AT THIS TIME THAT I DECIDED TO BECOME A WORLD famous comedy writer. I'd had enough of temp jobs and idiot line managers and scrabbling for the next bit of income, and the time had come to make comedy writing a reality. Of course, I had to get some work whilst I sorted it out and managed to get a job as a receptionist with the Bristol Youth Offending team. Answering phones gave me time to write, and it was here that I came up with a variety of sketches. These were odd, often dark affairs. Chris Morris's *Jam* had recently been on TV and was a big influence on my writing — having already heard the radio shows a few years before. It showed me that comedy could be dark and disturbing yet also very funny. I spent the next few weeks taking calls and writing, creating my own morsels of darkness in the form of *Security,*

Pride and Joy, and *Experience not Necessary.*[87]

Around the same time, the BBC launched a competition to find new sitcom writers and I jumped on the opportunity. In typical BBC style, they cited classics such as *Only Fools...* and *Blackadder,* their dedicated website exploring what made these particular shows so great. I was never going to write a *Blackadder,* so instead of dodgy market traders and historical figures, I decided to write about something I knew: temping.

Love Bugs was set in a dating agency, run by a mad, old woman (I had Lesley Joseph in mind) and her two office workers — both failed graduates desperate for fame, recognition, and a bit of love. Sound familiar? I devised a six-episode series and spent the next month writing just one of those episodes. It was incredibly hard work and by the time I came to sending it off it was well over 30 minutes and full of things I couldn't bring myself to cut. Unperturbed, I printed it off, bound it up, and sent it off to the BBC, eagerly waiting a response.[88]

Whilst working on *Love Bugs,* I would send snippets of the script to a couple of the girls from the theatre workshops. I figured that if it made sixteen-year-old girls laugh then it was hopefully reaching a target audience the Beeb were interested in. During this time, Simon (remember him from the Casino?) moved in with me — along with the gorgeous girl. They were now a couple, much to my joy and misery. In truth, I loved their company. We'd often go out and get absolutely hammered on jugs of Vodka and — something new to me — Red Bull. I'd never experienced a drink so full of chemicals

---

87 → Have a read — if you're brave enough! MWAHAHAHA!

88 I got a response. It was "Thanks but no thanks", delivered in that positive BBC way. I wasn't that bothered.

that you could smell it before you tasted it.

We were at a bar one night, indulging in our favourite tipple, when I heard a group of girls make their way in. I casually glanced over... and suddenly realised it was five of the girls from the drama workshop! They ran over to me, screaming as they did so.[89] I bought a round of drinks and we chatted about the fun we'd had, catching up on what they were doing now (GCSEs, mostly). A few drinks later and it was time for them to go. I asked them where they were off to.

"THE POWERHOUSE!!" one of them shrieked, and proceeded to make the 'Sign of the Horns' with her hands. I rolled my eyes: death metal. Eugh. They tried to get me to go but I politely declined, explaining that mosh pits weren't really my cup of tea. I promised that I would experience it some other time.

A week later and that time had come. I met up with a couple of the girls in town, had a drink, and headed to the Powerhouse. I can't deny that I was a little nervous. Beats and bleeps are my element and I was now suddenly thrust into a world of grinding guitars, shrieking vocals, and hundreds of long-haired goths, usually trying to smash each other to a pulp. I stood to the side, feeling somewhat old. An hour later and it was becoming clear that one of the girls had clearly engaged in a bit too much 'fun juice': she was slumped in the bogs, puke everywhere. I made my way over and managed to carry her out. It was time to go.

I ordered a taxi back to my flat. She was in a really bad way and I decided I had to do something I really didn't want to do: call her mum. One of the girls, Sara, gave me her mum's

89   In a good way.

number. I took a deep breath, punched in the digits, and explained the situation. She was very grateful to me for looking after her daughter and said she would be round straight away. I hung up and breathed a sigh of relief. Within a few minutes her mum arrived and I helped her carry her daughter out of the flat and into the car. As they left, Sara squeezed my hand, gave me a hug, and thanked me for helping out.

A couple of nights later, Sara and I went out for a drink with another friend, back to the Powerhouse to engage in more thrashcore. When I turned up to meet them, Sara was on her own — her friend couldn't make it. We bought a drink, went upstairs to some sofas and sat back, talking about the other night and how it could have been so much worse. And then silence. Comfortable silence. We looked at each other. And we kissed.

More silence. Comfortable silence.

We kissed again, this time for longer and we held each other tight. None of it felt forced, none of it felt wrong. In fact it felt very, very right. We left the Powerhouse and Sara got into a taxi to go back home. Our eyes locked again as we kissed each other goodnight. I stood on the pavement and watched as her taxi pulled away, a deep, rich smile growing across my face.

And then my mind went into overdrive.

How the hell did *that* happen?! Was it a one-off? She's seventeen and I'm twenty-four! What do I tell my parents? What do I tell *her* parents?! I just wanted to enjoy this moment, and so I temporarily erased those thoughts as I skipped back home.

* * *

I was still living in my rather wonderful basement flat in Bristol, but now with a new set of friends. I knew Josh from University and he had decided to make the wise choice to move down to the West Country. I also discovered that, literally over the road, friends of friends from Uni were living in a huge shared house too. My social network was expanding and I became really close friends with those that were living there. Indeed, we still are to this day, though most of them are now married with kids — so seeing them as much as I once did is difficult.

Our flat had three great assets: decks, music, and a pool table. We had all put some money together and bought ourselves an eight-foot American pool table that sat right in the heart of our lounge. Not ideal you might think, but we didn't care — it was immense fun.[90] What made it even more fun was when Obi, one of my flatmates, came back home after a night on the piss and challenged me to a game of pool. The rules: if I 7-balled him he would have to roll a joint and I got second goes on it. But if I 8-balled him (i.e. he didn't pot a single ball), he would have to roll a joint and then simply give it to me. It was like taking candy from a baby.

As well as losing at pool, Obi's other great trick was having no idea where he was. One night, at about four in the morning, Sara and I were fast asleep when suddenly my bedroom door burst open. I looked up to see Obi standing there with his cock in hand, pointing straight at me.

"What the fuck are you doing?" I blurted out, half asleep.

He mumbled something incomprehensible and then proceeded to piss all over my floor. I jumped out of bed and

90 → Oh how different I look compared to that cherub playing snooker back in Chapter 2.

pushed him towards the bathroom, piss arcing everywhere. The next day he had no memory of doing it — but that didn't stop me giving him a bucket and sponge to clean it up. A week later and he did it again. I've never hit anyone but this was the closest I came to knocking someone out. If he wasn't so out of it I probably would've done. When I woke him up the next morning with a bucket and sponge hovering above his face, he let out a groan of sorry realisation.

During those summer months, Sara and I tried to spend as much time together as we could, even though I had to work. I had found another temp job — this time at the Royal Bank of Scotland doing some audio typing and general admin. This was on a week-by-week basis and I was constantly concerned that I was going to be out of work again. I needn't have been. After a couple of weeks of being there my department found out that they were being closed down in three months time and that everyone was going to lose their job. I felt really sorry for these people who I had become nicely acquainted with and who now found themselves in a very precarious position. The only positive thing that came out of this (for me, at least) was that I now had a line manager who hated RBS with a passion, and was more than happy to sign off my time sheets without even looking at them. I'd often phone him up on a morning and ask, "Do I really need to come in today?" knowing that he knew I was in bed with my nubile young girlfriend.

"See you tomorrow," he'd chuckle.

As well as working at RBS I had also found some evening work teaching music production at a local Community Centre called The Park. It was only a couple of hours a week but it was a start. I was teaching all ages how to use Reason — the music making software that I had taught myself over the years. It was a great experience and it taught me how to work with learners of all age ranges and experience. I even got to work with a student who was severely deaf — a challenge I never thought I would face.

I was talking to one of the tutors one evening when he said, "Have you heard of Access to Music? You should give them a call." I hadn't, but a quick search on the Web showed me that they delivered courses in performance, music technology, and more. If only I could work for someone like that and leave the world of typing forever!

Spurred on by my desire to get out of the temping rat race, I sent them an email explaining who I was and what I was interested in. A few days later the Centre Manager called me up and asked if I would like to come in for an interview. I looked at my wardrobe and considered what to wear. Do I wear a suit for an interview at a music college or something a bit more... musical? I took the bold step to wear my Reason t-shirt — a somewhat geeky decision but one that I felt justified in making as it demonstrated my passion for music technology.

Upon arrival I was given a tour of the facilities, which were jam-packed with rehearsal rooms, a fully working studio, and a live room (where the likes of Massive Attack had recorded). And – much to my delight – there were computers everywhere. Myself, the centre manager and the assistant centre manager sat in the studio and talked about my experience. I explained that I had a degree in drama, that I had produced soundscapes for theatre and had been resident DJ at University too (coincidentally, the same uni that the centre manager had attended). I explained that I had taught myself how to use different software packages over the years, but had found Reason to be my software of choice. I explained that I was writing lots of music too: mostly drum and bass, but also that I was pro-active in getting tracks up online and giving feedback to other musicians. I also mentioned that I was doing little bits of home tuition as well as teaching at the Community Centre. They seemed suitably impressed and told me that there was a job available: course manager for the *Creating Music Through Technology* course. Wow! What a title! I wish I'd known about this before doing a drama degree! It all sounded too good to be true. And then it looked like it probably was. Without any real prior teaching experience they were a little unsure as to whether I was ready for a role as big as this. I emphasised just how interested I was in helping people learn how to write music on computers, and that my own self-taught skills and passion was all I could offer at this stage. We shook hands and I was told that they would let me know.

Two days later they did indeed let me know: I hadn't got the job. They were very impressed with my passion (they especially liked my Reason t-shirt), but they felt that I just wasn't quite ready for this particular role. They would keep my record on file though — just in case.

I was devastated. This was the first time in years I had found a job that I truly wanted to do, and I was now utterly resigned to a life of typing letters. My three months at RBS now up, I started to look for full-time secretarial work. I tidied up my CV, slapped on my suit, and ventured towards the recruitment agencies once more.[91]

As if that wasn't bad enough, our time at Pembroke Road

---

91   Those that I wasn't barred from anyway.

was about to come to an abrupt end. It all started when a massive water pipe burst at the top of our road — sending thousands of gallons of water into our flat. Whilst it was a quick and effective way to finally clean up the last few drops of Obi's piss, it totally ruined our carpets and some of our property. I was so enraged by Bristol Water's paltry offer of £250 compensation that I contacted the local paper. They came and did an interview and took some photos. I wish I hadn't taken magic mushrooms the night before — I looked terrible.[92]

Then, a couple of weeks later, I came home to find that we had been burgled. The bastards had taken my entire CD collection — a collection I had nurtured since I was a teenager at school. Rare gems from my favourite labels like Suburban Base, Moving Shadow, and Reinforced Records — gone. They were irreplaceable. I was mortified.

A week later and we came home to find that the scumbags had returned, this time taking Josh's hi-fi separates: thousands of pounds worth of equipment that he had spent months saving up for. We looked around the flat to see what else they had nicked and it slowly dawned on us that — not only had they made themselves some food in the kitchen — but they'd also sat down in the lounge and watched some TV too. We felt violated. It was time to live somewhere else.

* * *

It was now Friday and the end of an incredibly miserable week. Whilst looking at yet another student house I didn't

---

92   → It took me weeks, but I managed to track down a copy of the article. Not the best print ever. In many ways, it nicely epitomises just how my brain was feeling.

want to live in, I got a call on my phone.

"Hello. Is that Dan Jeffries?"

"Yes. Who's this?"

"Hi, it's John from Access to Music."

"Oh, hi!"

"I'm calling because, well, one of our tutors has had to drop out last minute and we were wondering if you'd like to come and work for us?"

"Are you serious?! What would I be doing?"

"Well it's not exactly what you were after but you'll be teaching our Performance students how to use 4-track recorders and how to compose using music software."

"But I've never used a 4-track before."

"You'll be fine — they're very easy to use. You could come in over the weekend and we'll show you how it works."

"Err, okay! Wow! I can't believe it! Thank you! And when do I start teaching?"

"Monday."

20. ATM

I hung up the phone, picked Sara up, and swung her around the room. The letting agent looked at me as if I had gone mad. I WAS EMPLOYED! I immediately called my parents (after putting Sara down first) to tell them the good news. I have no doubt that my dad went out and celebrated for the both of us that night — his wallet exhaling another sigh of relief. I was so glad that I had waited for the right opportunity. I was adamant that years of schooling and university would not go to waste.

The next morning I woke up, eager to get to Access to Music (known as ATM from this point on) to see what their set-up was like. I was very conscious that I had a new piece of equipment to learn. I didn't know much about 4-track recorders, having mainly written music on software, but I was keen to learn more.[93] As I still couldn't drive (I'd tried a few more lessons but I was never confident enough to continue), Dad had kindly bought Sara and me a car. She dropped me off at the Centre. I gave her a kiss and off I went. It all felt very grown up.

Once inside, I met with some of the tutors I would be working with and was once again shown around the premises, this time being more observant about the set-up and layout. I would be teaching Recording and Music Sequencing to the Music Performance students at Level 2 and Level 3, which was the equivalent of GCSE and A-Level respectively. I would also be teaching the Level 3 second-year students who had chosen to specialise in Music Technology. There were specific modules that I had to deliver and I would have to mark student assignments too. I was to be employed for two days a week. I quickly did some sums and realised that this paid the same as five days a week temping. Sweeeeet.

I spent that Saturday learning how the 4-track worked. Working with 90-minute tapes was fun and reminded me of all those mixtapes and compilations I'd made growing up. I spent some time familiarising myself with the software that the students would be using too. I hadn't used Cubase since Uni, but it didn't take long to get my head around it again and I felt confident about teaching it to my students. 'My students.' It felt like such an odd thing to say — I was barely out of education myself! I wondered if I was really up to the job. Would I cope? Would they fleece me? Could I manage a classroom of teenagers? I had no official teaching qualifications but I was told that this would come with time.

93 → They looked big and scary but were in fact really versatile tools, great for learning the basics of recording.

The ethos was: musicians first, teachers second.

Monday arrived and I nervously made my way to the bus stop. The 51 sat gently purring away, as if awaiting my arrival. As I looked at the timetable to double-check I was getting the right bus, a girl carrying a huge guitar case ran up and jumped on, asking to go to Hengrove shops. She could only be going to ATM so I jumped on too, made the same request and went and sat behind her.

"Are you going to ATM?" I asked nervously.

"Yeah!" she replied. "I'm a new student doing Music Performance. What course are you doing?"

"I'm going to be your teacher!" I beamed back and she high-fived me.

Unfortunately, not all of the students were quite as pleasant as she was. My first day was a proper baptism of fire. I had students who didn't turn up, students who left when they wanted to and — much to my dismay — students who just weren't interested in music technology. I had great fun watching some of the students compose melodies by simply drawing their name into the sequencer with the mouse. I'm not sure Mozart would have done it that way.[94] I finished the first day exhausted but elated.

Tuesday's timetable was predominantly working with the second-year Level 3 students. This was the session I was most nervous about. I knew that these students had been there for two years already, and they knew exactly how the place worked — far better than I did. I was a new teacher — fresh meat — and I awaited their arrival like a sacrificial lamb. The lesson was due to start at eleven o'clock. By five past, no one

---

94 Actually, he may well have done. Who am I to say how creativity should happen?

was there. And then slowly I heard the jangle of chains as a group of students walked into the room, hair like Sid Vicious and with clothes to match. They sat down, looked at me, and I gulped.

I needn't have worried — they turned out to be angels. All of them were there for a reason: to learn about music technology. They had chosen this pathway specifically as they felt they had enough performance skills already and they wanted to learn something new. We spent the next year exploring Cubase in depth, all of them producing a portfolio of music along the way. I got the feeling they were all grateful by the end of it. I knew I had made my mark when, one evening after class as I was waiting by the bus stop, they pulled up next to me and asked if I wanted a lift. I proudly accepted. Thanks to the joys of Facebook, I'm pleased to report that one of those students now runs his own studio, and another has worked with Geoff Barrow of *Portishead* fame. I'd like to think that I helped them a little bit in getting there.

My first year at Access to Music was coming to an end. What had I learned? Well, I'd learned that I had patience when teaching and was able to explain complicated things in a simple way.[95] I'd learned that I was good at giving feedback. I'd learned not to judge people by their appearance and not to be flustered by those students who aren't as interested as you'd like them to be. And I learned that — when it came to teaching — my eyes were a bit of a problem.

At the start of my lessons, I would often do some warm-up activities.[96] I would gather the students into a circle, and we

---

95 Having a techno-phobic family no doubt helped.

96 Once I'd taken the register, I hasten to add — just in case Ofsted are reading.

would play the Numbers Game: a game I had learned when doing drama workshops as a teenager. It involves closing your eyes and trying to count to twenty without two people saying a number at the same time. Doesn't have much to do with music I grant you, but it's a great little exercise to focus the mind and bond the group. After we'd done that a few times I would ask questions about what we had learned in previous lessons. The trouble was, when I pointed at someone, the person standing next to them would automatically assume the question was for them. Why? Because my left eye — the blind one — had drifted so badly that they thought I was looking at them. But what could I do about it? I wasn't going to start wearing an eye-patch and I wasn't going to stop these activities either, so I just had to learn to, a) say someone's name when I pointed and, b) point really specifically. It wasn't the end of the world and it didn't majorly disrupt my lessons, but I was conscious that it was an issue.

My end-of-year review was fast approaching. Those two days a week were not a guarantee and, if they weren't happy with my performance, I might find myself looking for work again. I met with the centre managers and we talked about the past ten months. They were — thankfully — very happy with my performance: I had settled in well, dealt with the admin work, and marked student assignments diligently and on time. How did I feel it had gone? I reiterated the same things: firstly expressing my gratitude at the opportunity to work within music and then saying how pleasing it had been to see students develop their skills at using technology — though sometimes I found it difficult because the music some of them were in to (grunge, death metal, hardcore) was not the music I was passionate about. I really wanted to work on the Creating

Music Through Technology course, and I reminded them that that was the role I had originally applied for. They told me they would be in touch.

* * *

During 2003, Sara, Josh, and I had finally found a new place to live. The two burglaries had turned us in to paranoid wrecks, now desperate to leave what was clearly a prime target. We moved to a house in Bishopston that was perfectly okay but nothing compared to that glorious basement flat I had lived in for the past three years. I remember moving all my stuff into my room, getting out my futon, lying on the bed with Sara and — thinking about what we no longer had — bursting into tears. Crying doesn't come easily to me, so I knew how affected I was by this. It was like the student flat burning down in Canterbury all over again.

However, it wasn't all bad. Bishopston was much closer to town than Pembroke Road and I was surrounded by shops, particularly record shops, which definitely eased the pain. Sara's parents were also nearby, so I would often call round for dinner, sometimes even staying over (something her mum was okay with but I'm not so sure her stepdad was). Our relationship was good though. We had lots of laughs and would often go out clubbing together as I had finally dragged her away from 'the dark side' of thrash metal and into the 'new frontier' that was drum and bass.

I was suddenly producing some of the best tracks I had made in some time — no doubt due to me being the happiest I had been for some time. Reason had released an upgrade with some great new synths and utilities and I was absolutely making the most of them, writing tracks like 'The Gong', 'Chromosome', 'Hijack (We're Alright)', and – a personal favourite – 'Inject Power'. These tunes felt more mature, more rounded.[97] I was starting to get more DJing work too, playing at some of the bigger nights in Bristol. I also took the decision to send off CDs to some of my favourite record labels in the hope that I might get something signed. I knew that lots of the big DJs and producers used AIM (AOL Instant Messaging) to send tracks to each other, but I didn't know any of their contact names — so physical CDs was the only way to do it. I burned twenty-five CDs with six of my best tracks, printed off covering letters, and sent them off, eagerly expecting to be the 'Next Big Thing'. I didn't get one reply.

My first year at ATM was over. I was on my summer break: great because I had six-to-eight weeks of freedom, but utterly terrifying because I had totally run out of money.

And then I got the call.

"Dan. We're really impressed with your first year at Access to Music. We know that you want to work more with the DJs and the Producers so, in light of this, we would like to offer you a full-time position as pathway leader for the Creating Music Through Technology course."

WHAAAAAAAAAAAAAAAAAAAT?!

"If you accept you'll be a full-time employee. You'll be responsible for recruiting and interviewing new students, deciding which level is best for them, and then keeping them on the course. You'll have a team of tutors and course managers that you'll need to help and support. You'll be responsible for organising local events and contribute to national events too.

97 ♫

You'll also be responsible for improving the success rates and retention statistics for the CMTT course, which have of late not been particularly good. You'll also be placed on a salary. How does that sound?"

I was in shock. I was only expecting two days a week, maybe three, and now I was being offered a full-time job with all the trimmings! This was a proper grown-up decision I had to make and I didn't know what to do. I loved the freedom of just working two days a week, but hated the fact that I was low on money during the holidays. Could I really manage a team of staff? Could I really be responsible for the education and development of Bristol's new musical talent?

"Well, I don't know. I'm very grateful for the offer. Can I think about it?"

"You'll get paid holidays."

Bingo.

"Really? Right, okay, that's good. But it's a big commitment. I'm really not sure if I'm ready..."

"Dan, this is a great opportunity. We really think you've got what it takes to push this course forward and bring it up to the standard required. We want you to lead the way."

How could I resist? A sucker for flattery, I duly accepted, hung up the phone, smiled to myself and immediately had a nosebleed.

21. BLOOD AND TEARS

LIFE IS A FUNNY GAME.
Some people have pets.

Some have imaginary friends.

I had nosebleeds.

For as long as I can remember, nosebleeds have been a constant throughout my life. I have no idea when I had my first one (my mum could probably tell you, I'll ask her in a minute), but when I got one, I got it bad.[98]

The pain and disruption was most pronounced throughout my time at school. Once, in my second year, I had a nosebleed that lasted four hours. Yes — four hours. The first hour was spent leaning over a toilet, letting it drip out. When that didn't stop it, I would blow my nose into the loo as hard as I could, hoping that force and dry air would bring it to a

---

98   I asked her. She can't remember either.

halt. Horrible, I know. When *that* didn't work (sometimes it did), I went down to see Matron who would put me in sickbay and instruct me to lean forward, pinching my nose. Y'know — the medical approach. But it was no use. The third and fourth hours were usually spent lying back, whimpering about how useless my life was whilst coughing up huge clots of blood. It was at this point we felt that going to hospital might be a good idea.

One of the boarding masters took me to Southmead Hospital for an emergency cauterisation. I had barely been there five minutes when I pulled the tissue away — to discover it had stopped. Typical. It felt like I had wasted everyone's time and we headed back to school. I'd lost so much blood that I was allowed fifteen minutes extra in bed the next morning. Small consolation but still gratefully received.

Nosebleeds managed to appear at the most inconvenient times and in the most inconvenient places. I've had them in supermarkets, school assemblies, church services, on holiday and more. I'm pretty sure I've even had one when trying to snog a girl. Thank you, Mother Nature. Thank you.

Peculiarly, nosebleeds at University were reasonably infrequent — remarkable considering the situations I put myself through. I assumed they were just part of being a teenager, and that my body had finally outgrown them. However, a couple of years after being back in Bristol, they started to return... and with a vengeance. Once I realised that blowing them out was no longer a successful remedy, I visited the doctor and was prescribed various lotions and potions to try and settle them down. They helped, but none of them stopped the bleeding outright. In July 2001, I was sent to St Michael's Hospital for further examinations but they couldn't find capillaries worthy enough of cauterisation, and so it was more creams and sprays for me.

In 2004, they got worse. I went to visit my GP and he wrote to the ENT Specialists (Ear, Nose and Throat) to see if they could find the cause of the problem. He wrote:

> '*Mr Jeffries' epistaxis [nosebleeds] improved following the use of Naseptin in the past but started again about one and a half month's ago, continuing on an almost daily-basis for about three weeks and then improving. He tried Flixonase for his rhinitis [inflammation of the inside of the nose] for a short time two years ago with little success. He admitted to some increased emotional stress in the last couple of months, and epistaxis [nosebleeds] as a child. He denies any nasal blockage or rhinorrhoea [a runny nose] or nasal trauma.*
>
> *On examination there is bilateral mild erythema [redness of the capillaries or skin] and crusting of both nostrils, more prominent on the left lateral wall. The Little's area is okay. There are some marked capillaries in the mucosa of the nose with no specific point for cauterisation.*
>
> *With a diagnosis of vestibulitis [inflammation of the tissue around the entrance to the nose] I have given him Naseptin cream and I have also advised him on nasal douching and epistaxis. We will review him in 3-4 months' time.*'

Reading other people's medical notes must be a bit weird, so I appreciate you sticking with me thus far. Please don't be too repulsed by the use of the word 'crusting'.

Whatever the reason for my nosebleeds, they were starting to make life difficult. I was beginning to have them at work. There I was, standing up in front of a classroom explaining the intricacies of LFO modulation when suddenly I would sense the slow, warm trickle of blood. The problem was, I would never know if these would last five minutes or five hours. If it was a long one then it would make me incredibly light-headed to the point where I could no longer work and had to go home. I tried every trick in the book but to no avail. It would be a couple of years until we looked to get this fixed once and for all.

When I wasn't a bloody wreck, work and life were generally going well. I was now fully immersed in my new role at ATM: spending lots of time interviewing prospective students, keeping existing students on track, teaching classes, and helping students develop their skills and get through the course. This was the first time in, well, forever that I had a job that I found truly rewarding. Long gone were the days of fruit packing and hanging on the telephone — I was in an environment I loved and I wasn't going to let it go.

And, as I was now a bit more solvent and reaching an age some might call 'mature', Dad wanted to look into the possibility of getting me my own place to live. This was big news. No more rent! No more landlords! No more arguments about washing up! I met with Mum and Dad to discuss the idea. Alix was with a long-term partner at the time and he had recently popped the big question. They were going to get married in the spring of 2005 and Dad was conscious that he had to help them find somewhere to live too. So, always willing to sacrifice my own needs for the good of others, I told Dad not to worry about my circumstances for the moment

— get Alix sorted and then we'd see where we were after that. I think he was somewhat moved by this gesture, as was my sister (and so she should be!). They were, as far as I was concerned, far more important than me. Well, that's not quite right: their *needs* were far more important than mine, and I wanted to make sure they got sorted first. I was fine. Shared living was good enough for the moment. Plus, I was used to this lifestyle. In fact, the idea of getting my own place was a little daunting. I wasn't putting it off, but I was in no great hurry either.

After it became clear that our landlord was a bit of a bellend, we decided to move house. Our new place was great. It was just off the Gloucester Road, had loads of space and — best of all — I had my own studio room for making music. My creativity had been going through a bit of a slump and I hoped that the move into a new house and the fact that I had my own studio space would help me get back into writing good music again. I also bought myself a dedicated music computer. Previously, my work computer and music computer had been one and the same, and — more often than not — work took priority. Having this dedicated space and computer gave me a much clearer frame of mind — somewhere to escape to when I needed a break from ATM. And so it was here that I wrote some of my best material, most notably 'I'm The Daddy', 'Inner Space', and the pleasantly-titled 'Suck Satan's Cock', my tribute to the late, great Bill Hicks.[99] I was also entering more and more remix competitions, where you're given a pack of samples in which you either make a new track or remix an existing one. The Drum and Bass Arena was probably the

99   By 'tribute' I mean that I sampled the arse off of his live CD. Bill's up in heaven now — it's what he would have wanted.

193

biggest drum and bass website around at the time, and I was pleased to win a competition for my track 'The Emperor', jam packed with samples from Star Wars. There was also a competition to remix the EZ Rollers tune 'Roadrunner'. I didn't win but, bumping into Alex Banks only last year (one half of EZ Rollers) through connections at work, I mentioned that I had entered that competition some years before.

"Ahh, the Powdermonkey remix! I remember that. It was really good!"

You had to scrape me off the ceiling.[100]

Sara was doing well for herself too. She was working in a shop just around the corner and had made her own group of friends by doing so. She was also studying a Foundation Degree in Art before making the move to London a year later. I knew this moment was coming but I didn't want to think about it. It might sound weird but I had really seen her blossom over the time we had been together. But now we didn't go out quite as much as we once did. Sometimes I wouldn't see her for a couple of days because she'd been out partying, and I had to be sensible and work. The divide was becoming more noticeable. I never resented her for it because this was *her* time — I had done the same when I was eighteen. But it was clear to me that the age gap — once not even a thought — was now becoming an issue. And so it was, in February 2005, that we finally separated. Or, to be more precise: she dumped me. I was distraught. I knew it was going to happen, but it didn't make it any easier when it did. I blubbed like a baby —

---

100 ♫ Have a listen to all of the above. As an aside, people often asked where I got the name 'Powdermonkey' from. I had my 'Eureka!' moment whilst watching the daytime TV quiz *15 to 1*. Question: *What was the name given to a young boy who would transport and load explosives into a ship's canon at times of war? Answer: Powdermonkey!*

not because I had been rejected but because it was the end of something amazing. I didn't want to let it go, but I knew I had to. She would be off to London in the summer to chase her dreams — I wasn't ever going to stop her doing that.

As with Anthe, I showed little resistance to the decision. Yes I was upset, but at no point did I beg or plead or grovel for her to reconsider. It wasn't in me. I spoke to my sister the next day, trying to explain it and justify it through floods of tears. She was sorry it had ended but explained that — because Sara was off in the summer — maybe it was better now than in a few months time. My dad's approach was a little less sympathetic:

"Fight for her! If you love her, tell her! Don't let her go! Be a man!"

But that was it: I wasn't a man. I didn't *feel* like a man. I didn't have that passion, that animalistic desire to *fight* like a man. I may well have done in my teenage years, but at that moment it just wasn't me. And it's not that I didn't want to, it was more that I *couldn't*. Instead I sat in my room, licked my wounds, and smoked myself silly. That weekend I wrote one of the best pieces of music I've written to date. It's called 'Sudden Sparks' and manages to capture just how I was feeling at the time. Most of my musical output up to that point had been tough drum and bass — this was reflective, melancholic. Once I had written the main melody, I wanted to find a vocal sample, something that reflected my emotional state. I looked through my DVDs and found one in one of my favourite TV shows, *Dream On*: a sitcom that used old public broadcast movies so they didn't have to pay for the copyright. I wanted something that had a timeless feel to it, something that would strike deep into the heart of the girl I loved. I wanted something that would stop her in her tracks, make her think, make her reconsider her actions.

Sadly it didn't. Perhaps Ronald Reagan wasn't quite the voice of reconciliation I was hoping for after all.[101]

101　♫

22. SOLO

I NOW FOUND MYSELF TO BE SHARING THE SAME RELATIONSHIP status as a slice of processed cheese: single.

It took me some time to come to terms with the break-up. For once I had forgotten what being single was like — and I didn't like it. But it was more than that. I'd lost someone who had been in my life for four years — who spoke secret words that only I knew, whose feet rubbed against mine in the night. The whole had become a hole. I had lost my companion.

Life now started to feel like a bit of a daily grind. My days seemed to consist of getting up, going to work, coming home, preparing for the next day, and then going to bed. I felt tired. I didn't want to go out. My musical creativity had nose-dived yet again. And all of a sudden, drum and bass no longer had the same appeal. Why was everything deserting me! It had gotten 'silly': no longer the subtle, menacing force it once was. Clubbers were getting younger and I was feeling older.

Bristol's music scene was starting to change too, reflected by what the new intake of students were listening to. Being Bristol, students had tended to want to write mostly drum and bass and hip hop, maybe some house and garage. But now I was being asked how to write grime: an aggressive music that I had no awareness of and found difficult to engage with. I helped — of course I did — but I found it hard to teach something I didn't have much interest in. I was losing my touch. Maybe I was just getting old.[102]

Whilst drum and bass and my creativity had gone awry, music hadn't fully deserted me yet. After 'Sudden Sparks', I went through a phase of trying to write different styles: some experimental, some more downbeat. They were okay, but nothing to match the weight of previous compositions. I even forced myself to have a break from writing music altogether but that only made things worse. I just wasn't feeling creative and I still wasn't hungry for success, even though I recognised that I would never see success if I didn't try to find it. An opportunity even arose to write some music for a Natural History programme but after trying out a few ideas, I didn't produce what they wanted. "Oh well," I shrugged to myself, complacent in my now familiar lack of ambition.

This wasn't me. I was clearly in a funk.

Living arrangements were becoming more and more unbearable too. All my friends had moved on. The people I was living with were lovely, but I was now twenty-eight and fed up with emptying two-day old clothes from the washing machine and arguing about whose turn it was to put the bins out. So I stayed in my room, listened to Detroit techno, and

---

102   That's twice I've ended a paragraph with the feeling of getting old. Hmmm.

watched old box sets of *The West Wing*.

* * *

A few months after splitting up with Sara, my sister tied the knot. And it was with great pride that I was asked to be best man. I'd never given a best man's speech before and I had a feeling it might be my one and only opportunity, so I decided that this was going to be the greatest best man's speech ever. I spent weeks jotting down anecdotes and evidence and gathering defamatory pictures, determined that this would not be your run of the mill 'stand and read' experience. The night before the big day I went to the hotel where we were having the reception and set up my projector and screen. I chuckled to myself with macabre delight.

There were serious duties to perform too. I had to look after the ring (most people put it on their finger for safekeeping but mine were far too big to do that), and I sat at the front of the church, sweating more than anyone else — including the groom. I had been asked to read a passage from the Bible during the service, something I was used to doing from my days at school. I made sure that I enunciated every word and that I caught the eye of every person there. This was important to me.

After the ceremony, it was time for photos and the reception. At the venue, I checked that the computer and projector were still set up and ready to go. People looked at it inquisitively. I smiled inside. And so once the groom and father of the bride (Dad, in other words) had made their speeches, it was time for me to deliver mine. This time I didn't have socks on my hands.

I looked round the room, took a deep breath, and delivered my opening line:

"My Lords, ladies and gentleman, the bride and groom, friends and family, honoured guests... and Ken."

Now, you obviously don't know who Ken is, but trust me — that's a funny line. It got a huge laugh and a round of applause. Not a bad opener, I thought. I then spent the next few minutes reminiscing about times gone by, cracking jokes about my sister and her new husband. And then I moved on to the real jewel of the speech: my PowerPoint presentation. Yup — a PowerPoint presentation. It had struck me that this would be the most visual way of making more jokes at the expense of my sister, and proceeded to deliver a volley of images, each one funnier than the last. Those years of after-dinner speaking and standing in front of a classroom were finally paying off. Twenty minutes later I got to the last slide and — upon saying my final words — the room rose to its feet, toasted the bride and groom, and then burst into rapturous applause. Friends and strangers approached, telling me it was the funniest best man's speech they had ever seen — and they'd seen a few. I felt like I was the one who had just gotten married! Even though I was acutely aware that I wasn't, I was still on cloud nine.

23. PLUMS AND GUMS

Now that the wedding was over and Dad's bank balance had had a chance to recover, I got the phone call I had been waiting for.

"Dan? It's Dad. It's time we found you somewhere to live."

Fan-bloody-tastic. At last I could escape from living with other people's noise and pubes. I wasted no time in contacting all the estate agents in Bristol, and suddenly I was a bit more awake again — I had something to strive for.

However, as has always been the way with me, give me too many choices and I'll end up picking none of them. I wanted something that was reasonably central if possible because — if I was too far out — I wouldn't be able to get anywhere. But I wanted something with a bit of space and character too. I'd lived in bedrooms for long enough — I wanted to be able to swing at least one cat, preferably two.

The first property I looked at was a house in Filton. On

paper it sounded amazing: separate lounge with real fire, huge kitchen, dining room, three bedrooms (always thinking of space for my studio), and a 100ft garden. Okay, so it was a bit further out than I wanted, but if I had to sacrifice that for space then so be it.

Mum and Dad came with me for a second viewing. I'd already had a look around a few days before and was perfectly happy with what it had to offer. I could tell Dad thought differently.

"Dan, are you sure about this? Yes, it's nice and big, but it's a bit out of the way, isn't it?"

He had a point. It was further out than I had realised, plus there were no bus stops nearby. And, looking around, it felt like the average age of my neighbours was eighty years plus. Was this really where I wanted to live? I weighed up property over location and, after a few minutes consideration, I told Dad it was. He advised the agent to take the property off the market — we wanted to buy.

That night, I couldn't sleep. My brain was working overtime, awash with pros and cons, desperate to figure out if I was making either the best decision or the biggest mistake of my life. Did I want to live that far out? Did I want to be surrounded by the elderly and a plethora of cats? Did I want to commit myself to living somewhere that I might regret in six months time? For hours I wriggled away, tossing and turning as my frontal lobe went into meltdown. I eventually fell asleep, dreaming of garden gnomes and welcome mats.

The next morning I awoke and immediately knew that buying this house was a huge mistake. I phoned Dad, nervous that I might get a bollocking. Instead, he said:

"That's the best decision you've made yet. I'll call the estate agent and let them know. You start looking again."

What a relief! I put down the phone, suddenly excited again. And, for once, I had made a decision — a decision about something big and important — and it felt good. I turned on the computer (who am I kidding, it was already on), and started my search once more. I was fully prepared for days of wading through websites, but was stopped in my tracks on the very first page. "No!" I exclaimed to myself: this was too good to be true. I immediately got on the phone and arranged a viewing for that afternoon.

Sat on the bus heading into town, I smiled to myself — I knew exactly where I was going. This flat was just a few minutes walk from my old school. At one end of the road was Park Street: arguably a contender for the most famous road in Bristol, whilst at the other end was Brandon Hill: a park I had frequented as a schoolboy.[103]

I got off the bus and walked up Park Street, familiarising myself with the shops and bars that I hadn't seen for a while. I turned left onto a little road that I'd never really noticed before and found the flat in question. It was a gloriously sunny day. I looked to my left and saw people strolling about in the park. I looked to my right and saw the hustle and bustle of Park Street. I closed my eyes and could hear nothing but birdsong.

The estate agent arrived and led me down a small flight of steps. In my excitement I had forgotten that this was a basement flat — which meant I had my own entrance. Swish! I had nothing against communal living — but after seven years of sharing a dorm at school, four years of university, and six years of shared houses, I was ready for my own front door.

---

103   And where I had tried my first cigarette: Silk Cut, given to me by a boy in the sixth form — swapped for half a Bounty.

Within thirty seconds of being inside I knew this was the flat for me. It was probably a fifth of the size of the other place, had no real fire, only one bedroom, and no back garden — but suddenly that didn't matter: I was right in the heart of Bristol. I looked around the flat and saw a small room towards the back, too small to be a bedroom. Amazing — I had my own studio too.

The estate agent explained that this was part of a block of flats maintained by a management company, which meant I had to pay maintenance fees. Hmmm, not ideal. But then he reminded me that I also had a parking space out the back, and that this could be rented out for up to £1000 a year. Suddenly not being able to drive had its benefits! I gave the flat one last look around, went outside, climbed the little flight of steps, and rested my chin on the gate. I looked to my right and noticed there was a tree in a tub. It was covered in plums.

"You're my plums now," I whispered to the tree and laughed. I had finally found my home.

* * *

Over the next couple of months, we did a lot of work on the flat.[104] It was looking a little tired, and some of the decor needed an update. What I wasn't expecting was a full-on makeover, but when my dad gets his hands on a property, there are no lengths he'll stop at to make it as wonderful as possible, and I can't express my gratitude enough for helping me out with that. Oh, that and laying down the initial deposit. The flat was transformed from a slightly dingy box to a magnificent,

---

104   I say 'we'. I didn't lift a finger.

modernistic man-pad. The stud partition walls that had divided up little sections of the flat were now gone — giving the layout more room and light. A central wall that had been covered in plasterboard had been taken back to its original brick, pointed out to reveal a stunning centrepiece. Reading the deeds of the flat it became clear this was, once upon a time, a wine cellar — which meant it was lovely and cool in the summer and reasonably warm in the winter. The work took about two months in total, which meant two months of kipping on my mate's lounge floor, but I didn't care. My own flat was being built and I was one happy bunny.

The flat wasn't the only thing undergoing reconstruction however. Whilst between houses I was — for some reason — finding it more and more difficult to eat. My teeth had always been pretty well looked after (a few fillings, I'll grant you), but on the whole, no real issues. The problem was that my lower back-right teeth just couldn't chomp on food. This meant that everything I bit on and ate took place on the left-hand side of my mouth. I went to see my dentist who advised that I had two molars on the bottom right-hand side of my mouth that were in trouble: they were going to need removing. She wrote a letter to the Dental Hospital, eloquently outlining my situation:

Please would you see this very pleasant patient of mine. He unfortunately had not been for a little while[105] and his lower right mesially impacted wisdom tooth has been causing food to build up under it and the lower right second molar, 7⌐ , has a very large distal cavity. Please would you

---

105   Clearly, my claim that my teeth had been 'pretty well looked after' wasn't quite true.

*remove both these teeth as I do not think the prognosis for
them is at all good and [nor is] a long protracted course of
treatment on them [in] which the outcome is not good.*

*Interestingly he feels that his bite has changed and he is
only able to bite on the ⌐8 and I think that he is right
and that his bite was different two years ago. He has been
having pain and swelling in the lower right area around
these two teeth.*

She was right: my bite *had* changed. I too had noticed that
I could no longer eat on the right-hand side of my mouth.
Nor could I do simple biting actions that one might take for
granted: I couldn't bite my nails, I couldn't bite Sellotape to
rip it off, I couldn't gnaw logs (I would have made a useless
beaver). And because of this I had to use the left side of my
mouth for everything. When I looked in the mirror I started
to notice my lower jaw was in front of my upper jaw. That
can't be right, I thought to myself. It's these bastard molars!
They had to go.

I've never been particularly afraid of the dentist, but I can't
say that the prospect of having two huge molars removed
filled me with glee — and right in the middle of moving house
too. But they were causing me problems so they needed to
go. I hoped it would be worth it, just so it would allow me
to eat on both sides of my mouth again. So in October 2005,
I visited Southmead Hospital, closed my eyes, gripped the
chair, and had two large molars removed. A letter from the
surgeon to my dentist confirmed the results:

Thank you for referring the above named patient regarding

the removal of the lower right second and third molars. Daniel attended our outpatient clinic on 17 October 2005 for surgical removal of the two teeth. This treatment was carried out quite straightforwardly under local anaesthesia. We are not anticipating any post-operative complications and we are now happy to discharge Daniel back to your good care.

No post-operative complications? Little did we know that this was the first indication of something much, much bigger.

24. RINGS, FINGERS
AND NOSES

LIVING ON MY OWN WAS GREAT. ALL OF A SUDDEN I HAD THE freedom to do what I wanted. I could roam around naked. I could listen to my music — loud. I could poo with the door open. I hadn't had my own space since the First Year at Uni. I was looking forward to self-sufficiency.

As for the flat itself, it was finally coming together. The small room at the back — my studio — was fitted with a new false ceiling and foam was put over the walls to help dampen the sound and catch any low-lying bass frequencies. I bought a new DJ desk to house my moderate collection of records (believe me, that's not something you want to move around too often), and I made the decision to buy myself a projector instead of a TV. I didn't want the 'One-Eyed God' dominating the room: so instead a £300 projector beamed its magic onto the huge wall in front of my sofa. I first heard Dad using the phrase 'One-Eyed God'. I don't think he was referring to me.

As soon as my studio was ready, I immediately got back into writing music, a sudden wave of creativity washing through my veins. Even though drum and bass had taken a turn for the worse, I wasn't going to let that stop my own output, and continued to write in my trademark style: catchy, lively and sometimes a little bit silly. Tunes such as 'Snigger', 'Kontrol', 'Heaven' and 'Are You My Mummy?' (using samples from the *very* frightening Dr. Who episode, made freely available by the BBC) showed a more developed – dare I say it - mature sound. It was good to be creative again.[106]

As my flat was part of a residential block, there was a committee that would meet every few months to discuss potential works, improvements, and so on. The first meeting was a few weeks after I moved in so — to show willing — I went along. Whilst I love my flat and appreciate the importance of it being in a Grade II listed building, I'm not overly fussed about the rest of it, so I sat quietly, taking everything in. Seated next to me was a big man holding a long, thin case — a case I immediately recognised as containing a snooker cue. Curious, I asked him if he played regularly. He said he was part of a league that played in the snooker club just around the corner. Was I interested in playing? Of course I was! I hadn't really played much snooker since my junior league days (a few casual games at Uni but nothing serious), and now was my chance to play every week, and for free. He gave me a contact number (this sounds a bit like *Fight Club* but I promise you it was nowhere near), and within a couple of weeks I was a member of the 'C' team — ready to do battle with my trusty weapon.

---

106   ♫ Please don't read too much into those titles.

My resurrected snooker career was, well, a bit of a limp cadaver. I played well on some days and couldn't pot a ball on others, and this made me rather angry. I wasn't renowned for getting angry over much, but this lack of consistency wasn't something I was expecting. Why was it I could play brilliantly one week and appallingly the next? Was it purely lack of practice or was there something else going on? One thing I was noticing was that my hands would get very clammy whilst playing: which meant the cue wouldn't glide properly and would stick to the inside of my fingers as I followed it through. I wasn't used to a poor performance in any of my disciplines (well, except for sex and writing music... hang on... that *is* pretty much everything), and I would leave the snooker hall sad and dejected.

One other thing that was really starting to become uncomfortable was my ring. Now, now, Matron, not *that* ring — I mean the one on my finger: the ring Anthe's mum had given me when I was visiting her in Greece. I could not — however hard I tried — take it off. I tried coating it in washing up liquid but it wouldn't come off. I tried sliding thin wedges and levers down the side but it wouldn't come off. I even hired a team of tug-of-war professionals to pull and pull and pull, and *still* it wouldn't come off. I looked at my hands and they looked at me — the ring was not for turning. My hands had always been big, but had they really grown so big that I could no longer take this ring off?! Dad was convinced it was 'water retention'. Not being medically trained I decided to bypass his advice, but I couldn't offer a solution to my large hands either. Maybe I was just fat. In the end, I resigned myself to the fact that I just had big hands, and that they had outgrown a ring that had fitted me when I was young and svelte.

So in the summer of 2006 — having spent hours tugging at a ring that wasn't going to budge — I went into a jewellery store in the centre of Bristol and asked them to cut it off. It's not that I wanted to get rid of it because I didn't, I loved it, but I didn't have the option to take it off, and that was somehow worse. The jeweller went to the back room and returned with a bag of tools. Once she had found the appropriate device she asked me to lay my hand flat on the counter and, with a good amount of strength, she cut one side of the ring, then the other. She stood back and beckoned me to take it off — but still it wouldn't move! My hands were so big that the ring was actually *stuck* on to my finger! I bent the band of the ring back (snapping half of it off in the process), and prised the ancient coin off my throbbing digit. At last — it was free![107]

* * *

My finger was not the only part of my body that was causing me aggravation. My nose was still spouting blood and it was becoming more and more of a problem. Cauterisation clearly had no effect. The creams and sprays that I had been prescribed did little to stem it either. Nosebleeds were happening at work. Nosebleeds were happening on the bus (ever used a *Metro* as a tissue? It's not a good look). To put it bluntly, they were making my life a bloody nightmare — pun fully intended. It was time to take action.

My visits to the Ear, Nose and Throat specialist during the past couple of years had been at a BUPA hospital called The

---

107 → And boy, did it look angry.

Glen.[108] I'd formed a good relationship with my consultant who was happy to see me ad hoc and carry out a quick cauterisation whenever needed. When the nosebleeds started to become unbearable, I went back to see him to find out if there was anything more permanent that could be done. There was: it was called a septoplasty.

A septoplasty always sounded to me like a mixture of Sellotape and Plasticine but I came to realise it was a bit more advanced than that. The operation involved going into the nose to straighten the septum. They do this by removing a bit of bone and then repositioning it to the middle of the nose. Maybe they *did* need Sellotape after all! Most people have a slightly bent septum and live a happy life regardless, but for some a bent septum can be the cause of a constantly blocked nose, or extreme snoring. Sometimes the septum is straightened to allow better access to the sinuses for further operations. Mine was to try and stop nosebleeds. I really hoped it would work.

Thanks to the generosity of my Dad, we were able to go private and book the surgery through BUPA. Now, I'm a huge fan of the NHS (and you'll find out why later) but in this instance, there was a real case for going private. The main benefits were:

a. We didn't have to wait months for surgery
b. We could choose the date that was best for us
c. The hospital was five minutes up the road
d. I had my own private room
e. I didn't have to pay

108   It was up near 'The Bus Shelter' — an infamous hangout for QEH and Red Maids teenagers to meet up before finding a secluded spot on The Downs.

That last point was particularly useful for me. Not so much for Dad, but at this stage I don't think he really cared — the nosebleeds were bad and he wanted me better.

On November 9th, 2006, I checked in to The Glen. Mum came with me (as she so often does in times of medical need) and they explained the procedure in detail. I would be under for about forty-five minutes to an hour, in which time they would go up the nose, remove a bit of cartilage, reposition the bone structure, and then come back out again. It all sounded very straightforward and — ever the stoic — I wasn't worried about the operation one bit. This wasn't life or death, this wasn't cancer or a tumour: this was just the removal of a little bit of bone in the nose. Simple.

With that thought in mind, I was wired up ready for anaesthetic and wheeled off for surgery.[109]

* * *

When I woke up an hour or so later, the first thing I noticed was that I couldn't feel my face. My entire head was wrapped in bandages, save for a small hole for my mouth. I felt like Jimmy Durante with a cold.[110] I reached up to touch my nose but couldn't feel a thing. I looked across the room and saw Mum sat there, pleased that I was okay.

"Water!" I croaked.

Mum came over and held a cup to my lips so I could gently take a sip. Within a few minutes it felt like the Sahara desert

109 → If you'd like to watch a video of a septoplasty in action (and who wouldn't), check this one out. I strongly recommend eating a bowl of strawberries while you do.

110 → For anyone under the age of 80, this is Jimmy Durante and his nose. Legendary.

again.

"Water!" I croaked.

I went to feel my nose again but a nurse stopped me. She advised it was going to be uncomfortable but, should it get any worse, I could always have some painkillers. Never one to turn down the opportunity to stop feeling sore, I mumbled that that would be nice. I put the tablets in my mouth and Mum fed me water again.

"You're to stay in overnight," the nurse told me, "and in the morning we'll take the wadding out of your nose. Then you can go home. Now... would you like something to eat?"

I was, as always, starving and said I would. Ten minutes later, dinner arrived. It looked lovely: far nicer than I had experienced in other hospitals years before. Yet, whilst it looked delicious, I couldn't taste a bloody thing — my bunged-up nose put a stop to that. Never mind. I was alive. I could eat tomorrow. And with that I fell asleep.

* * *

The next day I awoke — sore, uncomfortable, and with a mouth like a camel's arse. The nurse brought me breakfast which I wolfed down and, yet again, couldn't taste a thing. She told me that after breakfast they were going to remove the packing in my nose and then I could go home. 'Hooray!' I thought, even though I was quite enjoying lying in bed and watching daytime TV.

The moment of truth had arrived. Have you ever see a magician pull out a stream of handkerchiefs from his pocket? That's pretty much what happened with my nose. The nurse snipped gently at the delicate material and then proceeded to pull out yards of blood-soaked bandages. When she got to the final few inches, it felt like a golf ball going through a straw. When it finally popped out I yelped with relief. The bandages were caked with blood and gristle — which was to be expected — but crucially, there didn't seem to be any blood flowing upon their exit. This was a good sign. I looked at the nurse and she read my mind:

"Yes, you can go home."

I gave Mum a call and told her that they had removed the bandages and that I was okay to leave. Naturally pleased, she called the rest of the family to tell them the news. We're very good at that: we always keep each other updated. Before I left, the nurse gave me some advice about how to keep the area clean and, if it was still hard to breathe through my nose, not to worry as this would clear up within a few days. I thanked them all for their efforts, gently got into the car, and set off home.

Mum, as mums do, mothered me for the next couple of days — cooking me lots of lovely food and nipping out for painkillers and the like when I needed them. I hadn't been (s) mothered like this for ages, so I absolutely made the most of it. To be fair, I was still sore. I didn't want to make any sudden movements in case I bashed my shnoz by mistake, so I felt justified in having my own private help for a short while. Within a couple of days I was feeling much better and — mothering duties done — Mum made her way back to Weston.

25. WOOF

I HAD MADE A PROMISE TO MYSELF A FEW WEEKS BEFORE THE septoplasty that, once surgery was over and I had recovered, I was going to get myself a dog. We'd never had dogs growing up. We had a cat called Peanut and a few goldfish won at the local fairground, but nothing that ever went 'woof'.[111] My only real involvement with dogs was when I used to stroke those beautifully well-trained guide dogs at the Lauriston Hotel for the Blind. But aside from that, dogs rarely featured. So, whilst I was perfectly content with my own company, I felt that my life could do with another soul of some sort, and — as there was no immediate sign of a girlfriend on the horizon — a four-legged friend might be just the solution.[112]

I didn't want a puppy — that much I knew. Puppies are

---

111   I was terrible with goldfish. I used to scoop them out of the tank and hold them in my hands until they jumped back in. I think I liked the power.

112   I am not, repeat, <u>NOT</u> comparing dogs to girls.

like babies, and whilst I was nearing thirty and starting to have some paternal twinges, a puppy required twenty-four hour attention. I couldn't do that. Teaching was a full-time commitment, and I was sometimes out of the house 8-10 hours a day. I didn't want to come back home to find chewed up wires and my records floating in wee. If I wasn't going to have a puppy, I figured the best move was to adopt a dog. I went online and found the Bath Cats and Dogs Home. I looked through numerous doggie profiles and started to notice a trend: they needed lots of exercise, could be destructive, and often required an experienced trainer. I was definitely *not* an experienced trainer, and for a second I put the whole idea to one side — thinking that this was too much of a commitment and that, more importantly, it wouldn't be fair to the dog. Or to me. Yet... still I wanted one. A few days later I called Mum and asked her if she fancied a trip to the Dog's Home. She said she did.

Some weeks had now passed since the surgery, and my nose was clearing up nicely. The swelling had gone down and I could breathe through it again — allowing me to indulge in the olfactory delights of a home built for dogs. I'd never been to a place like this before. I felt excited and sad in equal measure. As we walked around we could see all kinds of dogs — big ones, small ones, yappy ones, quiet ones. All had notes explaining their behaviour and their conditions and — as I had seen on the website — they all needed regular exercise, constant company, and an experienced trainer. I didn't stand a chance.

Just as we were getting ready to leave, I noticed two dogs quietly lying in the sun. I looked at their notes: Norman and Millie. Norman was an eleven-year-old Tibetan Terrier, Millie a ten-year-old Shih Tzu x. They had been found abandoned in their owner's garden some years ago. A little light bulb came on in my head. Two old dogs. Now surely *they'd* like a nice, warm home? I asked one of the helpers if I could take them for a walk.

As she put their collars on, I could see that Norman's legs were shaking and his back was bereft of fur. As I walked them towards a field, Norman started barking at the other dogs around him. Millie, however, was oblivious to it all and trotted along quite contentedly. We spent a good twenty minutes walking around the field — just getting used to navigating two OAP dogs. My brain was weighing up all the ramifications. We walked them back to their cage where they had their collars removed and the gate was closed behind them. I looked at Mum and she smiled. And suddenly, this became an incredibly easy decision to make.

"I think I'd like to give them a new home."

A couple of days later I had a call from the Dog's Home. They wanted to come and visit: to see my surroundings and make sure I was fit and decent to look after them. When the lady from the dog's home arrived, she looked round the flat and observed that there was no outdoor space.

"I have one of Bristol's biggest parks at the end of my road," I pointed out.

She asked what I did for a living and I told her that I was a teacher. How long would I be out of the house? I said sometimes eight hours a day. This was the crunch part. I knew that leaving dogs alone for long periods of time wasn't healthy, but I promised that I would do all I could to find people to walk them at lunchtimes. She was, thankfully, very relaxed about it. Her attitude was that they were old dogs: they didn't, in reality, need a lot of walking. And, because there were two of them, they could keep each other company. In her eyes it was better that they lived here with someone that loved them than spend the rest of their days cooped up in a cage. She turned to me and smiled: I could adopt the dogs.

The next day Mum and I went to Bath to pick them up.[113] I was nervous as hell. I suddenly had responsibility! I would need to feed them and water them, walk them and entertain them. But this was, in truth, exactly what I wanted. We arrived at the home and, whilst they were collecting the dogs, we bought some new beds, some toys, and some food. They told me that we would have to bring Norman back every couple of months for a check-up, as he had an overactive thyroid gland. They gave me some cream to rub on to his back and some tablets to put in his food. Clearly, this was a dog that needed looking after, and the responsibility was suddenly becoming very real. I signed a document to say I was now their legal owner. It was done. And as I folded the paperwork to put it in my pocket, I could hear the sound of eight sets of nails scampering across the floor. I bent down and gave them both a cuddle. I now had a family of my own.

---

113 → We took some pictures of the first time we took them out and the car journey back. How could I not give them a new home?

26. FROM SLUMP
TO SALVATION

THE NEXT MORNING I AWOKE TO THE SOUND OF BARKING dogs, desperate for a cuddle, a treat, and a poo. This was more like it! Millie jumped up and down, howling like a wolf crossed with an Ewok. Norman tried to jump up too but eventually ended up sprawled on the floor, coughing and spluttering like an old man with the flu. Bless. I was clearly looking after a geriatric dog and his younger, fitter girlfriend.

(By the way, I ended the last chapter by stating that I finally had a family of my own. That's not to say I didn't have a family already, of course I did. But adopting the dogs now gave me a level of responsibility I hadn't really experienced before.)

Speaking of family, it's probably an opportune moment to fill you in about the fact that there had been some changes in our own infrastructure. About a year earlier, Mum and Dad decided not to live together anymore. It wasn't a divorce, it was just time for each of them to have some space. I was — as any offspring would be — upset that the dream of marriage had ended, but mature enough to see the reasons behind it. It also demonstrated to me that adults were perfectly capable of being civil to one another too, should they choose to be.

That Christmas I took Norman and Millie down to Weston. As they were my surrogate children, I showered them in dog toys and treats. The treats they couldn't get enough of, the toys they couldn't give a shit about. I remember standing in the garden with both of them beside me, showing them a stick and shouting "FETCH!" as I threw it halfway across the lawn. They looked at me like I was an idiot. Food was their master and I was merely their slave.

Toys aside, they loved the festivities: mostly because the house was full of the smells of cooking. Norman, for all his ailments, could sniff out a joint of beef a thousand miles away. Millie, with her bright, beady eyes and gurning lower teeth, took a more subtle approach and was perfectly happy to just sit and wait — staring up at you like she'd never been fed before — desperate for a scrap of food to fall from your fork and onto the floor. Norman was less patient. So much so that on Boxing Day, as Dad was tidying up after the night before, he dived into the fridge and pulled out a piece of pork big enough to feed a small army. Dad tried to catch him but he was gone, scarpering into the dining room to chow down on his bounty. "Norman you bastard!" yelled Dad, understandably irked by the fact that his dinner for the next few nights was now in the jaws of a salivating dog. But Norman didn't care and the pork was gone. As fragile as he was, Norman was like a ninja when it came to scoffing food.

Christmas was over, New Year's Eve was on its way. I was feeling particularly ambivalent about the festivities that year:

I just really wasn't that interested. I still went out, still got drunk, still pulled no one, and still came home to an empty bed. Perhaps it was the certainty of 'same shit, different year' that made the whole thing feel lacklustre. Besides, work was starting just a couple of days later and I had lessons to prepare. Jesus. Had my life really come to this — that the thought of planning lessons seemed more important than celebrating New Year's Eve? Obviously it had. I now saw work as the focal point of my life and almost everything else paled into insignificance. The academic and musical success of my students was paramount to me, and I was starting to put my own musical endeavours to one side. Even with my new studio, I just wasn't feeling inspired. Once again, drum and bass had gone in a direction I had no real interest in: morphing into a softer, more melodic style known as 'liquid' drum and bass. It didn't take long for this more palatable array of sounds and rhythms to find their way into the Top 40 and inevitably ended up becoming the background music to virtually every holiday programme on TV. This wasn't drum and bass for me: I liked it dark. I was trying to write new material, just to keep my creative juices flowing, but the tunes just weren't happening, and nothing's worse than forcing creativity. Another new sound had flooded the Bristol scene too: dubstep. It felt like the emerging generation had taken over. I was no longer 'in the scene'. My time had come and gone.

I was — to put it mildly — in a slump. I was going to be thirty that year, and what had really changed? Sure, I'd found a good job and yes, I was helping people chase their dreams, but what about *my* dreams? My focus only ever seemed to be on everyone else. All around me, friends basked in the warmth of long-term relationships, the smell of impending babies hanging heavy in the air. I had no partner and I had no kids — my parents had done all that by the time they were twenty. Was this how life would be now, a life spent on my own, curled up on the scrapheap of singledom? This was not me. This was not the Dan that I knew.

And then in February I received a letter that would change my life forever.

It was from Bristol Eye Hospital. I'd already been to see them towards the end of 2006 for a regular check-up and had been told that everything was as it should be, so it was a surprise when the familiar brown envelope appeared in my letter box. This letter was somewhat different. It asked if I was free in March to be part of an observation process for students undertaking their final-year exams. It would involve coming in for the afternoon and having my eyes looked at by a small group of student doctors. I smiled to myself. I'd been visiting the Eye Hospital for as long as I could remember and almost every visit ended up with a small queue of consultants wanting to look at my eye. I knew just how rare my condition was (one in three million people, don't forget), so to be a test case for a group of graduating students felt more like an honour than an inconvenience. Plus, they would pay me £15. Result.

* * *

March arrived. I made the familiar journey to the Eye Hospital — now only a ten-minute walk from my flat. It was never intentional but it felt very handy living so close to the Eye Hospital and the Bristol Royal Infirmary — just in case. I didn't plan on having any sprains or illnesses or broken bones, but I still wasn't able to drive and — knowing my eyes and knowing they *could* deteriorate at any time — I felt safer being only ten minutes away. Paranoid maybe, but I was living on my own now. I couldn't take the risk.[114]

I arrived at the Hospital and was directed to the waiting room. Twenty to thirty people of all ages and backgrounds were sat there. They had closed down appointments for the day purely so the space could be given over to the exams. I took a seat and picked up a magazine: *Gardener's Friend*. The magazines at the Eye Hospital had always been terrible and *Gardener's Friend* was no different. I politely put it back down, took out my phone, switched it to silent and popped my headphones in, keeping the music down low. Twenty minutes later a doctor appeared from one of the consulting rooms and called out my name. I stood up, removed my headphones, and followed him in. There in front of me was the big chair that I had sat in so many times before. He beckoned me to take a seat and I duly obliged.

"So, Daniel. Hopefully you understand why you're here today."

"Yes, I do."

"As you're no doubt aware, these are exam conditions. We will call in one student at a time, they will look at your eyes and try and diagnose your condition."

"I hope they know their stuff!" I joked.

"You're a bit rare, aren't you," he quipped back. "We would ask that you don't say anything to start with. Is that okay?"

"Absolutely," I replied, and with that he left the room.

---

114   There was no medical evidence to suggest that my eyes *would* get worse, it was just a feeling I had. Better to be safe than sorry and all that.

I sat there alone, excited by the prospect of whether these students could correctly diagnose my Wyburn-Mason syndrome or not. A minute later he returned with the first student. She smiled at me, shook my hand, and thanked me for coming. I smiled back, so wanting to say, "Good luck!" but figuring that it probably wasn't appropriate. She brushed herself down and stood in front of me, turned to the examiner and awaited his instruction.

"So here is the patient. A twenty-nine-year-old male living in Bristol. He works as a teacher. What do you see?"

What do you see. I'll never forget those words.

She paused, no doubt summoning all her years of training for this very moment. One last breath to steady herself, and then she began her diagnosis.

"The patient would appear to have very large hands. He has a protruding jaw and high zygomatic bones. He has an oversized forehead and noticeable receding hairline. His facial features are somewhat sunken."

"And what do you think might be the cause of this?" the examiner probed.

She thought for a moment, turned to him and said uncertainly:

"Pituitary adenoma leading to excessive release of growth hormones?"

He said nothing.

"Now please examine his eyes."

'Oh dear — she's got that wrong,' I thought to myself as she assembled her ophthalmoscope. I found it odd that he asked for her to look at me as a whole before looking at my eyes: I wasn't expecting that at all. But this was an exam, and I guess the ethos was that you looked at the patient overall

— not just the one area of interest — so I thought no more about it. Ophthalmoscope assembled, she bent forward and looked at my right eye, zooming in and out to get a better view. She commented on the reduced sight and examined it a little more. Then she moved over to the left eye. I felt a shift in the room, a sense that she had spotted something. She stood back up, thought for a bit, and made a tentative diagnosis — but it was wrong. I was loving this. It was like my own little game show. And then it was time for the next contestant.

"Here's the patient — what do you see?"

Again, I heard the diagnosis the previous student had given: large hands, an oversized forehead, and protruding jaw. When that student was asked what he thought the cause might be, he gave the same response — pituitary adenoma causing excessive release of growth hormones.

By the time the third and fourth students had made the same diagnosis, I was starting to get worried. What the hell were they on about?! I was here to get my eyes looked at, not to be told I had fat hands and a slaphead! By the time the fifth and final student had carried out his examination, I was worn out.[115]

Examinations over, I sat back in the big, black chair. The examiner made some notes and turned to look at me.

"That lazy eye of yours. You do know you can get that fixed with a simple bit of surgery?"

I took a minute to process this. What? I could get my wonky eye fixed? Why had no one ever told me! This was great news. But I had more pressing concerns.

"All these students... they've been talking about 'overly

---

115   He was, incidentally, the only one to diagnose the Wyburn-Mason syndrome correctly. Well done, sir: you'll go far.

large hands, big head and protruding jaw'. No one's ever said this to me. Well... not in a medical context. What are they talking about?"

He turned and looked me straight in the eye.

"I think you should go and see a doctor. You might have something called acromegaly."

27. HALLELUJAH

I LEFT THE HOSPITAL, MY MIND BUZZING LIKE A BEE IN A bottle. What had I just been through?! I'd only gone in to help some medical students with their exams, and suddenly I was being diagnosed with a condition I'd never heard of! I pulled out my phone, Google-searched 'acromegaly' and read as much as I could take in. I was stunned.

Acromegaly is an uncommon condition in which you make too much growth hormone. This causes various symptoms which slowly develop over several years. The most noticeable symptoms are that your hands and feet become larger, and features of your face may become more prominent. In over 99 in 100 cases, the excess hormone comes from a small tumour in the pituitary gland.

Wow.

I had a tumour?!

I read on:

This [tumour] is a benign (non-cancerous) growth called a pituitary adenoma. The adenoma may grow up to 1-2 cm across. However, as it is benign, it does not spread to other areas of the body. The abnormal cells in the adenoma make lots of growth hormone. It is not known why the adenoma develops.

The most common symptoms are:

- *large hands and feet*
- *thick, coarse, oily skin*
- *enlarged lips and nose*
- *protruding tongue and brow*
- *widely spaced teeth*
- *deepening of the voice due to enlarged sinuses and vocal cords*
- *excessive sweating and body odour*
- *fatigue and weakness*
- *headaches*
- *impaired vision*
- *abnormal periods (in women)*
- *impotence (in men)*
- *excessive height*
- *loss of sex drive*

This was it. I knew this was it! All those years of lethargy and sexual disinterest and changing shape and fat hands and sweating and eye problems — this was the reason why! And all because a little tumour had been growing in my pituitary gland, causing it to produce excessive growth hormones!! I was — very weirdly — the happiest I had been in a long, long time. I immediately called home.

"Mum? Dad? I think I know what's wrong with me!"

Their reaction was, understandably, somewhat different to mine. I explained what had happened at the Eye Hospital and how all these students were looking at me and saying that I had big hands and a big head and funny features, and that this might be because I had a tumour in my pituitary gland. I quickly emphasised that this was a *benign* tumour: I didn't have cancer. But in the same breath I waxed lyrical about how happy I was that I had finally found a reason for my malaise.

Of course, I said all this without any medical proof whatsoever. I remember reading on the website that the first step was to visit a doctor, and get a blood test to see what the growth hormone levels were like. As soon as I got home I rang them and made an appointment for the next day. It couldn't come soon enough.

* * *

I sat in the doctor's waiting room, playing over in my mind the events from the day before. It was incredible to think that if I hadn't accepted the invite to be a part of the examination, I would undoubtedly be sat at home, none the wiser about what was wrong with me. That is *if* anything was wrong with me — I might not have acromegaly. Maybe I was naturally a lethargic, fat-handed nobody? My name was announced over the Tannoy. It was time to find out.

I knocked on the door and was called in, whereupon

I shook hands with the doctor. I noticed my hands were sweating — one of the symptoms, I recalled. I sat down and told the whole story from the beginning. I explained that I had Wyburn-Mason syndrome, a really rare eye condition that meant I was blind in my left eye. I explained that I had had nosebleeds throughout my life. I explained how things had started to change during my twenties: that my personality seemed different, how I had to have a ring cut off my finger because my hands were so big, how my shoe size had changed from 9 to 11.[116] I explained that I didn't want to go out, that I wasn't interested in sex, that I had no drive to be creative — something I found torturous as I was a musician and a DJ. And then I explained what had happened the day before and that, through a chance encounter, students had all pointed out that I had enlarged features and this might be caused by something called acromegaly. I stopped. The doctor looked back at me, his mind clearly trying to take it all in.

He moved his mouse, loaded up the Web and typed 'acromegaly' into Google. I was glad to see I wasn't the only one to do research in this way! He found the most common symptoms and went through them with me, and I checked each one off as applicable.[117] He then read up on what the next course of action should be and advised me that he would need to do a glucose blood test. The glucose test would indicate how high my levels of growth hormone were. If I had a small tumour in my pituitary gland, then it was likely to be pumping out loads of extra growth hormones — hence the change in

116   I hadn't really considered this as something strange until I read the symptoms. Obviously it's not normal — I thought I just had big feet.

117   One of the questions was 'Could I wear hats?'. I hadn't even considered this a symptom but, no, I could no longer wear hats any more. None of them seemed to fit.

appearance. All we had to do now was wait for the results.

In the blink of an eye my life had drastically changed. Waiting for the blood test result was a formality: somehow I knew I had acromegaly. I tried to carry on with the usual processes of work and living and walking the dogs, but until I had this confirmed it was pretty hard to function normally. So rather than hide away, I read up as much as I could about my newfound condition.

My research was showing me that acromegaly was pretty bloody rare. Who would have thought it! Me? With a rare condition? I wouldn't have it any other way! My research also showed that acromegaly tended to happen in middle age. However, if you developed a tumour as a baby, then that's what caused you to become a giant. Famous sufferers of acromegaly were Andre the Giant and Jaws from the *James Bond* movies. It was thought Abraham Lincoln may have had it too.[118] But because the tumour formed when I was a fully-grown adult, instead of growing 'up' as a child would, I grew 'out': bigger hands, bigger nose, bigger lips, bigger feet. And that wasn't all. It wasn't just the extremities: my internal organs would be growing too. If left untreated, acromegaly could cause serious heart problems. If left untreated, it could displace limbs. If left untreated, it could take up to twenty years off my life. Wow. This was pretty sobering stuff, and I kept reflecting on how lucky I had been to be a case study at the Eye Hospital.

* * *

Two days later, my doctor called to confirm what I had been

---

118 → Looking at his face, you can see why.

expecting: the glucose test did show an excessive amount of growth hormones. Looking through my medical records (yes, I got them all to help me write this book!), it would appear he wrote to an endocrinologist at the BRI that day:

Thanks for seeing Dan Jeffries who has some classic features of acromegaly with raised GH [growth hormone] levels on GTT [Glucose Tolerance Test] - see attached sheet, lowest level 59. He cannot find a hat to fit his head and has had to increase the size of his shoes. He has a temporal visual field defect and Wyburn Mason syndrome with tortuous vessels in his one eye and blindness. I would appreciate your assessment.

On the phone, my doctor advised that the next steps were for me to see someone at the BRI. A week later I was sat with a consultant. We discussed my case and the next course of action. Here's what he wrote to my GP surgery:

Thank you for referring this 30 year old music teacher at a music college. He is currently single with no girlfriend and smokes cannabis on occasion. He does not drink alcohol. He has Wyburn Mason syndrome which has resulted in blindness in his left eye. He was invited to participate in your opthalmology exam and he was noted to have large hands and the students were mentioning acromegaly. He came to see [me] and has read about acromegaly. He does not complain of any joint pains or headaches, but has noticed sweating. His shoe size has increased over the years and he's currently shoe size 12. He's had no dental problems, but occasionally gets parasthesie in his hands.[119] He has not noticed any problems with impotence but he tells me that his libido is not as high as he would like. He has electro pulse photos and hope it changes his appearance. He particularly has a problem with his forehead. He's not had any problems with his high blood pressure or hypoglycaemia [diabetes]. There isn't a family history of endocrine disorder.

On examination he has a right temporal hemianopia in his right eye. He had large sweaty hands and large protruding tongue and prominent jaw. Cardiovascular examinations were normal. I note your glucose tolerance test which is consistent with acromegaly. I have arranged for him to have an MRI of his pituitary and I've also arranged for him to have a visual field test. I will also arrange for him to have a screening colonoscopy. I will discuss with my colleagues whether we should start him on treatment at the moment, or wait for the MRI and I will append this to this letter.

Pretty succinct explanation of my life at that time. So I had to have an MRI scan to look at the pituitary tumour and a field test to check my eyes. Oh, and I also had to have a colonoscopy at some stage too. I hadn't had one of these before but anything involving the word 'colon' could only mean one thing: fun.

* * *

A month later and it was time for my MRI. I arrived at the

---

119   I'd obviously forgotten to mention the two teeth I had taken out some time before or, more likely, hadn't linked that to the acromegaly.

hospital at 7am — the perfect time of day to be subjected to head-mangling rattles and whirs. I did ask why it was so early and was told that it was because I lived so close. I couldn't really argue with that. I climbed up onto the bed, this time ready with my iPhone to drown out the noise. What do I listen to at 7am? Do I go nice and mellow or opt for banging techno, a sensible accompaniment to the mechanical environment around me? I decided upon neither and opted for The Smiths, which seemed to make sense. Twenty minutes later and the MRI was over. Still half asleep, I got changed out of the gown and into my clothes. The consultant told me that I would receive a letter in the post with a date for my meeting with the endocrinology team to discuss the results. She thought this would be in about a month's time.

* * *

Lunchtime at work. I was taking a well-deserved break when my mobile phone rang.

"Hello. Is that Dan Jeffries? This is Professor Lightman from the BRI."

Oh shit. I wasn't supposed to be seeing him for another three weeks.

"Oh, Hi! Yes, this is Dan. Is everything okay?" I asked tentatively.

"Well, there's some good news and some not-so-good news."

Shit shit shit.

"As you know, you had an MRI scan last week on your brain. The MRI has shown that you have a tumour in your pituitary gland, which is creating excessive growth hormones.

The good news is that the tumour is about 1cm long and we will be able to remove it. The not-so-good news is that the MRI also shows a lot of blood vessels around the tumour area, and we are concerned that the complex surgery might damage these vessels. We want to discuss all the options with you. Can you come in, please?"

"Yes of course. When?"

"As soon as possible. Are you free next week?"

The endocrinology team had a weekly meeting and asked if I could come to that. I could then meet all the people involved and if I had questions they could be answered. I thanked him for the call and hung up the phone, numb with the news. This was getting serious. Not only did I have a tumour, I had a mass of blood vessels surrounding it. That must be the Wyburn-Mason, I thought. I called Mum and Dad and gave them the update. I couldn't quite imagine what they were going through. They said they would be there.

* * *

One week later — the waiting room of the Endocrinology Clinic. By this time I had done some more research online and found blogs that had been written by those suffering with acromegaly. They documented their experiences, including the life-changing moment of finding out. Their advice was to go to any appointments prepared with a list of questions because, in the reality of the consultancy room, it was easy to forget what you wanted to ask. I took their advice and noted a few questions down, going over them with Mum and Dad as we waited to be called in. They made a couple of suggestions too. This was a team effort.

I didn't have to wait long. As I entered the room I was greeted by what felt like a committee. Three people stood up: Professor Lightman – Endocrinology Consultant at the BRI, Dr Richard Nelson – Consultant Neurosurgeon at Frenchay Hospital, and Samantha Cooper – Skull Base Nurse Advisor[120], also based at Frenchay. It was clear to see that the 'big guns' were in. And the atmosphere was very unique. We all knew we were here to discuss something special, something life-changing. My parents were on edge — my dad especially so. All through my life they've had to handle difficult news: finding out I was blind in one eye, having a heart murmur, the agony of constant nosebleeds, that I wanted to be an actor. Now they were here to witness potentially the most explosive development in Daniel Conrad Jeffries so far.[121]

Professor Lightman began by reaffirming what he had told me over the phone: a glucose test showed that my body was producing excessive growth hormones, likely to be caused by a tumour in the pituitary gland. The recent MRI scan did indeed show that there was a small tumour growth in the pituitary fossa, which was about 1cm in length. He opened my file and showed us images from the MRI scan that clearly highlighted that there was indeed a little white mass sitting in the pituitary gland.[122] He advised that, because of my Wyburn-Mason syndrome and the mass of vascular activity it produced, they had to really consider the best methods of removing the tumour. I'd read about this. There were three main options: transsphenoidal surgery (going up through the nose to get to the tumour at the base of the brain), medication to 'manage'

---

120   What a job title!

121   And there it is. 'Conrad'. Worth the wait, wasn't it?

122   → Amazing how such a small thing can have such a massive effect.

the tumour if it couldn't be removed, and radiation therapy. Whatever that involved, I didn't like the sound of it. Their opinion was that transsphenoidal surgery was the safest and most effective route. In days gone by, they removed tumours by going through the skull. How glad I was to be ill in 2007.

It was at this point that Dr Nelson explained how the transsphenoidal surgery worked. They would go up through the nose, enter a space called the 'sella', locate the tumour, dig it out, seal the point of entry back up and then fill the nose with wadding. He told us that recovery time was usually two or three days, assuming no complications, and then a period of rest at home for three to four weeks. Had he done this surgery before? He had, numerous times. Frenchay Hospital, I discovered, was one of the leading hospitals in the UK for brain surgery. This was a huge relief. It's amazing to think that this kind of stuff is like typing a letter, or driving a lorry for us: it's their work, it's what they're trained to do. But like driving a lorry (not so much with typing maybe), there are always potential dangers. This is where my vascular activity would come into play and, in order to give us a better idea of the formation of these vessels and where they sat in relation to the pituitary region, the next step would be to carry out an angiogram.

Sam introduced herself and said that she would be here to support us along the way. She'd explain the procedures and the treatments and would liaise between us, the consultants and surgeons. She was our guide through this rather dark tunnel, one that was — thankfully — starting to show a chink of light at the end.

My final question to the team was about the impact that removing the tumour would have. What changes — if any —

would happen when it was gone? The answer was staggering.

"Within days you'll start to notice your facial features returning to how they were. The size of your hands and feet will reduce as excess fluids are released. Any headaches you experience should vanish. If you sweat profusely, this should subside. Over time you'll discover that you have more energy and a greater sexual appetite. The changes can be quite profound."

I looked at my family as a smile worked its way to my oversized lips.

"What are we waiting for?' I asked the room. "Let's get this show on the road!"

28. PICTURES,
PAINS AND POLYPS

O N THE 21ST JULY, 2007, I TOOK A COURSE OF ACTION THAT would change my life forever. I joined Facebook.

The 'Uber-Lord' — sorry — Facebook was launched to the public in 2006, and I'd heard whispers about its existence. My online communication up to that point had primarily revolved around message boards like Hijack Bristol, Reason Station, and the Drum and Bass Arena, and Facebook sort of crept in. I was glad of it though. Recent events had ignited a newfound urge to reconnect with people I hadn't been in touch with for a while, so it made perfect sense to sign up. I could see the potential that Facebook offered that had been lacking in Friends Reunited, bolstered by the fact that this was free. Free, I tells ya! Why pay a subscription to another site when you could reconnect with all your old buddies at no cost to yourself? Oh, how naive that notion seems today.

I immediately took a liking to updating my status. Here

was an opportunity to show off a little bit of creative writing through small life updates. I hadn't written a play or sketch for ages and forums and chat rooms were a way to reach a small audience — but generally an audience of 'strangers'. Now my network suddenly grew and — look! — I could share thoughts and music and pictures too! Over the past year I had been pretty solitary. I didn't go out much. I preferred to have friends round to play poker than venture into the busy pubs and clubs of Bristol. The idea of going out and looking for love couldn't have been further from my mind. And it was whilst I was uploading some pictures to Facebook that I could really start to see the difference between the younger me and the current — what I perceived — disfigured me. I didn't like it. I felt ugly and warped: my cheeks looked terrible, my jaw looked huge, and my forehead looked like you could land a plane on it. Maybe this public platform wasn't that great after all.[123]

* * *

It was now August. 'A' is for August. And it's also for angiogram.

As much as it was a shock to find out that I had a brain tumour, it was also, perversely, a huge relief. I knew *something* wasn't right, but the likelihood of me putting it down to a tiny tumour in my pituitary gland was pretty remote. Now that the MRI had confirmed the presence of a mass it was time to get cracking with the various other tests that had been arranged for me.

We knew that there was a complexity of blood vessels

123   → See what I mean?

around my brain, no doubt linked to my Wyburn-Mason syndrome. The question was: how complex were they? Looking back at my medical records, there was a lot of discussion between the consultants as to the intricacy of this vital and fragile network. One paragraph in particular caught my eye:

> *Further formal assessment of the cerebral and neck vasculature, perhaps best with CT angiography, may be useful to assess the process further, depending on the clinical picture and proposed management. Indeed some of the branches of the external carotid artery in the masticator space [front of the face]... also appear fairly prominent and this clearly may be a hazard if surgery were contemplated in this region for example.*

Nobody likes a hazard, so the angiogram was a way to see just how complex it was.

I don't know if you've ever had an angiogram but it's a truly strange experience. After being wheeled into the radiography room, a thin tube was inserted into my body (in this instance the groin), and then fed up to my neck. The consultant then explained the procedure to me. He was going to pump a coloured dye through the tube then, when it had reached the area it needed to, he would take some photos — the coloured dye outlining the structure of my vascular system.

"Ready?"

I took a deep breath and nodded in approval.

Nothing can prepare you for the sensation. As the dye is pumped in, your face suddenly starts to tingle and your head becomes prickly and hot. Every vein in your face feels like it's filling with static electricity. And then it's over.

I took another deep breath.

"Ready?"

A few seconds later and I could feel the dye again, this time on another area of my head. I closed my eyes in submission. By the third time I was growing used to it, but I still didn't like it. It's a bit like when you're a kid and you have to have a plaster ripped off your knee: the expectation is usually far worse than the outcome.

During the angiogram, I asked if it was possible to watch what was happening. I was intrigued by this mass of vessels inside my head so, wherever possible, they pointed the monitor towards me. It was amazing. Once they had all the information and images they needed it was time to go back to the ward and head home. But as we left the treatment room I started to get a really sharp pain in my chest. By the time we got back to the ward, it had become worse: it felt like a tight band covering my whole upper torso, most noticeably around my heart. I'd sometimes felt this when I was sitting up in bed before I went to sleep but never this bad. The consultant was concerned. They put me on an ECG monitor to watch my various levels. Typically, within an hour, the pain had gone. Even though I felt absolutely fine, I was to stay in overnight for observations. I didn't mind. The heart's an important thing — I wasn't going to argue.

In light of the heart and chest pains, a letter was written to the Cardiology team outlining their concerns:

This 30-year-old teacher was admitted to Frenchay hospital for a diagnostic carotid and cerebral angiography following an MRI report which revealed a pituitary adenoma and a suprasellar arteriovenous malformation. He is being investigated with a view to surgical management.

Soon after angiography Mr Jeffries developed gradual onset left sided chest tightness, which lasted about an hour. An ECG did not show any evidence of ischaemia [restriction in blood supply to tissues] but did reveal LVH [Left Ventricular Hypertrophy - thickening of the heart muscle]; a 12-hour troponin was negative [Troponin is a protein released when heart muscle is damaged]. He has had similar episodes over the past two years. He is not hypertensive [suffers from high blood pressure] or has any family history of ischaemic heart disease; he occasionally smokes cannabis. An outpatient Echocardiography has been requested.

Scary stuff, but it could have been much worse. And the discovery of the thickening of the heart muscle was something that was going to need further investigation. I really hoped it wasn't going to get in the way of the surgery.

* * *

I had decided that — if I was going to be having a potentially life-threatening operation — I'd better make the most of my time between now and then. A promoter in Bristol asked me if I wanted to DJ at a club in the centre of town, and I thought this would be a great opportunity to get everyone together. And, to make myself feel better, I decided to play ninety minutes of drum and bass tunes purely written by me. That's a nerve-wracking experience, I can tell you. What if I cleared the dance floor? What if someone threw eggs at me? Thankfully no eggs were thrown, partly down to the club's strict 'No Egg Policy', and hopefully a little bit down to my great drum and bass. The night went off. Everyone loved it. And someone took pictures. I look awful in every single one of them.[124]

* * *

13th August, 2007. I haven't checked, but it wouldn't surprise me if the 13th August had been a Friday. For that was the day I would undergo my colonoscopy.[125]

A few days earlier I had received a package from the BRI containing all the things I would need to get myself ready for the bum invasion. It was not uncommon for people suffering with acromegaly to develop small, benign tumours in their colon and it was the intention of the hospital to get rid of them. So up the bum they would go — on the hunt for polyps to destroy.

Before I went in for the procedure I had to 'prepare myself'. I opened up the package to find a single surgical glove. Only joking! Instead there were numerous sachets of something called Klean Prep. The name hardly filled me with glee. I shook my head and read the instructions:

- Dissolve the contents of each sachet in 1 litre of water, store it in the fridge and drink chilled at a rate of 1 glass every 10-15 minutes.

---

124 → Probably not helped by having my photo taken with beautiful people.
125 It was a Monday. Balls.

- You should experience frequent bowel actions followed by diarrhoea 1-2 hours after taking Klean Prep.
- You may find that applying a small amount of Vaseline/ Sudocreme to your back passage (anus) prevents discomfort during the bowel preparation.

I decided to pass on the last suggestion: primarily because there was no one around to help, and it didn't feel right asking one of the dogs to do it. So I made up my litre of Klean Prep and drank the first glass. And, dear reader, I can promise you that it was absolutely disgusting. It was like drinking gone-off lemon-flavoured salt water. Ten minutes later, I forced back another glass, then another, then another. Within an hour I had drunk the whole lot. I looked at the instructions and read that, because I had an afternoon appointment, I had another sachet to take in the evening and then two more in the morning. Two more in the morning?! The dogs looked up at me — not an inch of sympathy between them.

An hour later and my stomach started to gurgle. Here we go, I thought to myself and made a dash for the loo. And that's pretty much where I stayed for the rest of the day. Knowing I was probably going to be in there for quite a while, I took some reading materials in with me and read up on exactly what this Klean Prep stuff was doing:

Klean-Prep sachets contain the active ingredient macrogol, which is a type of medicine known as an osmotic laxative. Klean-Prep also contains sodium sulphate, sodium bicarbonate, sodium chloride and potassium chloride.

Macrogol is an inert substance that passes through the gut without being absorbed into the body. It works because it causes the water it is taken with to be retained in the bowel instead of being absorbed into the body. This increases the water content and volume of the stools in the bowel, making them softer and easier to pass.

The sodium sulphate, sodium bicarbonate, sodium chloride and potassium chloride (electrolytes) are included in this medicine to help ensure that the laxative works without causing the body to gain or lose significant amounts of sodium, potassium or water.

Whatever it did, it did it with all the efficiency of a German car mechanic. By the time I was ready for bed I felt like a dried-up leaf. And worst of all: I had to do it all again in the morning.

When Mum arrived at lunchtime ready to take me to the hospital, I hadn't eaten for over twenty-four hours. This was not good for me. I had over the past few months been on a diet and successfully lost over a stone and a half and was probably the lightest I had been since going to University. But I still liked my food, especially breakfast, and right then I felt weaker than Olive Oyl's eyelids. We made our way down to the hospital, and all I could think of was the slap-up meal I could have once it was all over.

We sat in the waiting room, numerous people shedding all sense of dignity as they waited in their gowns — the backs of which hung loose like badly made tents. It's amazing how we adapt when we need to. Grown men sat and waited, their feet tapping up and down in nervous expectation. I wasn't nervous — I just wasn't really looking forward to it. Who would? And what exactly were they going to do? All I knew was that my bowels were the cleanest they'd ever been, and no doubt something would be heading in their direction to see what lay within. My name was called — it was time to find out.

As I climbed up onto the bed, surrounded by wires and screens, the nurse explained exactly what would happen. They would administer me with a light sedative and then ask me to lie on my side. They would then insert a thin tube into my bottom (or anus, if we're being technical), which they would then push deeper until it reached the colon. Whilst it was inside they would inflate the colon with some air so they could get a better look. They were on the lookout for polyps: little benign tumours (or adenomas) that, if not removed, could prove to be problematic in later life. I was asked if I understood the procedure, which I did, and signed a form saying so. Then a little scratch on the back of my hand and the sedative was in. I started to feel funny. And then I was rolled on to my side.

Initial entry didn't really hurt but I could definitely feel the tube as they pushed it up. It wasn't nice and I winced and moaned in pain. At one point it felt like it was in my chest. When they were satisfied it had been inserted properly, they pumped some air into my colon, which caused it to expand, giving them room to work. I turned my head to have a look at the screen, determined to make the most of my front row seat.

As the camera wended its way along my colon, it would stop at the first sign of a little lump. This is what the specialists were looking for: polyps. Pesky little polyps. They would relay something to the nurse and, instrument in hand, start to burn the polyp away. I watched in amazement as I felt this tiny twinge inside my stomach. Then it was on to the next one. And the next one. All in all, eight polyps found: seven rectal and sigmoid 5mm sessile polyps, and one caecal polyp, less than 5mm. Within twenty minutes they were gone — all 'hot biopsied and destroyed'. I felt no different, but I knew this was another step to getting me back on track.

They slowly pulled the tube out of my bum and then held it up to my nose to have a sniff. NOT REALLY! I rested for a few minutes, the sedative still taking its toll. After a while they wheeled me back to the rest area whereupon I was greeted by a nurse who asked me if I would like a cup of tea and some biscuits. Biscuits?! BISCUITS?!?! Hell yeah! I'll have a whole pack, please! Make it two! A Selection Box would be even better!

Mum arrived as I was dunking a fifth custard cream into my tea. The sedative had finally worn off and it was time to go home. The trouble was, I was incredibly bloated from all the air they had pumped inside me. I practically had to roll off the bed to stand up and, once I managed to remain upright, I looked like a Weeble.[126] As we left the ward it was obvious that walking was not going to be easy, and, even though it was only a ten minute walk away, we ordered a taxi back to mine.

Back at home and I laid on the sofa, writhing in pain, my belly rock-hard to the touch. All I wanted to do was fart. I gently pushed down on my tummy to try and coax them out but they didn't want to budge. Norman and Millie trotted over to check if I was okay. I advised that they might want to move away and, unsurprisingly, they did.

Two hours later and I started to feel a stirring deep inside.

126   → Pretty much like this.

Could this be it? I drew a deep breath and gently squeezed, releasing a fart only audible to bats. It must have lasted a good ten seconds. Mum was in the kitchen, holding on to the worktop as she descended into fits of laughter. I wanted to laugh but I was in too much pain. Oh, how pleasant that fart had been! I knew I had plenty more to come and — never one to miss a comedy moment — reached for my iPhone, loaded up the voice recorder, and hit the little red button.

You know what's coming.[127]

127 ♫

29. ECHO

NOW THAT THE FARTS WERE OUT OF THE WAY, IT WAS A CASE of waiting for instructions from the hospital. I figured there would be more tests to come before the green light was given for surgery. How long that would be, I didn't know.

I had two choices: sit and wait or do stuff. I decided to opt for the latter. One of the things I knew I had to do was tell work. I crafted a strong yet slightly emotional email and sent it to my managers and various other key people. I received a wealth of kind responses, including one from the HR administrator, Isla. It was to be the start of a close and supportive friendship that's still going strong to this day.

And then a couple of weeks later I got a call — some friends had arranged a holiday down in Devon, and asked if I wanted to go. I was initially a bit nervous. There were quite a few people going that I didn't know and at that time I wasn't feeling particularly sociable. I was also worried that the hospital might call with urgent news or an emergency appointment, but I figured it was futile to let my life be dominated by this. More worryingly, they were all planning on going surfing — something I couldn't even dream of doing. With my sense of balance and spatial awareness I'd be a death trap on the waves. Plus, trying to get into a wetsuit would be like stuffing corned beef into a condom.

The cars were packed and loaded and we made our way to the holiday park. As we arrived, a group of people were waiting for us. We got out of the car and those that were already friends greeted each other with hugs and kisses. I sort of stayed at the back, never one to dive in with, "HELLO! THIS IS ME!". One of my friends introduced me to the group and I sheepishly waved back before they all ran off, chattering as they did so.

The next day it was decided that it was time to hit the beach. Uh oh. I could feel my back starting to arch, repelled by the notion of rippling torsos and butch skills on display whilst I sat there, fully clothed and sucking on a lolly. As the lads were donning their wetsuits, I could overhear three of the girls saying that they weren't that fussed about surfing and did they fancy going shopping instead? My ears pricked up and I sheepishly asked if they didn't mind me tagging along. "Of course not!" they replied — I could be an honorary girl for the day! With my lack of testosterone, that sounded ideal.

The next few hours were spent strolling around the seaside town, exploring all the clothes and shoes it had to offer. The girls would ask my opinion on what looked good, and I offered as much sage advice as I could. It was really nice to be so easily accepted into a group of people that I hardly knew, and hanging around with three girls definitely gave me an internal boost that I had been missing of late. After a spot of lunch it started to rain, so we headed back to the car. I can't remember how, but the topic of conversation wended its way to me and the developments of the last few months. The girls sat there opened-mouthed, shocked at what I had been through. They were incredibly warm and sympathetic about my situation, and it made me feel a whole lot better. They all vowed to visit me when I was in hospital, one of them promising they would smuggle porn mags in to help me through the days. These truly were the best of friends.[128]

When I returned from Devon there was a letter waiting for me from Frenchay Hospital. I had a date to see the cardiology specialist to review my heart, a necessity after the recent scare with the angiogram. Good news! The trouble was, the appointment wasn't until late November, and it was only the middle of September! This seemed like a ridiculously long time to wait considering how urgent everything else had been up to this point.

I immediately got on the phone to speak to the department — eager to know why the wait was so long. I was told that there was simply a long queue of people in front of me, and there was nothing they could do. Annoyed, I said that, if this was the case, I would have to go to BUPA and be seen by a specialist there, because I really wasn't prepared to wait three months just to get the all-clear for an operation. A quick double-check of the schedule and — oh look! — there was in fact a free appointment next week. Result. I immediately called Mum and Dad to let them know the news. Out of all the consultations, this was perhaps the most nerve-wracking

---

128   → Don't worry — no porn mags. Just a picture of me on holiday and looking thin. Porn for some, maybe.

because — depending upon their diagnosis — I would know if I would be able to have the surgery or not.

* * *

A week later and we were at Frenchay, nervous with anticipation. Accompanying us was a family friend who'd had previous experience in some areas of cardiology and knew how the NHS worked. Her presence was vital in ensuring that we all remained calm, and that we all understood the implications of what was being said. I've often found that, in moments of importance, one's hearing can suddenly lose all function and five minutes after you've left, you have no idea as to what's been said.

We sat in the waiting room and we did just that: we waited and waited and waited. Waiting is difficult. I have no issues with it: I've waited long enough for numerous observations, eye examinations, and more. For my dad and sister, however, waiting is a difficult game and their nerves were visibly on edge. I offered them an edition of last year's *Woman's Realm* but they weren't interested. They were more inclined to pacing about and nipping outside for a quick fag, whilst Mum and I sat and held fort. Eventually my name was called and we made our way in.

After the pains in my chest from the angiogram, I had been asked to undergo an echocardiogram, to look at my heart in more detail.[129] The cardiologist explained the findings from the echo. My heart showed symptoms of a leaking valve, and that blood was flowing backwards into the valve. And here was the dilemma: was the leak severe enough to preclude me from surgery? Would I be able to cope with the pressures of anaesthesia? The cardiologist confirmed that the leak was 'mild to moderate', as commented on in the echocardiogram report:

Summary: Dilated ascending aorta. Probable mild to moderate aortic regurgitation. Mild concentric left ventricular hypertrophy.

But would this affect surgery? Based on all the evidence, the consultant had to make a judgement call. And whilst we respected the medical necessity to do this, it soon started to feel like we were battling against him. It was becoming clear that he was happy for the surgery to proceed, but was insistent that he write a full and thorough report to Mr Nelson before any surgery could take place. We all looked at each other, the same thought transmitting between us: write the report, send the report, wait for a response... how long would *that* take?!

Sitting at the back of the room was a lady quietly working away. She had been introduced to us when we had walked into the consulting room, and had commented that she knew of my case as she was a part of Mr Nelson's team. It was this

---

129   If you've never had an echo, it involves lying on your side and your chest area is covered in a cold jelly (raspberry, I believe). The cardiologist takes a probe and places it over the chest wall, pushing down and around that area to take images of the heart. It's a bit like an ultrasound for babies, just higher up. The results show thickness of the heart walls and how the valves are working. It also looks for something called 'ejection fraction' — which to me sounds like a maths lesson for dirty boys.

fortunate seating arrangement that caused our family friend to have a light bulb moment.

"You're part of Mr Nelson's team. Can't you relay this information to him in person so we can get the all-clear?"

The woman replied that Sam, the lady who had been at the initial meeting at the BRI, worked in the office next door, and she could go and tell her straight away. We all looked at each other, nervous anticipation etched on our faces. A few minutes later she returned, pleased to announce that Sam would be advising the team that surgery could proceed. Hallelujah! We were on our way.

I don't resent the consultant for wanting to be thorough, but at that moment it just felt like a huge wall was being placed in front of us, and I'm so very grateful that we were able to break it down. Whilst looking through my medical records I came across two letters of real interest about this encounter. The first was from Mr Nelson to the consultant — I think unaware of the fact that my appointment date had been brought forward:

We have recently received a report from your registrar confirming that this gentleman has left ventricular hypertrophy associated with mild to moderate aortic regurgitation.

You may be aware that he has recently presented with acromegaly due to a pituitary macroadenoma. We have offered him a selective transsphenoidal adenectomy.

I understand you are due to review him in November. Would you be happy for us to proceed with elective surgery before then? Are there any particular precautions that should be taken?

Yours sincerely,
Dictated but not signed
to speed delivery

I love that last line.

The second letter was written by the consultant cardiologist after we had visited him. I have to say that, despite our initial locking of horns, it's quite possibly the most thorough overview about my medical situation I have ever read. It's a long letter, but it deserves its place in the book.

Further to recent correspondence on this gentleman, in the absence of a response to my letter of 3rd October, I got the gentleman up for urgent review. He came up this afternoon.

He's now 30, a music teacher. He tells me he has a variety of problems including the Wyburn Mason syndrome for which he's been seeing Mr. Grey at the Royal Infirmary for the past 25 years, acromegaly, discovered only this year, and the pituitary adenoma for which you are offering him surgery. More about all that later. He gives no family history of note. Unmarried, no children but he does appear to be with a partner.[130] He doesn't smoke cigarettes, only cannabis once a week which he claims isn't all that frequent. Rarely drinks. No drugs at present, no known

---

130   I must have lied. Or — and I've only just realised this — maybe he thought my sister was my partner?!

problems. No known allergies.

The history is most intriguing. He's had eye problems since a child which is why the review at the Eye Hospital and the discovery of the Wyburn Mason syndrome. He tells me a murmur was spotted when he was a young man and was reviewed for a couple of years by Dr. Joffe at the Bristol Children's Hospital. His mother, who came up to clinic with him, was very helpful here because she filled in the details. Apparently he was told this was a normal childhood murmur which cleared at the time of discharge from review at the Children's Hospital. This would have been about 20 odd years ago.

Earlier this year he was examined by medical students at the Eye Hospital. I think their interest was his Wyburn Mason syndrome. Anyhow a couple of students noted his acromegalic features, large hands etc, and this is how the diagnosis of acromegaly was made. He was then referred to the Endocrine clinic at the Royal Infirmary, he believes he has seen Professor Lightman, perhaps also one of his registrars. I gather you attend that clinic as well which is where he first met you. The MRI scan shows a pituitary adenoma and hence the admission to Frenchay for the angiography. Although the reason for the original referral was the chest discomfort which developed after the angiogram, he actually tells me he's had this before, intermittent episodes of chest discomfort mostly occurring at rest and coming and going over the past year or so. The attack he had on the ward was therefore by no means new. Echo scan I think was organised simply because he has acromegaly and this unexpectedly showed evidence of aortic reflux. As far as he was aware he had no current cardiac murmur, the murmur spotted as a child had cleared at the time of discharge from review in the paediatric cardiac clinic. Apart from the occasional chest discomfort, which doesn't really sound cardiac in origin, he's symptom free.

Clinically he has obvious acromegalic features, a steady pulse, equal on both wrists. There's a soft aortic systolic murmur with a short aortic diastolic murmur. Clinically the heart isn't enlarged. Lung fields are clear. Resting ECG certainly shows tallish T-waves but there's no LV strain or hypertrophy pattern, there's no ST Segment sag or T-wave inversion. I note the echo findings that he has mild to moderate aortic reflux, clinically I'd pass it as being mild.

There should be no problems with your planned surgery.[131] Once he's had his operation he will need to be kept under review in a cardiac clinic, the aortic reflux may progress over the years, he may become a candidate for cardiac surgery. He should in any case be kept under review in a cardiac clinic with serial echoes to ensure that he doesn't develop cardiac dysfunction which is often associated with acromegaly. We've also got the dilated ascending aorta which needs to be kept under review.

All that is for the future. For now the important thing is there should be no problems with your planned surgery. I'll copy this correspondence to Professor Lightman at the

131   That's the money shot.

Royal Infirmary and Mr. Grey at the Eye Hospital.

I assume following surgery he'll be kept under review in Professor Lightman's clinic at the Royal Infirmary, perhaps in a joint clinic which you and he do together. If that were the case it may perhaps be more appropriate for Mr. Jeffries to be referred to one of the Cardiologists at the Royal Infirmary for on-going review. He does after all live in ----- -----, just off Park Street, a several minute walk from the Royal Infirmary. We can sort all that out later, for now the message is that his aortic reflux is trivial, I don't think his chest pain is anything to worry about so he shouldn't cause you any undue concern when he has his neurosurgery. Please let me know if there should be any further queries.

30. 'I'M ALL IN'

WHILST WAITING FOR THE OPERATION DATE I DECIDED TO start writing a blog. We knew the hospital were keen to get me in quickly but we had to be realistic: there was a queue in front of me and it might be a little while until I was under the knife.

The idea of the blog — called 'Dan's Magical Medical Tour' — was to keep a record of the various events during diagnosis and everything leading up to surgery and beyond. I also thought it might be useful in the future for anyone diagnosed with acromegaly. I had already announced my diagnosis on Hijack and received a wealth of support, comments, and questions from people interested in the condition.[132] The blog and Hijack allowed me to expand on my writing — Facebook was, after all, only really there for quick life updates. My

132   → Have a read. Isn't community wonderful?

input to Facebook was ticking along nicely though, and I was reconnecting with old friends and making new ones too. Lots of messages of support were coming in, wishing me well and marvelling at how mad the whole thing sounded. This was long before the days of people 'Liking' posts and when any messages were sent, they always appeared on your Wall — so everything was out in the open. I particularly enjoyed one comment from Josh, the guy I had lived with a few years before:

> "Hey lady-balls, did you realise that Jaws off James Bond has the same head-wonk disease as you? If you don't get metal teeth off the NHS after this you can forget talking to me ever again."

Who needs enemies with friends like these?

* * *

I HAD A DATE!!

The news we had been waiting for had finally arrived. Surgery date: November 15th.

I called the family to tell them, suddenly realising that Dad was actually on holiday! I told him not to book a return flight just yet as there was always the possibility that the date could change, but I advised that he might want to have his passport on standby, just in case. And now that I had a date it was time to have one final party. That sounds very dramatic, but I knew what I meant: I just wanted to see everyone before I went into hospital. I was confident that everything would be okay, but I was acutely aware that this was difficult, complicated surgery and with my mass of blood vessels potentially getting in the way, I couldn't conceive of this as just being 'routine'.

During that year, our group of friends had all, somehow or other, found ourselves mildly addicted to poker — specifically Texas Hold 'Em. The first home game I attended was above a sandwich shop in Bristol. Each player was given a bag of 'chips' (1p and 2p coins from the shop's petty cash), and with an air of excitement we started playing cards. By 3am everyone was still in the game and barely any money had changed hands. In truth, no one knew what they were doing and by 4am I declared that I really didn't care who won — I was going home. So after a bit of reading and a dabble on the Internet, we managed to set up our own home games — replete with poker table, chips, professional cards, and software that managed the game. Within a couple of months we knew who had won the most money, who had knocked out the most people, and who was top of the leader board. It wasn't me.

So organising a game felt like the best way to get everyone together. We drank and laughed. We spoke about the impending surgery. Norman guarded the food. Goodbye hugs were tighter than normal.

And the Gods of Fortune must have been smiling on me because, that night, I won.[133]

* * *

November 15th had arrived. Forget poker — Mum and I were now 'Grand Masters' at playing the surgery waiting game. We had hoped to hear something over the last few days but the

---

133   → And don't I look pleased with myself.

phone stayed silent. I called the hospital a couple of times to speak to the Ward Manager (she who is in charge of beds), and was told that she was doing her best to get me in as soon as she could. This sounded ominous. I had built myself up to this moment and I didn't want it falling through due to the lack of a bed.

To pass the time, we watched some videos on YouTube — mostly detailed footage of the surgery I was about to have. Nice, huh?[134] I do realise, dear reader, that to some the idea of watching a video of your impending surgery might not be the best idea ever, but I had no fear: I wanted to embrace it. And I'm pleased Mum did too. If we had shown it to Dad or Alix they would have run a mile. Plus, it passed the time, which now seemed to be moving ever slower in the wait for the phone to ring.

And then it happened. We got the call.

They had a bed for me and I would need to come in immediately. This was it. Mum and I breathed a sigh of relief: a sigh mixed with a *soupçon* of fear. I double-checked my bags to make sure I had everything. I bent down and gave the dogs a hug: Norman coughed up something unidentifiable, Millie jumped up and sniffed my face. I was looking forward to coming back to these two buggers. Dad was still on holiday, so Mum called to let him know the news and that we were going in. Fair play to him — he immediately booked a flight back to the UK. Mum and I hugged each other, loaded up the car, and gently made our way to the hospital.

---

134   → Go on. You know you want to.

31. SHOWTIME

"**W**ELCOME MR JEFFRIES! WE'VE BEEN EXPECTING YOU!" OK – perhaps not the exact words uttered by the Ward Manager upon our arrival, but I'd like to think that it was something similar. To be fair to her, she was very apologetic for the delays and the confusion. I was just happy to be there. She then promptly took us to the ward. There, upon my bed, was the open-backed gown I had come to know and love. Once on, I jumped into bed and warmed myself up — I was hungry and it was freezing. In front of me I could see a screen. Hospitals now had televisions? And what's this — the Internet too? I wasn't planning on doing much Web surfing: the necessity to update Facebook with every life moment hadn't permeated my soul by that point.

I asked the nurses what time dinner was. They told me that dinner had already been served, and that I wouldn't be able to eat after midnight. I pulled a puppy dog face and asked if there was any chance of something to eat now. One of the nurses disappeared and returned moments later with a spare meal. Aren't nurses amazing.

Just as I was tucking into my last supper, I could hear the unmistakable squeaking of shoes and the trundle of wheels. Dad appeared, complete with meagre suntan and badly packed suitcase.

"Perfect timing, son!" he grinned as he gave me a hug.

As I polished off my jam roly-poly and custard, we spoke about the past few months and the procedure for tomorrow. I could sense they were worried, but doing their best to hide it. And then all too soon a nurse popped in and apologetically said that it was time for them to leave. We hugged each other tight one last time knowing that, by the end of tomorrow, this tiny little growth that had changed my life and theirs would — fingers crossed — be gone forever. I lay in bed as I watched them walk away, and once they were out of sight, fixed my eyes on the TV screen.

* * *

I woke up. Or at least I think I did. I'd barely slept. The poor chap in the bed next to me spent the whole night coughing and gurgling, and there was nothing I could do to stop it. I lay there, mind on overload, desperately trying to drift off but simply unable to. All around me machines bleeped and lights blinked. I love to sleep in total darkness and I was fast realising this was not a luxury that would be afforded to me whilst staying in hospital. I made a mental note to ask Mum for a sleeping mask. My stomach rumbled: I was starving. But of course I couldn't eat. Balls. What I'd have given for a bowl of Coco Pops, a mug of tea, and a pile of chocolate biscuits.

9am and the anaesthetist arrived to talk me through the procedure. He told me that they were going to operate later that afternoon. He asked if I'd had any issues with general anaesthetic in the past and I replied that I hadn't. He went on to explain that, once I was asleep, they would prepare me for surgery. After clearing the nose from obstruction, they would make their way up the nostril to carry out a transsphenoidal adenomectomy — so named because the procedure takes place in and around the sphenoid sinus, one of the facial air spaces behind the nose. There they would make a small incision whereupon a fiberoptic endoscope would be fed up the nose: giving the surgeons high-resolution images of the area and thus allowing pinpoint accuracy in order to remove the tumour. The surgeon then had access to the pituitary fossa where the tumour resided. Using a range of implements called curettes, they would then proceed to scoop out the tumour.[135] It was their intention to remove all of the tumour — but he made me aware that this was not always possible and it depended upon the size of the tumour — however there were follow-up procedures that could take place to remove any excess. Once removed, they would then seal up the area they had cut in to and pack my nose with wadding and bandages. Understandably, my nose would feel sore afterwards. Some time after surgery they would then remove the wadding and — if everything was okay — I would be able to go home. If I had no further questions, I would need to sign a patient consent form agreeing that — should anything go wrong — the hospital was not at fault.

---

135 → Probably no good for ice cream.

So… did I have any questions?

I paused for a moment and took a minute to think. There was nothing I needed to ask. The time spent reading blogs, watching videos, and talking to sufferers of acromegaly had prepared me for this moment. I was comfortable with what was about to happen — so I took his pen and signed.

* * *

An hour later, a young man approached my bed. He explained that he was a student specialising in neurosciences and wondered if he could talk to me about my experiences and follow up how I was feeling after the surgery. I said he could, always happy to further medical research and — if truth be known — just happy to talk to someone for a bit. I explained my medical history to him and how I ended up being diagnosed with acromegaly. Like everyone else he was amazed, frantically scribbling down notes as he listened intently. He asked if there was anything he could help with. Having seen videos of the surgery on YouTube, I asked if there was any plans to film my procedure, considering how unique the circumstances were. He laughed and said he would check with the surgeons. I then suddenly had a ridiculous idea and asked if it was possible for me to keep the tumour. He thought that unlikely.

* * *

1pm. Nurses approached my bed, looked at my notes, and then smiled sympathetically as they realised I wasn't allowed to eat. If only Facebook had been mobile at that time — I could have told everyone about how hungry I was and received lots of 'Likes', well-wishes, and a picture of a dog eating cake. Instead, I had daytime television to keep me company. As I was just about to switch channels to endure another programme about houses, a team of nurses turned up with a hospital porter. The moment had arrived. I took my glasses off and lay down, arms by my side. It's such an odd sensation as you're being pushed down the corridors towards the operating theatre, people moving out of the way as you feel their eyes peering down at you. I know it happens all day every day but when you're lying there, in that moment, you feel like you're the only one that matters. The doors of the theatre bumped open and we were there. A few minutes wait as the team prepared themselves. A nurse took my arm and advised me that there would be a sharp scratch. I winced as a cannula was carefully inserted, the vessel by which my anaesthetic would be administered.

"Is there anything you want to ask before we start?"

"Yes. Could I see Mr Nelson?"

"We'll see if we can find him."

"Please," I replied. "I just have one question."

A couple of minutes later, Mr Nelson came through the doors, scrubbed up and ready to begin.

"Is everything okay?" he asked.

"Yes. Everything's fine. I just have one question. The tumour: how big is it? That's the only thing I don't know."

Even though I had been told it was around 1cm in length this, for some reason, at that moment, seemed massively important to me — and I wouldn't feel comfortable about proceeding until he told me.

"It's about 7mm long so it's not very big at all."

With that I smiled, looked at the anaesthetist and nodded,

ready to be put to sleep.

I lay back down, nervous and excited in equal measure: excited because of the possibilities that lay ahead — nervous because they were operating on my brain. I started to feel the cold trickle of anaesthesia running up my hand and into my arm. I enjoyed trying to fight it, trying to stay awake — knowing that within seconds I would be out flat. In a couple of hours time it would all be over. Would it be okay? I wondered. Was my eye condition finally going to get the better of me? How would I feel? Would I wake up?

Would I...

would I...

gone.

I try to open my mouth, but my lips are glued together. Someone dabs water on them as, slowly, my eyes start to unstick themselves. Through the foggy haze of anaesthesia I can make out shapes around the bottom of my bed: Mum... Dad... Alix... Maddie? They are all smiling at me. A voice asks how I'm feeling and I croak something back. Everyone tells me not to talk and I duly oblige. For some inexplicable reason I have a primal urge to rub my fingers together: they are bone dry. All my life my hands have been clammy and sweaty and now they aren't. Now they're dry. My brain takes a moment to compute this. If my hands are dry then that means the sweating must have stopped — and that means they must have taken the tumour out. I reach out towards the shadows before me and, with the conviction of a born-again Christian, utter the words: "Feel... my... hands!" before my eyes roll upwards and I make my way back to La La Land.

32. TWO STEPS FORWARD...

"FEEL MY HANDS."

Was that really the best I could do? After months of worry and stress and expectation, was "feel my hands" really the best I had to offer my anxious family as I emerged from my post-operation slumber? Apparently it was, but it was an important observation: my hands really *had* stopped sweating. Rubbing them in my morphine-induced slumber told me straight away that the tumour was gone. When I awoke properly some hours later, I rubbed them again — just to make sure. They were still dry — no longer the sweaty, clammy trowels I had grown accustomed to.

It's hard to explain, but I immediately felt different: somehow... lighter. My vital stats all seemed okay. I was passing urine too which was a good sign. All being well, I would be able to go home in a couple of days. The main hurdle now was the packs up my nose. Because of my past history with nosebleeds there was some concern about the impact of these and also the possibility of something called — wait for it — spinal fluid leak, or a 'CSF leak' to give it its proper title (Craniospinal Fluid). These leaks occur if there has been a tear in the membrane surrounding the brain. Pulling out the wadding up my nose would reveal if this had happened.

* * *

I spent the rest of the day drifting in and out of consciousness. There's no denying that surgery can really knock you about and sleep was pretty much all I could manage. At moments I would awake to see my family sat next to the bed or, indeed, to see no one at all. Either way, I was pretty oblivious to the world around me.

By early evening the anaesthesia was starting to wear off, and I found myself sat up in bed, quietly tucking in to some simple foods. It was good to eat something, anything. Like the septoplasty before, my taste was limited and, as I ate the last little bit of my pudding, a nurse approached to tell me it was time to take them out.

I put down my spoon and prepared myself. She approached the bed with what looked like a huge pair of pliers and asked me to lie down. She gently entered my nostril and caught hold of the end of the bandage and slowly started to pull… and pull… and pull. It was painful: not too dissimilar to that moment in *Total Recall* when Arnie pulls that huge, red tracking device out of his nose.[136] Finally the last of the bandages came out and with that, blood. Ahhh shit. I quickly

136 → Like this.

took up the nosebleed position. Within a couple of minutes it had stopped. Wow. That never happened. The nurse checked my nose again and was happy to report there was no sign of a CSF leak. Good news. If everything stayed like this I could go home tomorrow.

* * *

I awoke the next morning feeling good. The prospect of going home had perked me right up, helped by the fact that I was no longer consumed by the heavy weight of anaesthesia. As well as that, there were still no signs of a CSF leak. There was a little panic the night before when it felt like something was dripping down my nose but after an inspection by the nurses they reported that there was no sign of the clear, white fluid. However, they still applied a nasal dressing — just to be safe. After breakfast they removed the dressing and reported there was still no leak. Things were looking up. They advised me that, once Mr Nelson and the team had been to check on me, I should be able to go home.

The day seemed to drag on forever. I was bored of daytime TV now. There was little point in the family coming to visit if they were picking me up later that day. I updated Hijack with the news that I would be home soon and was greeted with messages of "Well done!" and "Good for you!" But apart from that I had very little to do but lie in bed and wait. I didn't mind though. The prospect of being back in my own flat and in my own bed was enough to keep me motivated. And of course, I'd be going home without a tumour in my brain. That was pretty motivating too. Dan 2.0 was ready for action.

Around 6pm the team appeared on the ward. I sat up —

aware that this was hopefully the moment where they would sign me off and send me home. I watched them as they walked round, spending a few minutes with each patient. After what seemed like forever, they made their way over to me. They inspected my notes and asked how I was feeling. I said I felt fine. They told me that the surgery had been a success and that they had removed — as far as they could tell — the entire tumour. This was amazing news. They asked the nurse how the removal of the wadding had been post-surgery and she told them that, after a small nosebleed, all seemed okay — with the exception of me feeling like I had something running down my nose. However, they couldn't see any evidence of CSF. Mr Nelson bent forward, removed the bandaging and… trickle. I furrowed my brow as I felt a substance run down my nose and onto my lip. It didn't feel like blood. As I put a finger to it and bought it close to my eyes, I could see it was white and thin. Spinal fluid, I presumed. Great. I looked at Mr Nelson and the team and they took a minute to discuss the situation. Their conclusion was, because I lived so close to the BRI, I could still go home. However, if there was any change in my health or if the leak got worse, I was to come back straight away. I wasn't going to argue: I was ready for my own bed and if they were confident that this wasn't an issue then so was I. I called Mum and told her the good news and she told me she was on her way. I packed my bags and sat on the edge of the bed, looking around the ward one last time as I waited for Mum to arrive.

* * *

Back home I was greeted by Norman and Millie who, after

their initial attempts to jump up in excitement, went back to bed. All I wanted to do was eat, eat well, and eat loads, so we ordered a massive Chinese takeaway. I was finally sat on my own sofa, in my own flat, indulging in spare ribs and spring rolls and quietly reminiscing about the past few days. Mum told me what had happened from their side of the operating theatre: about how nervous everyone was whilst I was undergoing surgery. I hadn't really thought about this. The rest of our family has generally been illness-free — I was always the one needing the treatments. Mum told me that, as they waited for the operation to finish, her closest friend Maddie turned to look at them, tears welling up in her eyes and exclaimed:

"The things you Jeffries' put me through!"

But now I was home and everyone was elated. The surgery had been a success and the tumour was gone. Gone! The hospital had given me some medication too: Codeine for the pain and Hydrocortisone tables to manage my hormones. These were more precautionary than a long-term treatment, just in case I needed them. I went to bed happy. Tender, but happy.

* * *

Having stayed at my flat for nearly three weeks, it was time for Mum to go home. She too was happy but knackered: and understandably so, what with looking after me, the dogs, and living the trauma of watching her son undergo life-threatening brain surgery. My sister took over 'Dan duties'. On the menu that night: another Chinese takeaway and a couple of films on TV.

During the day lots of friends had come to visit. This was just what I needed. They bought chocolates and grapes. We spoke about the surgery, about how I was starting to feel better, and the impact this would have on my life. They asked me if there was anything I needed and I politely replied that I was okay. By 3pm I was starting to feel tired and getting a bit of a headache. I apologised and announced that visiting time was over. They understood and quietly made their way out, hugging me as they left. I lay down on the sofa and closed my eyes, the dull headache making its presence known. I took some Codeine and fell asleep.

A couple of hours later I awoke to see my sister sat reading a magazine. I looked at her and realised that I felt worse than I did before. I wiped my nose. The CSF leak was still producing its thin white discharge and — whilst it hadn't gotten any worse — it was definitely more of a constant 'drip drip drip'. Alix suggested that I go and lie down in bed for a few more hours to see if I could get rid of the headache. I took a couple more Codeine, and duly obliged.

* * *

In the pitch black of my bedroom, I suddenly awoke. The throbbing in my head was now a brutal pounding. I lifted my fingers to my nose to find more white fluid. I slowly pushed myself up and sat on the edge of the bed. I reached out for the wall and moved my hand towards the door handle and gently pulled myself towards it. As I opened the bedroom door, glaring white light screamed into my eyes. I immediately shielded my face and for the first time realised that I could barely see. I could just make out the figure of my sister walking towards me, and — as she put her face to mine — her mouth dropped: she could see my head pulsating.

"I think I should go back to hospital."

She immediately called a taxi. Now, I realise how ridiculous this sounds but for some reason it never entered our heads to call an ambulance. Why would it? I only had a visibly throbbing head having undergone brain surgery — a taxi would be fine! In a way I think we subconsciously did this as calling an ambulance may have caused panic and elevated the situation. But for whatever reason, a taxi was ordered and a few minutes later it arrived and I slowly made my way out of the flat and into the car. I felt utterly dreadful. My sister made small talk with the driver but was keen to emphasise a sense of urgency about our journey. He duly obliged, the Traffic Light Gods clearly smiling down on us as every light we approached turned green. I sat on the back seat, head resting against the window, my eyes slowly opening and closing.

We pulled up outside the main entrance to Frenchay[137] and made our way to reception. My sister explained who I was and the surgery I had recently been through. They told us to sit down and we'd be called through shortly. The waiting room was packed and I said to my sister that we'd probably have to wait a while. Within seconds my name was called. I was guided into a room where I climbed up onto a bed. The hospital lights were agonisingly bright. I looked around for my sister but couldn't see her: I couldn't see much. But I could hear. And all I could hear was the urgent voices of the doctors and nurses around me, trying to keep me awake, as I slowly closed my eyes and drifted out of consciousness.

---

137   Why didn't we go to the BRI? I can't figure that one out either.

33. CSF

Two days later and I'm awake. All around me, a network of wires and machinery. I'm lying on my side, my knees tucked up into my chest. Fingers prod at the base of my spine. I try to lift myself up, but a nurse gently lowers me back down.

"Please be still, Mr Jeffries."

I feel the cold tip of a needle press against my spine as anaesthetic is slowly injected in. My brain throbs. My spine burns. I feel pressure building up around the injection area. Headaches come and go, I don't know what's going on. I'm still woozy as hell and — for once — a little scared.

"Can you tell me what's happening?" I ask nervously.

"Two days ago you contracted viral meningitis. Don't be alarmed: it's not the dangerous type and you're out of the woods now. We're about to insert a thin needle called a lumbar puncture into your back, which is going to drain off some of the CSF fluid that has built up around your brain. It's this fluid that has become infected and caused the meningitis. We believe that happened because the area where we performed the surgery to remove the tumour didn't seal properly and consequently became infected. Now be strong — I can't deny, this is going to hurt."

I close my eyes and clench my teeth as the needle slowly makes its way in. Meningitis. Fuck. I cry out in pain as the needle penetrates further. For the next thirty minutes, the consultant moves and tweaks the needle, making sure the spinal drain is secure and in place. I bite my lip and try to think of nothing. Finally, it's over. The consultant and nurse ask me if I'm okay and I whimper that I am. I ask if my parents have been contacted and the nurse tells me they have — I will be able to see them soon. She rubs my arm and leaves with the consultant but returns a minute later with a small syringe of liquid. I ask her what it is. "Oromorph. Liquid morphine. Now open wide." I duly oblige and she squirts the liquid into my mouth. Minutes later and I'm melting into the bed, the pain in my back slowly starting to fade.

* * *

I'm awake. The past two nights are a total blur. I remember the taxi ride up to Frenchay Hospital, I remember the waiting room and being called in, but after that… it's hazy. I vaguely remember being violently sick. When was that? Last night? The night before? A nurse comes over to give me a bed bath. Poor woman. A sign on the wall tells me that I'm in the High Dependency Unit. It must be bad. I have just been given a bed bath though. Swings and roundabouts.

* * *

7.30am. I'm feeling brighter this morning and able to eat some breakfast. I still can't move very well though: my back is tender. I look over to the drain and see the slow, steady drip of spinal fluid. Thank God they don't serve porridge. The lumbar puncture is draining 5-10ml of spinal fluid per hour in the hope that — when they take it out — the dripping from my nose will have stopped. Let's hope so.

As I finish the last mouthfuls of toast, I lie back and think about the past few days again. I still can't believe that I caught meningitis. Of all the bastard luck! I chuckle to myself that we called a taxi and not an ambulance. But no matter — I'm here. And if my sister hadn't been bright and alert then I might not be. I can't quite imagine what she had to go through: seeing her brother's head throbbing and then being taken away by the nurses as soon as we arrived at hospital. Not only that, she had to call Mum and Dad at 3am to tell them the news — to tell them that I had meningitis. That's not a phone call I would ever want to make, and I'm forever indebted to her rational thinking and strong resolve. Thank you Ali. Thank you.

After breakfast I talk to Mum and Dad on the phone. They've been to visit but I honestly don't remember much about the last few days. I remember the lumbar punch. I remember waking up and puking everywhere. I vaguely remember a catheter being fitted to help with draining excessive urine due to the wonderfully named *Diabetes Insipidus*.[138] But apart from those memorable activities, that's about it. I'm still in the HDU where my bloods and vital stats are checked every hour,

138   I always think this sounds like a spell Harry Potter would cast – 'DIABETES... INSIPIDUS!'

so I know I'm not totally out of the woods. The nurses tell me that I can move into a lower dependency ward soon, once my vital stats have stabilised. I ask how long I might be in for. As long as it takes, I'm told.

As I'm talking to the nurse, I start to notice that the vision in my right eye is fuzzy. Not all of it: just the very far right-hand side. It's wavy, distorted, blurry. This worries me. I've only got one working eye — the last thing I need is to lose sight in that one too. One of the consultants does the rounds at 7pm and I talk to him about it. He orders nil by mouth for the rest of the evening.

* * *

I wake up the next morning feeling better than I did yesterday. I hope this trend continues. I'm finding sleep difficult though: so many bright lights and beeping machines. I ask Mum to get me a sleeping mask and some earplugs. She'll be in later today, along with a couple of friends who want to come and say hello. Great news as I haven't seen anyone since I've been in. I'm now out of high dependency and in the 'normal' ward. This means less hourly checks, but it also means no more bed baths. Harrumph.

My right eye is still fuzzy. I don't like this at all. A field test is arranged and soon a specialist comes to collect me. My back is still in pain, so a wheelchair is my mode of transport to the other side of the hospital. Frenchay is a network of lengthy corridors and old-fashioned outhouses and it's a small trip to the necessary department. I haven't tasted fresh air in days and, though it's bitterly cold, it's nice to see the sky. I take the field test and instantly know there's something wrong. I'm just not seeing the little white dot when it's over on the right-hand side of my eye. Something has definitely happened.

Back on the ward and I'm refreshed after my little jaunt to the outside world. The one thing I am now absolutely desperate for is a shit. I don't think I've laid a cable since coming into hospital, and I feel more blocked up than a tube train in rush hour. I tell the nurses and they ask if I want a suppository. Hmm, not quite yet I advise — let's see if I can plop one out today. I text Alix that I haven't pooed since being in and that I might have to stick some tablets up my bum to help it out. She laughs.[139]

* * *

It's 4pm. I'm starting to get a bit bored. Daytime TV has yet again drained me of all humanity. Phone signal is really bad so I can't get online to post updates — though I have managed to inform everyone on Hijack and Facebook that I'm back in hospital, which is met with lots of sympathy and messages saying "get well soon" (still no 'Like' button — who would want to 'Like' this?). The ward itself provides some entertainment. I love watching the day-to-day activity: nurses doing their work, consultants talking to patients, patients talking to family. One old lad opposite me has regular visits from concerned family, but he seems to be doing okay. On the other side of him a man — late teens? — refuses to talk to the nurses or accept any form of medication or treatment. I have no idea what he's in for but I find this attitude absurd. I don't care how 'strong' you are — if you're in hospital, it's

139   Actually, she LOLs.

probably best to listen to the people that want to help you. But he doesn't and instead pops out for a cigarette. I inwardly roll my eyes, more upset for the nurses who are simply trying to help him get better.

Dinner arrives and I eat with gusto. I'm definitely starting to feel better. As I finish my pudding I feel a rumbling down below. Is this the moment I've been waiting for? I call the nurse over and tell her I think I'm ready. A minute later she returns with a commode and gently helps me out of the bed and sits me down on the loo. The lumbar drain is temporarily turned off and wheeled over next to me. I thank her for her assistance and close my eyes, willing my bowels to relieve me of this burden. Within seconds of sitting on the loo, Mum turns up. The curtain around my bed twitches as Mum calls "Hello!" and I tell her I'm on the loo, finally trying to have a poo. I ask if she can wait a minute and she says she will. Two minutes later, Pete turns up. I can hear Mum telling him not to go in as I'm "on the loo." He laughs and asks if I'm okay. I strain out a "Yessss" but I'm not. It feels like I'm trying to squeeze the last bit of toothpaste out of a tube that has nothing left to give.

Thirty minutes later and I'm still pushing for England. Mum and Pete are patiently waiting outside, talking to me through the curtain. I can hear them laughing at the situation and if I was that side of the curtain I would be laughing too. Five more minutes pass and, whilst I know something has come out, I haven't felt that final 'plop' to tell me that the ordeal is over. I decide to investigate and see what the problem is. I gently lift myself up to review the situation. What I see is a shit so large that it's filled the entire commode: so big that it actually has nowhere left to go! It's now my turn to laugh and I tell Mum and Pete that they should see this but unsurprisingly they decline. I decide to stand up a little further and, with a final push, the beast falls out. Victory is mine.

"I've finished!" I call out like a three-year-old, and they make their way in. We cautiously look into the commode to see a poo so big that it pokes its head out over the top. And — if that isn't fascinating enough — it's the exact shape of my bowel. We stare in wonder and disbelief. It is in fact so impressive that I take a photo.[140] I climb back into bed, feeling like a new man. Mum and Pete go to sit down just as the nurse announces that visiting time is over. I tell her that I've just been sat on the loo for the past forty-five minutes and was there any chance they could stay a bit longer? She laughs and agrees they can. We do our best not to talk about my poo.

* * *

I wake up the next day feeling goooood! Mum brought in some earplugs and a sleeping mask when she visited last night, which really helped me get some deep sleep. Not only that — the commode-based antics of the day before have left me much lighter. I feel like I'm getting back to normal. The nurse comes round and asks me if I want any breakfast. Do I?! I tell her I could eat a horse but instead opt for four slices of toast. I wolf them down and feel like I could eat more, but considering I've only just emptied my bowel I'm not sure eating half a loaf of bread is the best idea.

About 9am I feel the urge to have a wee. I look around for a nurse to help me but there doesn't seem to be one nearby. Now that I'm feeling better I decide it's time to fend for

140   You're lucky — it's lost.

myself, and slowly get out of bed and make my way to the toilet, dragging the lumbar drain behind me. I lift the toilet seat and steady myself to wee. Suddenly, there's a bubbling sensation at the top of my nose and a huge shooting pain fires up into my brain. I am in agony and pull the red cord next to me, feeling like I'm about to collapse. I lean against the wall, the bubbling sensation getting worse and worse. My eyes start to close. A nurse rushes in and adjusts something on the drain, takes my arm and slowly walks me back to bed. In my haste to show that I was getting better I had forgotten to turn off the lumbar drain — an essential action to perform if you're no longer lying down. I feel absolutely awful. As I lie in bed, Dad calls on the internal phone. I can't pick it up. This no doubt worries the hell out of him but within a couple of hours I'm feeling better and I call to explain what happened. I learnt a valuable lesson that day.[141]

I spend the next few hours quietly resting in bed, drowsy from the morning's experience. In the evening the girls from the Devon trip come to visit. As promised, one of them has brought me some porn mags. We giggle as we flick through them, trying to keep them hidden from the nurses. Whilst I am grateful, I don't think keeping them in the hospital is the best idea and I say I'll collect them once I'm out. One of the girls winks and stashes them in her handbag.

* * *

The young guy in the bed opposite me has gone. I ask one of the nurses what's happened and she tells me that he discharged

---

141   That lesson being: Don't run before you can walk. Or, to put it another way, don't walk unless your spinal fluid machine has been turned off.

himself during the night, not advising anyone that he was leaving. We look at each other, bemused. How someone can abuse a free service — and themselves — is beyond me.

I spend the day watching TV. Dad and Alix come to visit at lunchtime, which is very much needed. I can't express how vital these visits are, and knowing that people will be popping in makes the days much more bearable. Dad arrives with two magazines (not porn — that would be weird) and tells me to look through them and find some music equipment that I want. He promises me that, when I'm out of hospital, he will buy me some new gear for my home studio. Wow. How lucky am I? I know this is his way of keeping me motivated and positive but still — I'm extremely grateful.

"Is your TV working?" he asks.

I tell him it is and he asks me to put on Channel 4: the horse racing is on. I laugh and suggest this isn't really the time or the place but he's adamant — Kauto Star is about to run. Not only that, he's also going to put a bet on for me, certain in the knowledge that Kauto will win. How does £100 at 5/4 sound? I say it sounds great and he nips out of the ward to call the bookmakers. Alix and I look at each other and laugh. Minutes later he's back and tells me that the bet's been placed. We anxiously wait for the race to start and, once it does, we do our best to shout as loud as we can whilst recognising we're in the confines of a hospital ward. And, as predicted, Kauto Star romps home and we all punch the air in delight. After all the exertion I'm starting to feel a little tired, and Dad and Alix give me a kiss and make their way out, Dad reminding me to look at those music tech magazines and choose the equipment that I want. I say that I will. I can't explain how important these moments are in keeping me sane.[142]

* * *

It's time to find out if the spinal drain had done its job and whether the CSF leak has stopped. Before that, the nurses want to take some bloods. This means putting a cannula into a vein. Three different people try to fit one: in my arms and in the back of my hand. None of them are successful. By the end I look like a dartboard. I have no idea why, but my veins don't want to play ball, and the idea of fitting a cannula is temporarily abandoned. Later in the day a different nurse has a go and thankfully she's successful.

Lunchtime. My appetite has really come back and I accept the offer of food with open arms. As I'm quietly tucking in, a loud buzzer goes off in the High Dependency Unit, and nurses rush over to a patient. They pull the curtains around him and suddenly the ward goes into overdrive, consultants and nurses urgently at work. Minutes later and the curtains gently open and the team slowly leave. It doesn't take a genius to work out what's happened. Someone goes to inform the family and a few minutes later they walk into the ward, faces red and blotchy. As they approach the bed, loud cries and wails can be heard and the curtains are pulled round the bed for the last time. This is the closest I have come to seeing someone die before me and it is a thoroughly sobering experience. It re-emphasises the fact that, whilst I have my own set of problems, there are people out there with far greater issues than mine. I

---

142   It wasn't until a year later that Alix revealed to me that, because of the poor phone signal in the hospital, Dad never actually made that bet — he had to give me the winnings out of his own pocket. How I laughed.

look at the old guy in the bed opposite me. No words are said.

That evening a nurse comes to tell me that they'll be taking my spinal drain out tomorrow. I text the family and let them know.

* * *

Morning arrives. I'm looking forward to finally having my back back. Around 11am, a team make their way to my bed, ready to remove the drain. Removing it is far less painful than fitting it and it only takes a few minutes until it's out. A nurse peers under the bandage wrapped around my nose and it's good news: there are no immediate signs of CSF leak. I update Facebook.

That afternoon the team return to see if the lumbar drain has finally stopped the spinal fluid leak. The bandage is removed from beneath my nose and... drip... drip... drip. The familiar white fluid is back: the treatment hasn't worked. They advise that they will check later tonight and tomorrow to see if the dripping has stopped but deep down I know they'll be going back in to fix it.

* * *

I awake the next morning and can taste the fluid in the back of my throat. The dripping hasn't stopped. Even before they tell me I know that surgery is inevitable. Whilst I'm obviously happy that this will (finally) fix the problem, I'm somewhat disconsolate too. For the first time in weeks I am feeling really good: strong, lively, sharp. I know that — if I do go back into surgery — I'll become slow and sluggish with the after-effects of anaesthesia. It can't be helped, I know that, but I still don't like the thought of it.

Midday, and the team returns. They remove the bandaging again and within seconds the white fluid drips onto my bed sheets. It's confirmed: surgery will take place. The procedure is the same by going up through the nose, but this time they won't be hunting for tumours. Instead they will take a strip of fatty tissue from my thigh and use that to 'plug' the hole where the infection occurred. There is still the complicated network of blood vessels to negotiate however but they are confident that this is a routine procedure.

That evening a nurse confirms that I will be having surgery tomorrow.

* * *

I wake up to find it's a gloriously sunny day. And it's a Saturday too. I figure that — if they're operating on the weekend — this must be important. I talk to the family who are naturally concerned but pleased it's going ahead. At 11am, the porters come to collect me and wheel me to the operating theatre. I'm not scared, just sad at how groggy and low I know I will feel post-surgery. I have no questions this time. I see this simply as an intricate puncture repair job.

* * *

4pm and I'm back on the ward. As expected, I feel crap but I'm just pleased that it's all over. I can't taste any salty fluid. This is a good sign, but the nasal packs will have to stay in for another forty-eight hours before we truly know the results. I want to sleep. I call over a nurse and croakily ask for some Oromorph. She duly obliges. Night night.

* * *

The next day. Still no drips. Have got a headache though. Not sure why — they're keeping an eye on it.

Nose packs out tomorrow.

* * *

I wake up, not feeling too clever. Still got headaches. I wonder if it's the pressure of the nose packs? I hope and pray it's not the evil, thin, white liquid making a return. I can't taste anything as yet but we'll know later on today.

1pm. Another inspection by the team. I've still got headaches so I'm given more medication to help. They'll take the packs out tonight.

7pm. The moment of truth. As luck would have it, my mum and grandad pay me a visit just as they're about to take the wadding out. They decide not to watch and wait outside until it's over. The nurse gently pulls the material from out of my nose until there's nothing left. The team watch with anticipation. No white liquid. But then there is blood. And lots of it. For the next hour, I'm rendered useless by one of the worst nosebleeds I've had in years. Mum and Grandad stand by my bed as I gush and cough up blood, unable to talk. I guess this wasn't the visiting hour they were hoping for. I feel sorry for my grandad as it's something of a wasted journey, but he understands.

Later that evening a nurse comes to check on me. The

bleeding has stopped. She looks at my nose and asks me to lean forward: there's no white fluid. Happy days. Drained from such a loss of blood, I don my eye mask and earplugs and quickly fall asleep.

* * *

Oh frabjous day! I'm going home! It's been three days since the surgery and all reports indicate that the hole at the back of my nose has been fixed. My intravenous drugs are replaced for oral ones. I start to notice that the area around my right thigh where they took the skin graft feels numb. I'm advised that this is to be expected. The team come to visit me. I can go home tomorrow.

* * *

After nearly two weeks in hospital, I'm finally given the all-clear. There's no sign of the CSF leak anymore, and the consultants are happy with the treatment area. A nurse writes up a prescription of drugs for me: Hydrocortisone and Codeine, just in case. Mr Nelson, Sam, and the rest of the team come to visit me in the afternoon, happy to sign me off, giving me advice about how to look after myself for the next few days. I thank them for all their work. They smile and walk away, ready to look at the next patient. To them it's another day's work — to me it's a life-changing experience.

Conscious of how much travelling Mum has done these past few weeks, I call a friend and ask if he can come and pick me up. I slowly pack my bags and say my goodbyes to the other patients and nurses whom I have grown so fond of during the past few weeks. My friend arrives and he slowly escorts me down the now familiar corridors, my back and legs still aching from the surgery. The outer doors swing open and I step into the cool night air. He unlocks the car door for me and I gently ease myself into the passenger seat, whereupon a smile hits my lips as we pull out of the car park, finally heading for home.

DAN 2.0

34. CAUGHT BY THE FUZZ

I'M HOME.

I gently make my way down the steep flight of steps outside my flat. My back twinges with every step I take. I walk through the door to be greeted by two mad dogs… plus Norman and Millie. (Sorry Mum and Alix — couldn't resist!) It's good to be back home. Mum asks if I want anything, but all I want to do is sit and feel the cushions on the sofa nuzzle into my back. I familiarise myself with my surroundings, recalling that the last time I was here I could barely see. One thing I notice is that the flat is immaculate. Mum and Alix have clearly been busy whilst I was away — no doubt a coping mechanism to keep them sane. I slowly push myself up and head to my bedroom — to find it has been completely rearranged. The bed is now against the wall, giving me much more room to move. Alix really *has* been hard at work. She asks me what I think and I smile, a little unnerved by the change. I promise to try it out.

That night I barely sleep. My back is in utter agony and I'm not totally enjoying sleeping next to the wall. Mum and Alix both stay over to make sure I'm okay. In the morning, we call the hospital to say that my back is in pain and that it aches every time I move. They tell me to take some painkillers. God, how stupid. The simplest things are often the most effective and that night — after moving my bed back to where it was — I sleep like a baby.

The next morning, I awake to find my sheets soaking wet. Oh God... have I wet myself? As I get out of bed I notice that the skin on my hands is completely shrivelled up, like when you've been in the bath for too long. The next morning it happens again, the mattress now soaking wet too. I can only conclude that this must be all the excessive fluid in my body making its way out of my system. I try on an old pair of shoes, ones that I could never get into before. They fit. This is incredible! Within a few weeks of the tumour being removed my body was now morphing itself into something new. Dan 2.0 is being born.

* * *

I'd now been home for a few days and was slowly starting to get back to normal — well, as normal as leaking fluid from your body can be. Mum and Alix were there to look after me since the start and I'm indebted to them for their support, but it was time for me to fend for myself. My back — with the help of painkillers — was slowly starting to recover, and I could move without the need for someone to hold me upright. I'd even managed to take the dogs for a walk — thank goodness they're senior citizens. So at around 8pm, once Mum had cooked dinner for the last time, we hugged and looked at each other and smiled, relieved that it was finally over. Life could start afresh. She left and I sat on the sofa, slowly becoming aware of how eerily quiet the flat was. I'd been living on my own for years but I hadn't been on my own for weeks — since we were waiting for a bed to become free back in early November. And now my own company seemed a little alien to me. I decided that I quite fancied a pipe — partly to ease the pain but mostly because I hadn't had one in ages and, quite simply, I fancied one. I wasn't a big smoker but it seemed like the right time: a mini celebration if you will. I loaded up the pipe with a little bit of weed and reached for the lighter, but it wasn't there. I checked a couple of drawers and then looked in more abstract places, but I just couldn't find one. I started to panic, refusing to be denied the one thing I really wanted. I frantically searched some more, but I knew it was hopeless. I plonked myself on the sofa and — for the first time in years — started to cry. Now this might seem like a ridiculous reaction but I think it was an escalation of lots of things: not being independent, not being able to walk to the shops, and not being able to do what I wanted. A minute later I was fine, and I recognised, for that night at least, getting stoned was not on the cards.

Speaking of cards — it was nearing Christmas. Unsurprisingly, I hadn't had much time to get any presents sorted, and I was in no fit state to traipse around town, fighting my way through the marauding crowds of Bristol. The Internet came to my rescue, and I ordered all the presents I needed. I still wasn't back at work yet, and I was now on statutory sick pay. I had kept everyone at work informed of my progress and the messages of support and sympathy had been brilliant. Dad chucked a little bit of money my way to help me out of the slump. And as Christmas approached, there was a definite sense that this was going to be a special one. And it was. We celebrated the day quietly but determinedly, the focus — unsurprisingly — on me and the past few weeks. After lunch, Dad stood to talk about recent events, his voice breaking on occasion. I stood too (did I? Maybe I didn't for once, my back being in so much pain), and talked about how brilliant the family had been, and what an incredible journey we'd had. I joked about how much this was going to cost Dad as I'd finally decided on what music tech equipment I wanted. We all raised our glasses and toasted to better days.

With Christmas done for another year, it was time to face the impending misery that was New Year's Eve. Did I say that? I mean… it was time to face the joy and exultation of New Year's Eve, and for once, I was up for it. Back home after Christmas, I decided to venture into town to buy some new clothes. I was the thinnest I had been — down to fourteen stone — and I felt I deserved some new threads. My back was still sore but painkillers were helping, and I refused to stay at home forever.

Sunday morning. Time to hit the sales. Bristol was nice and quiet as I made my way down Park Street and though the centre, quietly strolling towards Broadmead. I'd missed walking through Bristol. I reached a set of traffic lights and waited for the signal to cross. When it came, I slowly made my way over, in no hurry to race against the lights. As I reached the other side of the road — BANG! — I walked straight into two homeless guys.

"Watch where you're fuckin' going!" they shouted, and I apologised profusely for not seeing them.

I walked away shaken: not because I had walked into two winos but because this was further proof that something had affected my eyesight, either during the surgery or after it. These guys had simply walked towards me from the right-hand side of my vision and I just hadn't seen them. Upset but unperturbed, I made my way into Broadmead. Town was busier now and the right-hand side of my eye was getting fuzzy again. People walked in front of me and I only saw them at the last minute — making me jump out of my skin every time. I finally made it to the shops where I bought myself a new suit: beautifully cut and sporting a size thirty-four waist! Mama mia! Someone was going to look dapper for the New Year's celebrations.[143]

Normally I would spend New Year's Eve out clubbing or, even better, DJing, but this year I wasn't up for anything too strenuous. My back was still delicate, and it was more important to have close friends around me than to party with strangers. I made my way into town, dressed to the nines in my particularly dashing suit. I felt self-conscious but confident, carrying an air of someone that had just undergone brain surgery and survived meningitis. The party was at The Grain Barge, a well-known boat cum restaurant. As I walked on my own to the harbourside, groups of people laughing and joking passed me by. It reminded me of my own single existence and — even though I knew I was going to meet friends — I guessed I'd probably be going home alone. The tumour had gone, but the damage to my testosterone hadn't.

As I climbed aboard the boat, I was greeted with hugs and whoops and cheers — people genuinely happy to see me out

143   → Me.

and see me healthy. As we welcomed in the New Year, I made my own little toast to the powers that be, thankful that I was here to see in 2008.

35. EYES RIGHT!

AND 2008 GOT OFF TO A FLYING START.

First off: music equipment. I was toying with the idea of a new synth or a keyboard but it didn't take me long to realise what I really wanted: an iMac. I had never been a Mac fan, but just before I went into hospital I was asked to do a demonstration of Reason software at a big music tech conference at the Birmingham NEC. One of my work colleagues was showing Logic in another room. I popped in to see what he was doing and instantly fell in love with the software. As well as that, ATM were now introducing more and more Macs into the classroom — so it felt like a natural progression. My PC had served me well but it had been struggling of late and I wasn't feeling that inspired. I was hoping that a new approach would give my creative arse the kick it needed. The iMac arrived just after New Year's Day — the best present I could have had (besides the successful removal of a brain tumour, of course). Thanks, Dad. Love you!

Between Christmas and New Year, I received a call from the BRI, wanting me to make an appointment with the endocrinology team. This was merely a routine check-up, just to see how I was feeling after the surgery and to monitor my medication. Alix came along and we were lucky enough to see Professor Lightman again — the man who had guided us through this from the start. We discussed the past few weeks: surgery, meningitis, the CSF leak, how my shoe size had decreased, and how I had stopped sweating so much. We also discussed the fuzziness in my eye, something that had settled down but was still noticeable. And then we started talking about sex.

"And how's your sexual activity?" he asked.

I looked at my sister, slightly embarrassed.

"Err… it's okay. Not great though." I could feel my face getting hotter.

"And do you get erections in the morning?"

This caught me off guard. How did I answer that with my sister sat next to me?! I turned to her.

"Sorry you have to hear this."

"Oh, don't be sorry," interrupted the Professor. "This is something that needs to be addressed by the both of you."

I looked at Alix and we burst out laughing.

"Dude… she's my sister!"

Now it was his turn to go bright red. Embarrassment over, he suggested that I try something that might help: testosterone injections. It was true — I wasn't feeling much in the love department and morning wood was barely a morning twig. An immediate injection was requested and then another one in six weeks time, followed by regular injections every three months. As well as discussing my testosterone, we looked at the recent results from my blood tests. And it was good news: my glucose levels had dropped. This was a direct result of the tumour being removed — the pituitary gland was no longer producing the excessive hormones as it had been all those years before.

I am delighted to say that the glucose tolerance test you [my doctor] performed on 3rd January shows that all his growth hormones are markedly improved, starting at a basal level of 0.7 and falling to 0.4.

All in all, it was a successful consultation, incest *faux pas* aside. It was confirmation that I was on the mend and that my body was responding to the surgery. I commemorated the day by writing a new blog post and making an appointment to see the nurse, eager to get some red-hot testosterone inside me.

* * *

A week later and I was in the treatment room at my doctors, pants round my ankles, and bum on full view. The Nebido injection was huge: a 1000mg ampule of liquid that had the consistency of treacle. The injection — right in the meat of my bum — took around a minute. That is a BIG injection and the next day I could barely walk. I soon got over this, however, when, a few days later the magic started to happen. My morning twig had now become a mighty oak. I'd wake up, peer under the duvet, and laugh to myself at how powerful it was. It was like a diamond cutter on steroids. And it wasn't just the pants department that was improving either: I was also feeling more confident, more sociable. Music and creativity were on the up too, which made me very happy. But it was mostly about the nether regions, and it was a huge boost to my masculinity.

* * *

Now that my brain tumour had been removed, it was time to undergo the second phase of Dan 2.0: straightening my eye.

All my life I have suffered from my left eye not looking straight ahead. It *was* blind after all and therefore surplus to requirements so, understandably, it just did its own thing. But after thirty years of blindness the drift was now particularly noticeable.[144] Compared to a brain tumour it might sound insignificant, but I knew this cosmetic tweak would make me feel a whole lot better. I was initially going to have it done mid-2007 after that pivotal visit to the Eye Hospital but — because of the imminent tumour removal — it was put on hold. Now the tumour was gone and it was agreed that squint surgery could go ahead and an appointment was made for March. I couldn't wait.

Happily, life had pretty much returned to normal. I went back to work in the first week of January (which may seem somewhat soon after major surgery), but, in truth, I had missed it. Weeks in hospital and sat at home had turned my brain into putty, and I was eager to be back with my fellow colleagues and students — enveloped in the hustle and bustle of the classroom. But something was different. I still loved teaching but I felt like I needed a new challenge. I was, after

---

144 → Especially in photos. See what I mean? (No pun intended).

all, Dan 2.0 and something inside me was stirring. I just got the feeling that life — from this point on — needed to be about *me*. I loved my job, don't get me wrong, but I had come to the conclusion that my pesky little tumour had undoubtedly contributed to me being utterly focused on my work, almost to the point of fixation. Something had to change.

In 2005, myself and another colleague had started to explore something called Moodle. Moodle is what's known as a Virtual Learning Environment (or VLE), a place where students could upload work and access resources, whilst tutors could give grades and feedback and create activities like quizzes and discussion boards — activities students could undertake outside of the classroom. I was finding this angle of education more and more interesting as it combined my love of all things tech whilst helping students develop their skills. My mind was a muddle: I didn't want to leave ATM but I did want something new.

It was therefore a stroke of luck that, a couple of weeks after starting back, a new position became available within the company. It was for a Curriculum Advisor. The role involved working with colleges who delivered our qualifications by helping them get set up, making sure they were teaching the right combination of units, and moderating/approving the work later in the year. It involved travel to different parts of the country and a not-to-be-sniffed-at pay rise too. This definitely sounded like the kind of change I was after. I had already helped the curriculum team with some unit rewrites a couple of years before and my work with Moodle meant that I was becoming more and more involved with wider aspects of the curriculum. I decided to apply.

Whilst waiting for a response, March arrived. This was

my first birthday since coming out of hospital and I was determined to celebrate in style. I've always put a lot of stock in birthdays, and still do, and this one felt like the most important yet. I was, after all, ALIVE! and Dan 2.0 was out to party. It was spread over two nights: the first was a raucous game of poker, whilst the second involved ridiculously strong cider and clubbing. It was exactly what I needed. I looked trim and felt confident, no doubt helped by the testosterone that was now starting to surge through my veins. The difference it was making was really starting to show.[145]

A week later I received two letters. One was from ATM, asking if I was available in mid-April for an interview. Yes! The second was from the Eye Hospital, asking me if I was available on March 26th for squint surgery. Double yes! Things were starting to move — I could feel the wheels of change in motion. ATM asked me to prepare a short presentation about my role in the company and the latest educational initiatives around apprenticeships, the Eye Hospital asked me to prepare by not eating from midnight. I was happy to do both.

* * *

Time for surgery. I needed to be at the hospital for 7am — not ideal, but as it was only ten minutes down the road, I couldn't really complain. I had already spoken to my consultant who had explained in detail what would be happening. This was a routine procedure in which the muscles attached to the outside of the eye were moved to a new position. By doing this, the eye is straightened. He advised that he would

145 → Man, I look good!

probably overcompensate and bring the eye a little further in than normal because, after twenty years or so, the eye would inevitably drift out again. Surgery would take around an hour and — all being well — I would be home the same day. Wow. Compare that to the fun and games of last year and this was going to be a breeze. I got into my gown (how I had missed these), climbed into bed, and waited to be wheeled in. Mum sat by my side, as ever.

Twenty minutes later and I was on my way to surgery. Whilst I was being wheeled through the corridors of the Eye Hospital, I thought about how many years I had been coming here and... wait a minute... they do surgery?! Of course they did: it was a hospital. I was being silly and I blamed my lack of breakfast for my rare moment of stupidity — mixed with the mild excitement at finally getting my wonky eye fixed. That familiar sensation of the operating theatre doors being pushed open greeted me once more. I said hello to the team. I always enjoyed coming in to surgery. Is that strange? Final checks were made before that cool tingling sensation made its way through my veins. I thought about making a joke about how I had forgotten to mention something important but that was…

it was…

shouldn't I…

gone.

* * *

An hour later and I was awake — a massive bandage wrapped around my head. The family were sat by the bed, gently welcoming me back into reality. I felt groggy as hell but the smiles on their faces soon perked me up. Behind them stood the surgeon.

"Welcome back, Daniel. Everything was a success. We'll leave the bandages on for a little while and, once you're feeling better, we can remove them, look at the eye and — assuming everything's okay — you can go home."

Just the news I wanted to hear. I reached up and felt the bandages. Thankfully this time they weren't shoved up my nose. An hour later, a nurse approached the bed and told me it was time to take them off. There was a noticeable air of excitement in the room. It was like that moment in *Batman* when The Joker has his reconstructive surgery: hopefully I wouldn't look quite so demented or respond in the same way. Mum, Dad, and Alix stood round the bed as the bandages were slowly unwrapped and — as the last strand of material left my face — I tentatively opened my crust-laden eye and looked at the people around me. An audible gasp could be heard... I WAS A MUTANT! Of course I wasn't. The gasp was because — for the first time in years — my eyes were looking straight. I was handed a mirror and I looked for myself, a grin spreading over my face.

I'd just been upgraded to Dan 2.1.

36. HORMONES

THE SURGERY WAS A SUCCESS. THE TEAM WERE VERY HAPPY with the results and after giving me some medication (eye drops and a bit of cream), I was released — just in time for lunch. I was keen to share the news with Facebook (this was becoming standard procedure for *any* life event now), so I asked Dad to record a video of me moving my eyes. Yes, it hurt a little as I rolled them around for the camera, but I was so pleased to have both eyes looking in the same direction that it was worth the brief bout of pain.[146]

Over the next couple of weeks my time was divided between watering my weeping, bloodshot eye and preparing for the upcoming job interview. I had done some research on the new apprenticeship, and built a pretty effective PowerPoint that covered these details and outlined the work

146 → Excuse the slightly poor video, but you get the eye-dea (I'll stop soon).

I was doing with Moodle and other areas of the curriculum. I was even able to include a couple of pictures from a recent marketing photo shoot – something I was sure would seal the deal.[147]

Interview day arrived and I made my way to the Head Office in Leicester. Keen to make an impression I donned the suit I had bought at Christmas. Before 2007, a three-hour train journey combined with a sea of nerves would probably have left me sweating like a monk in a nunnery, but now I was cool and fresh — like an advert for chewing gum or a well-known men's deodorant.[148] I arrived, signed myself in and waited to be called. No sweating. No nerves.

A few minutes later and I was called in to the interview room. Because of the work I had done recently with the curriculum team, I knew the two people doing the interview pretty well. Indeed, I had interviewed one of them a couple of years before about the early years of Access to Music as research for a teaching qualification. I shook hands with them both and sat down. Knowing them didn't do me any favours though, and I had to work hard to answer some challenging questions and consider difficult scenarios that were presented to me. When the time was right I opened my laptop and delivered my presentation — talking about the changes in education, my work with helping to write new units and how I was managing the online system I had introduced a couple of years before. I could sense it was going well.

Interview over, I shook hands and walked out, a big smile plastered across my face. I had done it. I don't know

---

147 → Nothing says 'teacher' better than pointing at a screen.
148 Sponsorship deals gratefully considered.

how I knew, but I just knew that I had nailed it. I called home, excited about the interview and — with as much caution as I could muster — stated that I thought it was mine. I hung up the phone and made my way down Leicester High Street, on the hunt for some lunch. A few minutes later my phone rang: it was one of the interviewers. She congratulated me on a particularly impressive presentation and was delighted to offer me the post. I thanked her and hung up the phone, beaming from ear to ear. Would I have been as confident in my interview if that horrible little tumour had still been inside me? I think not. I decided to celebrate with a particularly sinful cream cake.

To be honest, I would have probably bought that heart-clogging cake even if I had been told my interview was awful and I should never work in education again. Since coming out of hospital, I could not stop eating. I accepted that I was going to pig-out a bit over Christmas — everyone does — but this was next-level gorging. I could eat the biggest meal on offer and, fifteen minutes later, start to feel peckish again. And this saddened me because, just before going in to hospital, I was the leanest I had been in years. It amazed me how much weight I lost in hospital too, considering I just lay in bed all day. I guess a controlled diet and no temptations meant I shed the pounds. But now I was piling them on. Why was this? Did I just have appalling self-control? Or was my new medication — the testosterone injections — responsible for my weight gain and appetite?

If the injections weren't responsible for making my stomach grow, they were definitely responsible for giving me major backache. Days after the injection my body would sob in agony and I'd find myself clutching the base of my back every time I stood up. Was the promise of magnificent erections worth this terrible pain? I wondered if there was another way to get the testosterone inside me. I had a consultation coming up with Professor Lightman — there was no harm in finding out.

It transpired that there was: it was called Testim, a gel that was rubbed onto the shoulders morning and night. It wouldn't be as powerful as the injection but being able to walk properly was, at that time, more important than getting a stalwart stiffie. I was, after all, sadly using my legs far more than I was using my tackle. Professor Lightman made a note of this at our consultation:

> In terms of his testosterone replacement, he was tried on Nebido but gave this up as he was concerned that the effects wore off a bit quickly and quite severely two months after the injections, and also he was getting quite severe pain in his back two weeks following the injections. He was switched to testim gel which he has been using as per normal and I have checked his testosterone level with the bloods that I am doing on him. I have encouraged him, after this to increase the dose to two sachets a day so hopefully this will lift his testosterone levels and improve the symptoms of lack of libido, lack of drive, and fatigue. If not and his testosterone levels are still low we may have to reconsider.

There definitely was a lack of drive. Even with a new job and even with my musical output being the best it had been for ages, I had started to feel sluggish again: nonplussed, disinterested. Was this my hormones or was it just me?

Erections out of the way, we spoke about my hunger levels:

> *In terms of his increase in hunger, certainly post operatively he had good growth hormone levels to glucose stimulation but l have elected to repeat this in case he is having an early recurrence of his Acromegaly. l will also repeat his thyroid function to make sure that this can not be the causing [of] his problem.*

The suggestion of a return of the tumour was somewhat worrying but (and I appreciate this sounds daft), I didn't think that was the reason. Somehow I would have *known* if the tumour was returning. My hunger was due to something else, but right now we couldn't put our collective finger on it.

Next up for discussion: fuzzy vision. I stated that it hadn't gotten noticeably worse but it was still a bit fuzzy and I was still bumping into people when walking about town. Not only that, I was bumping into things in my own home too, particularly door frames. This might sound ridiculous but I just couldn't judge the width of my doors — crazy considering I had lived there for over two years. Professor Lightman noted that I had an appointment at the Eye Hospital coming up and an MRI scan too, so we would see the results of those before proceeding any further. Finally, he reminded me that I was due another colonoscopy — on the hunt for those pesky polyps. My mind shot back to 2007 and the farts I recorded on my phone. I wondered if this was a good opportunity to further expand my sonic repertoire.

* * *

As tempted as I was, I made the creative decision *not* to use farts in my compositions. During April and May I had started to write more house music — moving away from drum and bass — partly in thanks to Logic and partly due to a really strong house and techno resurgence in the UK, especially in Bristol. Bristol has always been at the forefront of pushing new music and whilst house had never gone away, dubstep had really taken over the city: a sound I was not particularly keen on. I was also hungry to push my DJing again and looked into online radio stations. I contacted a website called Brap FM with an idea for a show called 'Welcome to the Bleep Seats'.[149] It wasn't a radio show *per se* — more me mixing minimal techno for two hours. But it gave me something to promote once a month, and I loved the thrill of discovering new music.

There was more creativity to come when, in May, I put myself forward for a Laptop Battle. "A *what?*" I hear you cry. A Laptop Battle! No — I'd never heard of it either.

Basically, a Laptop Battle involves nerds on horseback, jousting with their MacBooks. If only. It was actually a live event where producers got together and 'battled' their musical and technical skills in front of a live crowd. Judges would rate their performance, awarding a prize to the overall winner. Feeling brave, I put my name forward and was duly accepted.

Round One saw me up against Severn, a producer who had modified his setup to use a PlayStation controller to trigger loops and sounds. Ableton (another music production package) had been around for a little while and was synonymous with beat mangling — ideal for this setup. I didn't have a laptop so

---

149   A brilliant pun on The Wonder Stuff's song 'Welcome to the Cheap Seats'.

I brought my iMac and a keyboard, which looked ridiculously large in comparison.[150]

Round One was two songs, two minutes each. Let battle commence!

My first performance, a house tune, went okay, but I could tell the crowd were after something else. Severn stepped up and produced an aural assault, PlayStation controller in hand. He did good — so it was time to bring out the big guns.

As worrying as this might sound, I had made the creative decision to include some porn samples into one of my tracks, like you do. In search of more samples on the net (honest, Mum!), I stumbled upon a website called... wait for it... *Porn for the Blind*. I kid you not.

The idea behind the site was that the good-natured folk of the Internet would describe pornographic scenes for blind people. Now, this sounds ludicrous but — if you're blind — I can imagine it being an invaluable service.[151] As I clicked through the descriptions my jaw dropped: someone had recorded a description of *Two Girls One Cup*. Now if you don't know what that is then <u>don't</u> go searching for it on the Net! It is famous for all the wrong reasons and yet, despite this, some brave soul had decided to explain every single detail.

Within a minute of listening, you could hear the mixture of shock and repulsion in his voice. Thirty seconds later and he started to crack — and so did I. This was comedy gold! Trying to explain to someone exactly what's going on in *Two Girls One Cup* was an exceptionally brave thing to do, and you could hear the disgust in his voice as he did his best to

---

150   → See?

151   And being half blind, I felt like I was participating in some serious medical research.

get through all three minutes. By the end I knew this was the sample I had to use.

So did I win? Watch the first round to find out![152]

Having won Round One (sorry for the spoiler) it was time for Round Two. This time it was two three-minute tracks against the brilliantly named Elastic Space Cat. He was playing drum and bass, which I knew would be a crowd pleaser — I figured I should too.

So did I win? Watch the semi-final to find out![153]

Back in the real world, I was moving ever nearer to the start of my new job. I was going to continue to manage the Music Technology pathway in Bristol, but my teaching hours had been cut, giving me more time to focus on curriculum, moderation, Moodle, and — at last — me. I knew that this new role was going to be difficult and would pose a lot of challenges. So, in July, I decided to do something I hadn't done in a long time: I went on holiday.

There had been murmurings about me and Alix taking a break but what with the past few months being somewhat hectic, it was always being put on hold. Now we felt ready and with my wonky eye fixed, I could finally ask the locals for directions without them wondering who I was talking to. I hadn't been abroad in years, not since my visits to Greece in my early twenties. We eventually settled on Tunisia: it was hot, relatively cheap, and there was stuff to do. Or we could do nothing. I've never been particularly adventurous nor had ambitions to see the world, but I did fancy getting away for a

---

152   → Oooh - how exciting!

153   → If you can't be bothered to watch, I can tell you now — I didn't win. Elastic Space Cat played better music and a three-minute house loop clearly didn't cut it with the judges. If you look at my face at the end of the video you can see just how disappointed I am which, in retrospect, was probably a good thing: it showed I cared.

bit. So we booked up, packed our bags, and set off for sun, sea, and sex — though not with each other.

Sun and sea were there in abundance. As for the sex — well, we probably shouldn't have booked a hotel for the over-60s. It was our own fault. We didn't want a place full of screaming kids nor did we want the Tunisian equivalent of Ayia Napa, so we settled for somewhere a little more serene. It was lovely during the day, but by night it turned into a madhouse of line dancing and bingo. I happen to love bingo, so I was in my element, and it won us three bottles of cheap plonk. Bingo aside, we went on a few trips, rode some camels, got ripped off by the local taxi drivers, and watched a man play tennis in his pants.[154] That was probably the highlight of the holiday. That and a certain photo. If anyone can hazard a guess as to what Alix is actually doing here, please let me know.[155]

Returning to Bristol, I was greeted by a whopping mobile phone bill. Oh silly, silly Daniel. Just before I left for Tunisia, I had bought myself a new pair of glasses. When I went to collect them, the person serving me handed me a slip of paper with a phone number on it.

"This is the number of the girl who served you last week. Give her a call."

Blimey. For the first time in years I had someone interested in me! Typically it had to happen just before I went on holiday so — in my excitable state — I spent the ten days there texting her. It cost me a fortune. When I got back I got cold feet. I don't know what it is with me. I think I start to question *why* someone might like me even though, deep down, I knew

154   → Classy

155   → Nope, we've no idea either.

I'm perfectly okay. And sometimes that person doesn't have quite the same sense of humour as I do, or doesn't share the same outlook on life — so I look into the future and quickly come to the conclusion that it's probably never going to go anywhere. Is that normal? Does everyone do this? And as well as a whopping great phone bill, the other thing to greet me was an appointment for my colonoscopy. Great. At least it gave me an opportunity to get rid of the free buffet.

* * *

Summer was over. October had arrived, and I was feeling tired. The new job had started, and I was doing a lot of travel. Tired I may have been, but I was loving every minute of it: the responsibility, the impact I was having, the reliance upon me to do a good job. But deep down I didn't feel great. I was slowly coming to the conclusion that the Testim Gel wasn't really working. I know, I know — I sound like a fussy bugger and I felt awkward going back to the doctors having said earlier in the year that the injections were too painful. But the gel was doing so little that I was prepared to suffer a sore back if it meant I could be more of a man again. And so it was agreed — I was immediately put back on a course of injections, one administered straight away. I would then receive an injection every twelve weeks.

Within a matter of days I knew I had made the right decision. Something inside me was stirring. Things were starting to happen. Testosterone was pumping through my veins like diesel at a petrol station. And it got to such a stage that I had to do something about it — something that would change the way I looked at the world forever. We're going to explore this in the next chapter and so a small note of caution: if you're my mum or dad, look away now.

37. LIGHT RELIEF

HAVE YOU EVER WOKEN UP IN THE MORNING AND FOUND yourself dry-humping the bed?

Now, I appreciate that not everyone will have experienced this (ladies, I hope I'm not being presumptuous in assuming that this is something you don't find yourself doing but please, correct me if I'm wrong), so I guess I'm aiming this more at the men. We're not talking about morning glory: we're talking about having sex with your mattress. No? Well good for you, because this was the oddly curious predicament I found myself in.

It was clear to see that the move from rubbing gel into my shoulders to a big, fat injection of testosterone was the right one. A couple of weeks after my second injection I could really feel things starting to stir. It was an odd sensation and hard to put into words, but I could feel this energy coursing through me, both in my head and in my loins. I felt sharper, more creative, and much more confident. I was also still eating for England but that was a side effect I could handle if it meant the rest of me was more finely tuned. But waking up in the morning and finding myself having sex with some bed sheets wasn't exactly what I had in mind. It was time to do something about it.

I guess most rational, normal people would resolve this issue by dressing up, going out, and finding themselves a partner. I've never found this easy. There's something incredibly difficult about going out merely to 'pull'. Whilst I was feeling more confident about my music and work, when it came to my own self-worth in terms of how I looked and how I thought women would find me, I was still a bit of a mess. My face had changed so much since I was that ravishing, sought-after teenager that I constantly assumed that no one would find me attractive. My features had settled down since the removal of the tumour, but the damage had been done: my hairline had receded, my forehead looked bigger than ever, and I had a jaw that stuck out like a Neanderthal's. What woman would look at me and think — Phwoar! He's a bit of alright! None. So in my mind, I was defeated before I'd even started.

So what were the options? Well, I could do what people had done for thousands of years and pay for sex, but I knew deep down that this would never happen. I could say this had something to do with my testosterone and perceived manliness, but in reality it just didn't feel right. My need for gratification was immense but this was a resolution I just couldn't entertain. Nothing against those that do, but I'd had sexual relationships in the past so I knew I was good for someone — it was just going to take a bit of time to find them.

And then there was always the option of going to Thailand and finding myself a bride. This was a complete and utter no-no. Again, nothing against those who do, but whilst all the sex and subservience might be brilliant, it was no substitute for shared childhood stories, and late night discussions about 80's children's television.

I needed sex. I needed uncomplicated, guilt-free sex.

It was at this point that I turned to the saviour of mankind: the Internet. It occurred to me that women had a plethora of toys at their disposal, designed for a wealth of experiences and a world of self-pleasure. I wondered if there was anything out there for the men. The only thing I could think of was sex dolls and I'd rather travel to Thailand before buying one of those. So I booted up the computer, interested to know what developments had taken place in the male sex toy market.

It didn't take long to discover that things had come a long way from the days of inflatable sheep. The online sex shops were proud to shout about a new range of toys specifically designed for men: most noticeably a brand called Fleshlight. These were discrete devices built for penetration — their name coming from the fact that they resembled flesh, and that they lived in a container that looked like a flashlight. I was intrigued. Further investigation showed that they came in a range of colours, textures, and experiences. There were ones modelled on the inner workings of porn stars, for example. They even came in fake beer cans for maximum discretion! Ever the cautious shopper, I read up on numerous reviews (a truly weird experience) and every one of them said it was as close to the real thing as you could get. My finger hovered over the 'Buy Now' button. Was this okay? Should I be ashamed? Was I a sordid little pervert who had to resort to sex toys because I couldn't find a woman? Let's not dwell on that one... But my mind raced back to those mornings humping the bed, and so — with a deep breath that was tinged with fear and excitement — I clicked the 'Buy Now' button. I couldn't wait.

I didn't have to. The next day, there was a knock at the door. I opened it to see my postman stood there with an innocuous cardboard box in his hands. I immediately got the fear that he knew exactly what was inside, and that he would be telling all his mates back at the sorting office what a dirty little boy I was. But of course he didn't. How could he? And by now I didn't care. The saviour of my sexual sanity had arrived. I ripped open the packaging to find another box inside containing the hallowed device. I slowly pulled it out, unscrewed the cap, and looked at the soft, pink sleeve. It winked at me suggestively. This was it. The moment of truth had arrived.

* * *

A minute later and it was all over. For the first time in years I felt like smoking a cigarette. Wow. WOW! Why had I not bought one of these before? Why were these not available on the NHS? Any guilt I'd felt had now completely evaporated: the sensation was like nothing else![156] An hour later and I was testing it out again — something I know I would never have bothered doing if I was carrying out the usual methods. This time I really got to experience it, and all those months of gel and injections and surgery and frustration burst out of me

---

156   Apart from sex, obviously.

like Vesuvius on a hot day.

* * *

It's been a few years since I bought my first Fleshlight and I think it's fair to say that it has transformed my life. It is, of course, no substitute for the real thing. You can't stroke its arm before bed. You can't indulge in foreplay. You can't whisper sweet nothings in its ear. You can't cuddle it afterwards. But in terms of simple self pleasure — just as women get with vibrators — it can't be beat. And I urge any long-term single men reading this: do yourself a favour and buy one. Not simply because it's an incredible experience but because when the time comes and you *are* intimate with someone, it won't all be over in seconds.

If you think that this is wholly embarrassing and that I shouldn't be talking about it then I'm sorry, but the truth is: I should. Single men can have it hard, especially when you're not sexually confident. To feel like you're having sex again is a wonderfully luberating — sorry — liberating experience and so I proclaim to all the single men out there: GO FORTH AND BUY A SEX TOY! You'll never wank the same way again.

38. BUILDING BLOCKS

My body had — at long last — finally let out a massive sigh of relief. And now that the testosterone was properly pumping through my veins, I felt like I could conquer anything. I was, after all, KING OF THE WORLD! And 2009 turned out to be a particularly vintage year.

It all started off on New Year's Eve. I had been booked to DJ at a club in Bristol and, for me, there is no better way to see in the New Year than by making people dance. After my set, myself and a few mates made our way to another club where I was introduced to some of the movers and shakers of the Bristol music scene... and a guy called Bailey.[157] More on him later. The club was only five minutes from my flat — so once 6am arrived and the bouncers started kicking people out, I invited them back to mine to carry on the festivities. I had

---

157 Sorry mate.

been buying lots of new music during 2007, a genre called minimal techno. The term 'minimal' is usually associated with a sparse, introspective vibe but I had found a collection of labels and artists that were producing bouncy, cheeky, challenging tracks. I played a selection to my newfound friends and they were hooked.

Having established that this new sound was both effective and not widely known in Bristol, I immediately got back into production. I had spent most of 2008 getting to grips with using Logic and finding my sound: a sound I'd christened as 'party minimal' (an oxymoron, I recognise — minimal techno but with a fun and lively twist). It embraced the off-note baselines that I had so despised during the euro house days of the mid-90's, but gave it a darker edge: this was a bit slower, a bit more measured, and the soundscapes used felt more intricate and mature.

So it was a real shot in the arm when — on my birthday weekend — four of my tracks were released on the same day. 'Datum' and 'Zsa Zsa' were signed to a small label owned by a friend of mine, and the *Boom and Bust EP* was signed to a label in Bogota. The contract I received for that was ridiculously flimsy but in my excitement I just signed it and faxed it back. What I didn't realise was that I had signed the complete worldwide rights away to a label that I knew nothing about — meaning that they owned the tracks from now until the end of time. Ah well. I wasn't expecting it to appear on Radio 1, but losing control of your music is an annoyance, and one I regret.[158]

Before I could release any music though, I had to come

158 ♪ Sod it — have a listen.

up with a name. Artist names had always been a challenge for me — Dan Jeffries was not an option. I envied DJs and producers with names like Max Cooper, Boris Brejcha, and James Harcourt. These were strong names: names that would fill a press release or flyer nicely. Powdermonkey just didn't feel right anymore.

One night, whilst reading a book, I saw the use of the grammatical term [sic]. There was something about it that I liked: it had a slight street connotation (sick, bruv!) and, more importantly, it would look good on a poster. The only problem with it was explaining to people how it was spelt ('[sic], not sick!'), and websites such as Beatport often spelt it wrong. In hindsight, it probably wasn't the most sensible name in the world.

Having now released a couple of tracks, DJ work started to come my way. I was regularly playing events in Bristol, sometimes headlining, sometimes supporting. Whatever the circumstances, it was just great to be finally entertaining people with the music I loved. And nothing brings greater pleasure than dropping your own tune and seeing the crowd go wild. And, conversely, nothing is more heartbreaking than dropping your own tune and seeing the dance floor clear. Thankfully, that rarely happened.

Bleep Seats was going well too but it was still just two hours of music and I felt like I wanted to get more involved. I was talking to Bailey about it (remember him from New Years?), and we joked about the two of us hosting the show, just chatting about whatever we fancied and playing the music we liked. A few weeks later that spark became a full-blown fire as we reinvented *Welcome to the Bleep Seats* with our first 'talkie' show. It was hilarious. The chemistry between us was great.

Sadly we only recorded a few shows (Bailey had a baby on the way which I claimed was the worst excuse I'd ever heard), but what we did make was pure gold — albeit cheap and tacky gold.[159]

All of this activity made for a very happy Dan 2.1. I was buzzing off the success of the releases and the DJ work it was bringing in. The next natural step was to try and run my own night. Bailey was interested in helping out (not massively involved, baby duties considering), and with another Bristol DJ, Greg Shaw, we came up with the rather bizarrely titled *Let's Go Lego!* We spent days making giant pieces of Lego out of cardboard boxes and foam. We trawled the charity shops finding boxes of Lego for people to play with. We even made Lego heads out of giant plant pots! When the night finally arrived we decked out the club with hanging blocks of Lego and Greg, Bailey and I stood out on Park Street wearing our huge yellow heads in an effort to entice people into the club.[160] Whether it was too weird or too frightening, it didn't really work. The club was busy but it wasn't busy enough, and we didn't meet the bar takings in order to get our money back. We were a hundred pounds short and, even more depressingly, when we went to pick up all the Lego boxes the next day, we found that the club had been completely trashed — our cardboard Lego creations smashed to pieces and boxes of Lego thrown all over the place. What we didn't realise was that this was the last weekend the club would be open — the owners were going to do a runner. No wonder they wanted to keep our money. Like the Lego, we were broken.

---

159   I sadly can't find a recording of one of our shows — but if one turns up, I'll add it to the Bonus Content on the website.

160   → Even the police wanted to get in on the fun.

We moved *Let's Go Lego!* to another venue but it didn't really work and, after a couple more attempts, we all decided to hang up our Lego heads. It was a shame but you've got to try these things. I started to realise that I was not a natural promoter: I just wasn't ruthless enough. I told myself that there were people out there better at doing this than me, and that I should just stick to writing the music. I vowed never to promote another night again.

39. 'AFTER THE BREAK...'

F OR THE FIRST TIME IN A WHILE, MY HEALTH HAD TAKEN A back seat. I hadn't thought much about tumours, meningitis, or heartbeats. My nosebleeds had completely stopped. This was, quite frankly, amazing, and led me to conclude that they must have been caused by the acromegaly. Despite this, my interest in the condition hadn't dissipated. I joined some websites and Facebook groups to try and help support others who had recently been diagnosed with the condition, and to talk to those who had been through it and come out of the other side. I was starting to realise just how lucky I had been. For some, the tumour was never fully removed which meant a lifetime of tablets and, on occasion, radiation therapy. I was so glad I didn't have to experience that.

And then in May 2009, I was casually watching TV when a trailer appeared on Channel 4. They were launching a new series called *Surgery Live* in which four operations would be performed in front of a live studio audience. The first show was open heart surgery, the second, awake brain surgery, and the third, keyhole stomach repair. I gripped the sofa in anticipation. Could it be? Would it be?? And the fourth: pituitary tumour removal. I whooped with joy — an odd reaction I grant you — but I was so pleased that this was getting some exposure and that I would be able to see the procedure that I underwent. I called Mum and told her the news. She was just as excited as I was. Dad and Alix weren't quite so keen.

Transmission date: 28th May, 2009. I was so excited about this. Even though I was living on my own, I was able to share my viewing experience with others through the wonderful medium of Twitter. I don't think I'd ever engaged in a hashtag discussion before and this was an innovative way of getting people to submit questions and comments to a live show.[161] I discovered that the tag was #slive and spent a bit of time reading the tweets from the night before.

11pm arrived. I dimmed the lights, opened the popcorn, and settled down to an hour of fascinating television. We were shown the background history of the patient who clearly had the symptoms of acromegaly. We then went straight to the operating theatre where the surgeons explained the procedure and then began the transsphenoidal surgery: going up through the nose and into the pituitary fossa. I was gripped — though I have to confess it wasn't the easiest thing to watch. The worst part for me was, when clearing out the nasal passage, they used an instrument called 'The Hoover' — designed

161   Now you see hashtags on everything. #memyselfandeye

to remove cartilage from inside the nose. It looked like a medieval weapon of torture. I can't deny that my legs went a bit tingly at that point, even though they explained that they used cocaine to expand the inside of the nose. Annoyingly, I don't remember that bit.

One particularly funny moment came about three-quarters of the way through when someone tweeted in and asked, because the brain was so exposed, was there not the possibility of contracting meningitis?

"Oh no," exclaimed the expert, "that's incredibly unlikely."

I laughed to myself and immediately tweeted in:

#slive And I caught it! I got Meningitis 3 days after the surgery. The hole wasn't fixed - spinal fluid leak. Back in hospital for 2 weeks.

I have to say, kudos to Channel 4 for being brave enough to do something like this. It's incredible to think where we're at in the advancement of surgery that we can watch it on live TV and see life-changing operations performed in under an hour, ad breaks included.[162]

Whilst the first half of the year had been incident free, the same could not be said for the second. The fuzziness in my right eye had returned. Not only that, I was getting more and more retinal migraines — something I hadn't really had since that experience at Future World back in 2000. I went to see my doctor and two appointments were made for me at the Eye Hospital: one to see a specialist about the wavy lines, and one to see someone about the possibility of visual aids. In other

162 → You can watch the entire episode online. And check out the accompanying website too. It really is fascinating stuff.

words: a white stick. I wasn't sure if this was totally necessary. Yes, I bumped into people and of course people couldn't tell that I had impaired vision and would therefore happily walk across my line of sight, but a white stick? Really? After some discussion we decided that my sight wasn't bad enough to justify a stick quite yet. I was, to some extent, relieved but when I walk around town I do think how useful it would be, just as a warning to others if nothing else. Either that or I need a hat with a flashing pointy arrow saying: 'Mind the almost-blind person!'

One useful thing that did transpire from this meeting was that I was eligible to apply for a disabled bus pass. When I asked if I would, realistically, ever be able to drive, the specialist almost had to stifle a laugh. I couldn't fault him for his reaction: my field of vision was now so poor that it felt like I was looking down a tunnel. So what the hey — let's get some free bus travel. It would at least save me a few quid every week.

As for the wavy lines, well, they still weren't sure. We knew that they were retinal migraines, but what was causing them? It was decided that more tests would be required — and an appointment with the Stroke Clinic to see if my blood pressure had anything to do with it. Gulp.

It wasn't all eyes, however. I still had to see my endocrinologist, Professor Lightman, for check-ups, blood reviews, and general discussions. My next appointment was in September 2008. When I arrived at the BRI for my appointment, I was advised that Professor Lightman wasn't available that day, and that I would be seeing someone else. I looked at my sister. It wasn't the end of the world, but when you're used to talking to someone that knows your medical history, you feel a little concerned that this new consultant might not grasp all the nuances and complexities of your conditions.

But I needn't have worried.

I was going to see Andy Levy.

40. THE FEAR, THE FAME

I HAD ACTUALLY FIRST MET ANDY BACK IN MARCH 2008. A friend of mine sent me a message on Facebook telling me that there was a lecture at the University of Bristol about pituitary tumours: an inauguration speech by a Professor Andy Levy. Seeing as the University was only a few minutes away it felt wrong not to go and so I headed over. I entered the huge lecture hall to see a plethora of students and academics. I could have felt out of place but I didn't. I could have balked at the idea, frightened that I wasn't 'smart' enough to fully engage, but I didn't. The testosterone was clearly working.

Andy came on stage and presented a mesmerising insight into his work with pituitary research, particularly the pathogenesis of pituitary adenomas. Or, in simple terms: where they come from. What was most impressive (from a teacher's perspective) was that almost every slide he used had NO words on it: instead he let the pictures do the talking —

pictures that told a story and left Andy the space to elaborate. It was an exemplary performance and I was enthralled the whole time I was there, even if some of the medical references went over my head a little.

Afterwards, there was a reception with drinks and nibbles. Andy was surrounded by people, as you might expect. After a couple of minutes there was a small gap in the crowd and I tentatively made my way over.

"Hi. You don't know me but I'm a patient of Professor Lightman. I just wanted to say how much I enjoyed that."

"Thank you very much."

"I had acromegaly once, so it was of real interest to me."

"I thought you might have when you started walking over."

"It's that obvious is it?"

"Was the surgery successful?"

"Well, the tumour was removed but I caught meningitis afterwards. I was a complex case because I have Wyburn-Mason syndrome too."

"Ahhh yes. I'm fully aware of your case. We've been talking about you quite a bit!"

And with that we chatted for a little longer before I politely bowed out and made my way home — not before scoffing a few more of the free crisps and nibbles on the way out. And now, sat in the waiting room with my sister, the door of the consulting room opened and Andy Levy appeared, picked up my folder, and called out my name.

I think I'm rather fortunate in that I seem to be able to have very relaxed, casual conversations with highly skilled medical professionals. Perhaps by putting them on a pedestal we assume we can't engage in a normal fashion. Thankfully, Andy and I didn't have that problem. The conversation was instantly convivial, putting my sister at ease too. We spoke about that meeting at his lecture, about my various conditions, and we spoke about how I was feeling right then. I stated that — generally — things were okay, although I was a little concerned about my fuzzy eyesight. When Wyburn-Mason syndrome was mentioned, he commented that this really was a very rare condition indeed.

"I know. About one in three million people, or so I've been told."

He grabbed a book off the shelf and flicked to the back pages.

"Wyburn-Mason syndrome. Here it is. So, according to this book, there have only been approximately thirty reported cases in the last thirty years. Worldwide."

I was gobsmacked. Thirty cases in the last thirty years... worldwide?! I couldn't begin to comprehend how rare that was.[163]

Once I got over the initial shock of this statistic, we spoke about testosterone. I told him that I was feeling pretty good. He asked if I was sexually active. I looked at my sister, nervous about him getting confused, just as Professor Lightman had done. Thankfully, he was fully aware as to who she was. I said that, sadly, this area of my life was pretty quiet right now.

He asked if there was anything I was concerned about. I thought for a minute. There was one thing but was it really something that could be treated?

"Well... I don't like the way I look."

There — I'd said it. There was no getting away from the

---

163   Someone on *Hijack* worked out that 6,768,167,712 (the world's population) divided by 26 = 1 in every 260,314,143 people. I have no idea how accurate that is, but it looks pretty damned impressive.

fact that my facial features and cranial shape had changed due to the acromegaly and I was uncomfortable with the results it had left me with, particularly my smile. To me it was more of a grimace: exemplified by my protruding lower jaw, and overly large tongue and lips. I hated any profile picture that was taken of me. I didn't know how to smile anymore for fear of spoiling a photo. But really — what could be done? Was there really a problem or was it actually all in my mind? I wasn't expecting him to offer a complete and utter face transplant, but — as Dad would say — "you don't ask, you don't get."

Andy suggested that it would be worth looking into the possibility of maxillofacial surgery. This would involve moving part of my jaw to get a better smile and bite. For years we'd known that my bite wasn't correct, even before my dentist removed those two lower molars in 2005. And since then it had only gotten worse. When I tried to bite down on my back teeth, I simply couldn't. I could only eat on the left hand side of my mouth: there was simply no contact between the teeth on the right, just a huge gap. If I were to have surgery, they would break the jawbone and move either the upper or lower jaw so it was in a better position and consequently give me a better smile and better lower facial definition. It sounded pretty drastic but I was prepared to consider anything. The great thing about Professor Levy is his ability to explain very complex concepts in easy-to-understand language — whilst all the time reassuring you with humour and the occasional profanity. I liked that: it meant he was human.

It had been nearly two years since the tumour had been removed. Andy felt it was appropriate to request another MRI scan, just to make sure no naughty cells were trying to make their way back in. I was pleased to hear this — even though I knew it meant another 7am clang-a-thon. He would contact my GP to advise him of all we had discussed, and he would write to a maxillofacial specialist about looking into some reconstructive surgery. And, true to his word, he did:

I wonder if you would be kind enough to help me with the management of Daniel, who is a delightful music teacher who has acromegaly. He has another complication which is Wyburn Mason disease (of which there have about 30 cases in the last 30 years) which has manifested as vascular malformations at the base of his brain causing blindness in his left eye. Aside from that he has got a dense hemianopia [loss of vision] on the right-hand side, but fortunately, from a pituitary point of view and acromegaly point of view, is now completely stable.

The bottom line is that we usually get very side-tracked by the delights of his rare conditions and don't pay enough attention to his dysmorphophobia [fear of deformity]. He has got significant prognathism [protruding lower jaw] which is not progressive and clearly has some real problems with body image. He is a completely straight-down-the-line guy and I really feel that he could/might be helped by some maxillofacial rearrangement to improve his occlusion and also to make him more comfortable with his appearance. I would be really grateful for some assistance.

This last paragraph made me realise just how committed he was to the cause. His honesty and awareness were wonderfully refreshing.

* * *

The wheels had been set in motion for the next upgrade: not quite Dan 3.0 but definitely Dan 2.2. Whilst waiting for news about my jaw, an interesting and unexpected development was about to come to the surface at work.

It was a pretty normal meeting up at Head Office. A full day's agenda had been covered and we had moved on to Any Other Business. Someone held up a pamphlet and announced that the STAR Teaching Awards were coming up and did we have anyone we could nominate? The room fell silent.

"No one?" she asked again. "Okay then, I guess we'll just…"

"What about me?" I offered.

I suddenly felt half a dozen pairs of eyes turn to face me.

"I've managed our VLE for the past few years with pretty good success. And I've done this whilst having a brain tumour and catching meningitis too. I don't want to blow my own trumpet or anything, but I think that might be a story worth telling."

What had I done? Was this a really stupid idea — to put myself forward for an award? In truth, I didn't do it for me. Well, not *all* for me. I did it because I wanted Access to Music to have some representation and, at that moment, the only person I could think of that was eligible was me. I looked around the room to see gentle nods of approval. It was decided: I would be nominated for a STAR Teaching Award.

VLE developments had been going pretty well with work. We had gone from one centre running Moodle to every centre wanting one. As well as online learning, I was also interested in seeing how mobile phones could be used for better communication. A large number of our students had mobiles, so I argued that we should make the most of this. I looked into services that sent bulk text messages to hundreds of students at a time and found one that specialised in education. Perfect.

Before rolling it out across the country I wanted to do a test run in the Bristol centre. The Centre Administrator was going to be responsible for sending texts (e.g. 'The centre is closed because of snow' or 'Don't forget the gig tomorrow night!') and so I decided to spend a quick ten minutes with him, to show him what to do.

"Okay. So let's imagine you want to send a text. You load up this website... type in your message... choose the number and hit 'send'. Let's not send one to everyone — let's just send one to me. So you click my number... like that... and then you type your message... I don't know... let's put, 'You smell'."

We both laughed.

"Then choose the number you want and click 'send'. Simple!"

I picked up my mobile to see if the text had arrived. As I did, a chorus of phones started to beep around the centre. I checked the screen again: I had accidentally sent the message to every student in the college! I looked at the administrator in horror. What had I done?! Two minutes later the phone rang and an irate parent wanted to know why they had just received a text telling them that they smelt. I had managed to send it to every parent too.

For a moment I thought I might lose my job. And when I got a call from my manager a couple of weeks later, I assumed it was game over. In fact, she was calling to tell me that I had been shortlisted for the STAR Awards! Oh the irony. I was in the category of Support Role and would need to attend a regional event in London on the 9th October. To celebrate, I bought myself a new suit (the one I bought just after surgery was getting a little snug now), and a few weeks later made my way to London — specifically the very grand Gibson Hall. It was a fantastic day. We had a wonderful lunch, were entertained by a choir, and each nominee was presented with a certificate of achievement.[164]

Now that I was an awards nominee, the marketing juggernaut went into overdrive. Well, I got a feature in the Bristol Evening Post.[165] A journalist from the paper came to the Centre and we talked about the award and what it meant — and also discussed my medical conditions. Like most people who hear it for the first time, she was shocked. In fact, she was so taken aback by the story that she recommended I contacted some bigger publications, such as The Daily Mail, as they liked to cover interesting and different medical stories. This was a conundrum for me: I wanted to make the general public more aware of acromegaly, but did I want to do it through the soul-sapping rag that was The Daily Mail? I decided against it. She also suggested that I contact some 'life' magazines who might be interested, and who often paid quite handsomely for a good story. Again, I was a bit torn by this, but — in the pursuit of spreading the message — I got in touch with one of them. They requested to see some before and after pictures, which I sent via email. The next day I was told there wasn't a striking enough difference between how I looked before the tumour and how I looked after surgery, and consequently they wouldn't be covering my story. If that was their attitude then I was grateful for their rejection.

164   → Now THAT is a fine, fine suit.
165   → See that website in the background? I did that.

Awards day had arrived. My family and I made our way up to London. I can't deny, I would have loved to have taken someone special with me: an intimate affair for just the two of us, but it wasn't to be. The ceremony was held at Old Billingsgate in London, a particularly glamorous venue that had been home to ceremonies such as the British Independent Film Awards. As we walked in, we were greeted with free wine and canopies and — to my horror — a bank of TV screens showing interviews we had filmed back at the regional event. God, I had forgotten all about this. A few minutes after being there, someone tapped me on the shoulder and pointed to the screen — and there I was. I looked terrible. Or at least I thought I did. Dysmorphophobia was rearing its ugly head again. I turned to Mum and Dad who were beaming with pride. I mock-barfed in disapproval.

At 6.30pm, we were ushered in to the main hall. This really did feel special. Cabaret acts were all around, incredible light shows darted across the room, and there was more free booze than was probably healthy. We sat at our table and were served a delicious three-course meal. I could get used to this! And, once our bellies were full, the lights dimmed, the music started, and on walked our hosts for the evening: TV broadcaster Mike Baker and BBC political correspondent Reeta Chakrabarti. Mike Baker kicked things off by welcoming us all and congratulating us for getting this far. There had in fact been well over 2,000 nominations for the nine different categories — so to get to this stage was an achievement in itself. Mum patted me on the back.

There were four awards to be presented before I was up on stage. Dad and Alix kept nipping out at the end of every award for a quick fag break — they were more nervous than I was. And then my big moment arrived: the Award for Support Role. As my name was called out I stood up and made my way to the stage, gripped with fear that I would somehow trip over my own feet as I walked up the steps — thus making this the talking point of the evening. Thankfully, I negotiated them just fine. As we stood there on stage, Mike Baker picked up his microphone and spoke to a nominee at the start of the line. I've no idea what they spoke about — all I could see was the blinding lights beaming down onto my face. A few moments later, he moved down the line and — wouldn't you know it — decided to talk to me. He asked me my name and what I did, and I duly replied. So far, so good. He then went on to ask me what the challenges were with working in education. That's a pretty big question! I had no grandiose answer for this so, after a moment's thought, I said that administration and systems were often the challenge: especially TLAs. He looked puzzled.

"TLAs?"

"Three-Letter Acronyms," I grinned.

The audience chuckled. I was back on stage and revelling in the attention. Isn't it strange that, when under the lights and in front of hundreds of people, my fears of how I look fall to the wayside? It must be the actor in me: there can be no barriers in the pursuit of entertainment.

So did I win?

drum roll please

Nah. An IT support worker who had revolutionised the way their college systems worked got the accolade — and fully deserved it was too. Was I disappointed? Of course I was. But this award was given out based on impact and innovation, not how well an individual had coped with their illnesses.

Dad was upset, but then he's far more passionate about these things than I am. I just shrugged it off, pleased that I had been nominated and mildly famous for the past two months.

That night my sister and I stayed in the same hotel room, our evening capped off by the hilarious cacophony of noise emanating from the room next door as they proceeded to have non-stop sex until breakfast. Perhaps the world of awards ceremonies wasn't so glamorous after all.

ME, MYSELF & EYE

358

41. TEETH AND TRIBULATIONS

From: Dan Jeffries
To: Andy Levy
Date: 8 January 2010

Hi Andy. Hope you had a great Christmas and New Year! I just thought I'd drop you a quick email.

I was watching a documentary about dieting last night and they covered a story about a boy who — after having a brain tumour removed — found that he was constantly hungry. It transpired that his hypothalamus was damaged during surgery, which affected his hormonal balance. I myself am still experiencing massive issues with my diet — I still feel permanently hungry, even after eating myself stupid!

So I just thought I'd email you to see if there's anything that can be done regarding this. I've just had an MRI so perhaps there may be some indication on there? Even if there is, I still don't know if this is a treatable side effect or not.

Hope that makes sense.

Regards
Dan

It was true — I could not stop eating. Christmas was over and, aside from the presents, the 25th December felt like any other day: food, food, and more food. I was putting on weight at a rate of knots. I tried going back to Slimming World but I left after two weeks: the people were different, the vibe had changed and the group was now being run by a massively overweight man with no idea of how to run a class. Or that was my excuse. In truth, it wouldn't have mattered if Claudia Schiffer had been running the session — I was going to eat, and that was it.

So when I stumbled upon a TV programme about a boy who had put on loads of weight after having his hypothalamus damaged, it got me thinking that this might be the cause of the problem. But even if it was — what could be done about it? The hypothalamus lives deep at the base of the brain: it was highly unlikely anyone was going to dive in and fix it. At my next session with Andy he advised that, yes, possibly, it might have been damaged, but it wasn't worth focusing on. Nothing could be done to fix it and — besides! — I was looking fine and who cared about a few pounds? I did. My dysmorphophobia was once again rearing its (very) ugly head.

And my sense of body repulsion was only about to get worse.

Andy Levy's letter to the maxillofacial specialists had come up trumps. They referred me to Bristol Dental Hospital just before Christmas to discuss possible treatment for reducing my underbite and correcting my jaw. A team of specialists examined my teeth, discussing what the aims were, and what the methods of treatment would be. And I soon realised that their preferred method of treatment would be the thing I was dreading the most: braces. It was going to be the full set too — train tracks, top and bottom. I asked how long they would be in for.

"About two years."

Deep inside, I sighed. Here I was, fast approaching thirty-three and the most sexually active I had felt in years, and I now faced the prospect of a mouthful of metal.

As my next appointment wasn't until early February, I decided to do a little research into the possibility of going private. I wasn't concerned about using the NHS — far from it in fact — but the private route offered the option of white enamel braces, something the NHS didn't provide. These were lighter in colour and far more inconspicuous, but, unsurprisingly, that came at a cost: £8–10,000 to be precise. Ouch. More importantly, though, it was made clear to me that private dental clinics had very little communication with the NHS. This was something I hadn't considered. Did I want to risk the potential problems that a lack of communication could cause all for the sake of nicer-looking braces? I knew the answer. Considering all the complexities surrounding my eyes, brain, blood vessels, and heart, I decided to go with the

NHS. I would just have to ensure my charm and wit won over my shiny smile.

Early February, and I returned to the Dental Hospital for final discussions before the braces were fitted. It was explained that the aim of the braces would be to align my teeth so that, when it came to surgery, they could get the best bite and jaw position possible. They once again confirmed that this would involve the full set of braces: bottom and top. They also confirmed that another MRI scan would be needed to check that the mass of blood vessels around my eye and brain wouldn't interfere with the surgery. At the end of the meeting I signed an agreement form — recognising that the 'intended benefits' would be 'correction of incisor and molar relationships, correction of maxillary and mandibular positions' and that the 'serious or frequently occurring risks' would be 'discomfort, decay, discolouration, root length loss and tooth mobility'. Shit just got real.[166]

And so on the 12th March 2010, I finally had my braces fitted. Well, that's not quite true. I had the brackets fitted, each one carefully stuck on to each individual tooth, fixed with a foul-tasting adhesive that I could still taste days later. I remember one not fitting properly and it having to be removed and stuck back on again. This was no fun, and we hadn't even fitted the wires. Brackets attached, I walked home from the Dental Hospital in the rain, sad and dejected. Blind in one eye I could handle. Removing a tumour from my brain? No problem. But subjecting myself to a mouth full of brackets and wires felt like a real invasion of the self. And it played havoc with my own image perception. I knew I wasn't the

---

166   I really want to say 'brace yourself' but I'll resist.

most beautiful oil painting on the wall, and now someone has vandalised me even more. I decided to commemorate such an important event in the only way I knew: by putting it up on Facebook.[167]

A week after the brackets had been fitted, it was time to get the wires put in. Thankfully I was in safe hands: my shining light throughout the whole of this process was a lovely lady called Farnaz, who fitted my brackets and wires with great sensitivity and humour. As I lay there, mouth wide open, she tightened the wires ever so slightly and closed down the brackets. Job done. And no pain either! That changed when, the following day, I could barely open my mouth. I resigned myself to a diet of soup and mashed potato, such was the searing pain in my jaw. No more sweets, no more crisps, and definitely no more chocolate. Hmm. Maybe this wasn't such a bad thing after all.

A week later and I went back to have the wires changed, this time for something a little 'heavier'. Fitted and tightened I immediately felt the difference and the next day saw my jaw once again in lockdown. And as if that wasn't bad enough, the ends of the wires were starting to poke into the fleshy inner walls of my mouth. I returned to the Dental Hospital a few days later, the inside of my cheeks ripped to shreds. Farnaz trimmed down the ends of the wires, and gave me some wax to place on the sharp bits to soften the rubbing. Unfortunately, the wax was rubbish and just fell off in minutes. A quick search online and I found my saviour — 'BraceEze': a protective gel that was placed over the brackets and sharp wire ends. It was a godsend. I immediately ordered five tubes and it became an

167 → Mmmmm. Sparkly.

essential companion in my fight against cheek mutilation.

* * *

After a while, day-to-day living wasn't too bad. Eating was manageable once the wires settled down. Sleeping wasn't as bad as I thought it would be (though waking up with metal wire sticking into your cheeks wasn't the most fun). And — for the first time in a long time — I was about to discover that snogging was pretty doable too.

I had for the past couple of months been frequenting some dating websites, most notably Match and Guardian Soulmates. And, as per usual (well, at least for me), they were full of promise and disappointment. I had some encouraging interactions that would eventually evaporate into the ether and I even found myself blocked by someone when I merely suggested meeting up for a drink. Was it me? Or was this just a cruel game played by people who didn't really want a 'match' or a 'soulmate' at all? I was fast giving up hope on all this nonsense when a message appeared in my inbox. My heart raced a little as I clicked on the message. This person — a girl! — thought my profile was funny and that I sounded interesting. Would I like to chat some more? Of course I would! Little did I know what was to come.

Over the next few weeks we slowly got to know each other. We would talk about the music we liked, the TV we loved, our hopes and goals and dreams — the number of kisses at the end of each message growing in size over time. We definitely had a connection. And after a few weeks I tentatively suggested that we spoke on the phone. She agreed. We would chat almost every night: talking about our day, and just getting to know each other. It was nice to be preoccupied with someone again. The only problem was — she lived in Ireland and even with my terrible geography skills, I knew that was more than a bus ride away. But who knew? Maybe we were made for each other. Travel wasn't that difficult any more, webcams and Skype were commonplace and many a long distance relationship had survived with even more miles in between. And so, when the time was right, I plucked up the courage and asked if she would like to meet. She said she would. I checked my work schedule and could see that I was due a few days holiday, so I booked my flights and reserved a nice four-star hotel for two nights. I set my return flight four days after I arrived: not too long, but long enough.

Departure day arrived. I hadn't been on holiday since Tunisia but this wasn't really a holiday, was it? When you contact someone on a dating website and you agree to meet up, it's pretty clear what's on the cards, isn't it? I was cautiously excited. Would we get on? Might it be awkward? Could this be love?

I got off the plane and walked through the arrival lounge. It occurred to me that I had only seen a couple of pictures and a very grainy Skype video, so I didn't have the best idea of what she looked like. I scanned the airport, cursing my oh-so-familiar inability to find someone in a large, crowded space when suddenly a figure ran up to me and threw their arms around me. It was her. We hugged each other and I took a step back to say hello properly. As we made our way towards the exit — and this is going to sound absolutely terrible — I knew that this was a mistake. I just didn't feel a spark, I didn't feel a connection — and who's to say she didn't feel exactly the same way too? We didn't say much as we walked to the taxi and once inside we didn't say much there either. But I was here now and I was determined to make the most of it. I gave the address of the hotel to the taxi driver and sat back and smiled.

"When we get to the hotel I'm going to have to leave you and pop home for a bit, I'm afraid," she said. "I need to do a bit of work."

Whaaaat? I had come all this way and within minutes I was being abandoned in favour of work?! It was a good job I had my laptop and headphones with me. About an hour later, she returned and continued with her work, and I carried on writing some music. This wasn't quite how I imagined it would be, but I'm a patient man and a few minutes weren't going to make much difference. When it looked like she had finished what she needed to do, I shut my laptop and we made our way to the bed where things took their natural course. That's to say we had a snog and a bit of a fumble. We didn't have sex — it was a tad too soon for that. An hour later and we were at it again, this time exploring each other in much more detail. Warning: the next section is a little bit crude but very, very funny. Skip if easily offended. Mum and Dad — you should know what to do by now.

We were deep in the throes of exploration, undertaking an activity commonly known as the sixty-nine position (or the sixty-eight and 'I owe you one'). For the first time in years, I was entwined with a female form and it was fantastic. Whilst doing all the things you normally do in a sixty-nine, I did something that I think is… y'know… not that shocking… and I… err… I gently licked her bum.[168] Down by my feet I could hear light moaning and sighing. Encouraged by this,

168   Please don't judge me.

I continued. A few seconds later, she stopped what she was doing and turned her head to look at me.

"I'm sorry, but could you go and clean your teeth?"

I looked back at her, my hands full of bum.

"Excuse me?"

"Could you go and brush your teeth, please."

I couldn't quite believe what I was hearing. Either she was worried about her own personal hygiene or she knew something about mine that I didn't. Sure, ask me afterwards but don't ask me *during!* Maybe it was the braces. Whatever it was, I made my way to the bathroom, reached for my toothbrush, and lent against the sink, staring at myself in the mirror. I shook my head, rinsed my mouth, and took another moment to gather my thoughts.

"They've done a good job on this stonework," I mused to myself, desperate to think of anything other than going back into that room. It wasn't even the end of day one and I was ready to go home.

The next couple of days was a mixture of sightseeing, food, and failed sex. I really enjoyed the food and tourist attractions — I wasn't so happy with my lacklustre performances. Things would initially get off to a good start but as soon as we tried to put a condom on, it all went downhill. I hadn't even thought to bring condoms, that's how long it had been, and when she produced extra-thick ones from her bag, I knew it was going to be a calamity. It was like trying to put a jellyfish in a sandwich bag. Irritated by my disappearing erection trick, we tried everything we could to resolve the situation: female condoms, thinner condoms, even a bit of porn. Nothing worked and, try as we might, we were both pretty much resigned to not having sex.

By day three, I was *really* ready to go home. I called Alix to give her the update.

"There's nothing wrong with the girl — she's just not the one for me. She's a bit soft and delicate and I'm... well... not. I'm finding it hard to have conversations with her, even to look her in the eye. It's terrible I know and I feel really bad but I don't know what to do!"

"Just get on a flight and get home. Make up some excuse. Anything! But if you really need to get out of there, then think of something. I'll call you and pretend someone's died."

I laughed. "No, no. It's fine. I've made my bed. Anyway, I can't change the flight and I'm not paying for a new one. It'll be fine. It can hardly get any worse."

I couldn't have been more wrong.

The next day we were walking around the shops having just had breakfast when she said she needed to pop into the bank. I stood outside, watching the world go by, enjoying a brief moment of sunshine. As she walked back out, she looked at me:

"Well, I don't think you're going anywhere for a while."

"What do you mean?' I asked, slightly scared.

"I've just been watching the news. There's been some volcanic explosion in Iceland or something? All the airports are stopping flights. I don't think you're going to be able to get back home!"

WHAAAAAAAAAAAT?!?! I ran into the bank and stared up at the TV screen. She was right: news footage showed smoke and ash billowing from the Eyjafjallajökull volcano, followed by graphics showing the airspace it was covering. Virtually every flight had been cancelled. We hurried back to her flat and I turned on the news again to watch further coverage, reports confirming that all flights in and out of Ireland were cancelled. Airspace experts were interviewed, stating that there wouldn't be any flights for days. I couldn't quite believe what I was hearing.

"You can stay for as long as you need to," she offered kindly.

As sweet and lovely a gesture as that was, it wasn't an option — I had to get home. I immediately got on to the airline who confirmed that all flights had indeed been cancelled, and I would have to find alternative means of travel. That only meant one thing: ferry. I got on the phone and only just managed to get myself a seat, never mind a cabin, to depart the following day. I packed my bags and we spent one last night together. She kindly drove me to the docks the next day where we hugged and said our goodbyes.

Once inside the waiting lounge, I let out an almighty sigh of relief. I suddenly felt like myself again. For the past few days I just hadn't been able to be 'me'. Was it fear? Embarrassment? Or just purely a lack of chemistry? Whatever it was, I felt bad, really bad — more so for her. I think it was just a combination of misguided expectations, an underpowered sexual toolkit, and a friendship that was based on emails and telephones. I thought about the past few days, and where I was right now and chuckled to myself: only I could end up in such a calamitous situation. That night I slept on the floor of the restaurant, awoken at 6am by a swarm of truck drivers queuing for breakfast.

Back on dry land and it was another three or more hours on the train until I finally made it home. I walked through the door to see Mum there. I hugged her and fell onto the sofa, telling her about the past few days (well… not all of it). I asked what she was doing here and she explained that, whilst she had been looking after the dogs, Norman had become very ill — a possible stroke — and that she had brought them back to Bristol and decided to stay over until I returned. I looked at his melancholic face as he lay in his bed, too tired to even walk over and greet me. He was getting old and I feared the end was nigh.

* * *

A week later and I was sat opposite Andy Levy at the BRI for my annual check up, sister in tow. He asked me how I was and I said that I was good. I told him that I felt the testosterone injections were definitely helping with my mood and character, and that I was feeling positive about things. He asked if there had been any developments in my sexual activity.

"Funnily enough, that's what I spent most of last week doing."

"Mazel Tov!" he exclaimed, genuinely pleased to hear my good news.

"Yup. It was interesting!" I replied. "The only trouble was, after a few minutes or when we tried to put a condom on, things just fell flat. I was definitely 'excited' — but keeping it that way was nigh on impossible."

"I'm sorry to hear that. How about we give you some tablets to help you out?"

And with that he prescribed me a box of Cialis: little 2.5mg tablets to make things strong again. If I was with a partner then I could take one every day or, more appropriately, if I was lucky enough for the opportunity to arise, I could take one and thirty minutes later my soldier would be standing to attention. I always had the fear that Viagra and the like would leave me walking around with a crotch like a barber's pole, but this wasn't how it worked: the tablets only did their magic upon arousal.

What a pity I didn't get them the week before.

42. THE BOOK OF CLIPS

DESPITE THE CACOPHONY OF EMBARRASSING SEX AND dental work, 2010 turned out to be a particularly creative year.

Following on from the *Boom and Bust EP*, I was asked to do a remix for a new label called AUX, an odd little track called 'Nu Jakker'. What arose was a rousing behemoth that had all the trademarks of my bouncy techno sound: it was energetic yet friendly and got some nice reviews. After that I released the *Rise of the Misfits EP*, which included the title track, '23' and 'Stay Horizontal', plus a remix from an ex-student whose sound I had always liked. At the end of March, I released one of my best tunes to date: the strangely moving 'We Are Not Alone' which featured two remixes and a track called 'In The Flesh' — a cheeky, joyous exposition with a name that (thankfully) only I understood.[169] The EP did really well and received some nice reviews and support from well-recognised DJs. I was then asked to do another remix for AUX, this time a track called 'I Like to Party'. It took a while, but the end result was well worth it — especially when techno legend Gary Beck asked if he could have a copy.

October then saw the release of the *MuSic EP* on a new label — Re:Sound — which explored a newer, fresher style. 'Accesso Rapido' was born from a little arpeggio line that I had experimented with, which somehow turned into an epic tale of Latino vocals, trumpet melodies, and timpani hits. Everyone I played it to loved it, including the family (trust me, they didn't like everything I played them!). The B-side, 'Chew', had a totally different vibe but was technically more accomplished, with some really rich textures and little moments that made my (now receding) hair stand on end. Again, both tracks did really well, 'Accesso' reaching No.1 on the Track It Down minimal techno chart.

It was also during 2010 that a guy called Andy Basic — who I had met through *Hijack* — told me that he was thinking of setting up his own record label. He then asked if I would like to have the first release. Wow! What a nice thing to be asked! And so, on the 29th November, 2010, 'Chomp' was released to the world on the wonderfully titled Slime Records. It got a great review from local magazine Venue and other press too — no doubt helped by the massive Phaeleh remix, a veritable legend when it came to emotional and cinematic dubstep.[170] 2010 was finished off with the *Substance Abuse EP* on AUX

169   Chapter 37 may give you some clues.

170   → Venue's review. Makes me smile every time.

(more brooding, wobbly minimal techno), and a remix for The Sloppy 5ths entitled '1987'. Whenever I played it out, crowds tended to go a bit mad. There really is nothing better.

If you've ever read Homer's *Iliad*, you're no doubt comparing the start of this chapter to Book Two: The Book of Ships, in which Homer explains in meticulous detail all the ships present for the epic battle. I used to skip over that bit at school, and if you've skipped over the above then I fully understand why. But if you're curious to find out more about my own 'Book of Ships', there's a footnote at the bottom of the page just for you. I've made two playlists: one with the full tracks and one with small clips. Don't worry Mum — you don't have to listen to all of them.[171]

But why am I telling you this? What relevance does this have to tumours and eyes and testicles? Well, it's massively relevant because I get the feeling that if I hadn't found that naughty little tumour, none of this would have happened. That tiny little mass of cells really had been a plug on my creativity and removing it unleashed a torrent of musical outpouring that surpassed even my expectations. That's not to say it was all perfect, mind. Testosterone or not, I still struggled to finish ideas, or would find myself in a creative slump — something every musician goes through at some point. Thankfully, the slump wouldn't last too long. I was still a bit rubbish at pushing myself forward though. I was very grateful for the support from the labels and DJs within the community, but I wasn't making enough NOISE! I just wasn't promoting myself effectively nor capitalising on my recent success. Why? I dunno. Was this just how I was: a little afraid

171 ♫

to sell myself? Or did I have genuine self-doubts about what I was doing? Could I blame testosterone for this?

One way I thought of boosting my profile within the scene was to start promoting nights again. Had I not learned from the mistakes of *Let's Go Lego!*? Clearly not. A new club had opened in Bristol and were looking for nights, so, teaming up with a couple of other DJs, we launched *CODE* — a night dedicated to techno and minimal. I was a big fan of a duo from Ireland called Loco and Jam who played quite a hard, bouncy style, so we booked them to appear at our opening night in June. They arrived in Bristol around 11am, fully up for 'the craic'. We spent the day chaperoning them around town, buying food and drinks as and when required. This was the life of the promoter and, whilst it was fun, it was damned expensive. It was all worth it though: they played a great set and *CODE* was born.

* * *

Whilst I was struggling to find love, other members of my family seemed to be doing pretty well. My dad, for one, had found himself a new partner. Her name was Sharon and it's fair to say that she's one of a kind.

I first met Sharon when a group of us visited the town that she was living in at the time. She owned a pub and we were all invited round. As I walked through the door, two huge dogs greeted me — salivating like I was their dinner. Sharon called them to attention. As I looked up I could see nothing but tattoos and a purple Mohawk. This was my dad's new girlfriend?! My dad, who dressed in suits and listened to Radio 4, dating someone covered in tattoos?! She came over and hugged me and I immediately understood why. She was warm and caring and belied the 'challenging' exterior that you were first presented with — something I could identify with.

Meeting Sharon that night was a joy, however the rest of the evening didn't go so well. I really fancied one of the girls in the group and was hoping to somehow let her know. Whilst at the pub, I wondered where she was and opened the door to check outside — only to see her lips glued to someone else's. They didn't spot me and so I slowly closed the door and went and sulked in a corner. That night we all had to share the same room and I spent the entire time listening to them 'getting to know each other'. The next day I barely uttered a word.

I was approaching that stage in my life where everyone was either getting married or having babies, usually both. Consequently a large proportion of that summer was occupied with stag do's and weddings. It was always wonderful to get the invite — though it was often tinged with sadness as I'd inevitably be attending them alone. It was also a sombre reminder of my own singleton existence. Is that bad? It never took anything away from my joy at their happy day, but it was just a gentle prod to the soul: a little reminder that I was still on my own. Regardless of that, the stag do's that had been arranged couldn't have been more different. And — because I was there — incident was never far behind.

43. SUPER SHARP SHOOTER

Stag Do #1: Prague

FIFTEEN OF US MADE OUR WAY TO BRISTOL AIRPORT TO FLY out to Prague — known as the 'Mother of Cities'. This was going to be messy. Proceedings immediately got underway at the airport bar as someone pulled out a clothes peg from their pocket.

"OU EST LE PEG?" he yelled, and everyone cheered. I was bemused. He explained the philosophy behind the game: you have to sneakily place the peg on someone's clothing without them noticing and, when ready, shout "OU EST LE PEG?" If you couldn't find the peg on your person within ten seconds, you had to down whatever drink you had in front of you. I was at an immediate visual disadvantage but, mercifully, they didn't pick on me too much — downing a vodka and diet coke compared to a pint of lager wasn't that much of a challenge anyway.

Upon arrival it was evident that there wasn't going to be much culture. No touring the ancient streets or critiquing the local artwork. Instead, our culture was to be football and drinking. We arrived on the same day that England were playing the USA in the first round of the World Cup. After lunch, we congregated in the main square where they were showing the match on huge screens. I looked around to see armies of men draped in Union Jacks, usually with one poor sod dressed up in some ridiculous outfit. Prague was clearly the stag do capital of Europe.

Now, I'm no football pundit, but England were diabolical. They drew 1-1 and I could sense the tension rising. The rest were too bladdered to care, but I wasn't that keen and felt ready to move on. We had 'hired' two local girls (that sounds so bad) to show us round Prague and they turned up just at the right moment. We asked them where we were going to next.

"We're going to take you to a traditional English pub!" they exclaimed jovially, as they high-fived the rest of the group.

Fantastic. I'd come to Prague to get *away* from bulldogs and pasties but shut up Dan, go with the flow and enjoy the weekend. As we turned the corner to reach the *George and Dragon*, a chair flew past us as a massive fight erupted outside. This really *is* a traditional English pub, I mused, as I watched a group of lads try to kick the shit out of each other. Football was once again showing itself to be the beautiful game.

Plans for the rest of the weekend involved three key things: drinking, strip clubs, and shooting guns — a trio of activities I was far more interested in. Later that evening we made our way into the heart of Prague, chaperoned by our two local ladies. They got us in cheap to one of the many strip bars and, whilst we found ourselves a table, they went and sat at the back of the venue — something I was a little bit uncomfortable about. The place was pretty amazing. Beautiful women swanned around, approaching you with all the love and attention in the world. I wasn't really that interested and, funnily enough, neither were they. It annoyed me that, even amongst a group of my closest friends, I still couldn't let myself go and enjoy a private moment. Part of me felt sorry for their situation, part of me questioned whether I was 'right' for this (not now, dysmorphophobia, not now!) and so I never indulged. However, we did pay for two ladies to 'dance' for us on our table and when they both came over and smothered me in their boob-flesh, I melted a bit inside.

A couple of hours later we headed to a nightclub, which had five floors of music. The place was absolutely roasting and as I climbed the stairs to find a cool spot, I noticed that each floor had its own name. As I reached the fourth floor I saw the words 'Black Music' emblazoned on the wall. I decided that I had had enough and made my way back to the apartment.

The next day I awoke to find bodies strewn everywhere. The stench of dirt and booze filled the air. Ripped clothing hung over the edge of the bath. What had happened here?! Suddenly someone sprung up out of bed.

"Shit! Get dressed! We're meant to be at the firing range in half an hour!"

The prospect of firing actual guns filled me with dread. I hadn't shot a weapon since my days in the ATC, and they were merely simple little air rifles. We were now in Prague and I had visions of trying to shoot an AK-47 — the gun going wildly out of control, shooting everyone dead. After a quick breakfast of bread and alcohol, we met up with our guides and made our way to the train station. I looked around to see some of my friends hanging off the handrails like rhesus monkeys, and some sat motionless, heads between their knees. Sickeningly for them, even though I had barely slept due to it being over twenty degrees the night before, I felt great.

We arrived at the firing range and were shown into the waiting room. More alcohol was on offer and, much to everyone's delight (and confusion), so were a pile of porn mags. Whilst everyone chortled like a gaggle of schoolboys, I thought it best to warn the owner that I had really bad eyesight, and that I might need help now and again. He nodded. I wasn't sure if he understood me or not.

After giving some safety instructions that none of us understood, we made our way into the range. It was small, dark, and slightly exciting. He showed us the first gun and taught us how to load it, aim it, and fire it. We all had ear protection on because these guns were loud. A few guys went before me, which I was grateful for as I wanted to see how it was done. Now it was my turn and — trying to remember everything he had shown me — I gripped the gun tight and fired six bullets. He pressed the button to bring the target into view and... nothing. It was like new. I shrugged my shoulders, half-expecting that to be the result.

For the next hour we fired a range of weapons, each one more powerful than the last. My success rate at hitting the target was still pretty dismal. When we came to the end of the session he told us that, for a few extra Euros, we could have a competition: six shots each with the biggest gun they had. We looked at each other and nodded. He returned a few minutes later with a beast of a weapon and showed us how to use it. It had a real kickback so we had to be careful. Stag boy stood up to go first, took aim, and fired his rounds. The target returned to show he had scored 20 out of 30. Not bad! A couple more took aim and all hit the target, averaging around 20. There was room for someone to take the lead. And I was up next.

I took the shooting position, blood pumping in my ears. In the background 'Eye of the Tiger' blared out of the speakers.[172] I loaded the gun, squinted at the target, took aim, and fired. BOOM! The kickback was huge and my shoulder winced against the pressure. I fired again. BOOM! And again. BOOM! Six shots — done. Had I made it into the lead? Had I even hit the target? I was more concerned about that than winning the competition, and I waited nervously as I pushed the button of doom. As the target came closer I shrugged: I couldn't see any holes but then... hold on... no way! There *were* holes — massive, gaping holes! — and all near the bullseye! I whooped with joy, a huge smile beaming across my face, my braces flashing in the glow of my achievement. I had scored 26. Okay, so I was beaten by someone who got 27, but I was buzzing with my result. Even the owner was impressed and gave me a prize for second place. I don't think I'd ever felt quite so manly.[173]

Prague was over and we made our way back home tired and bruised. And, thanks to our demented state, the poor air hostess on our flight back discovered, much to our amusement, that the hem of her skirt had been littered with clothes pegs. She didn't find it quite as funny as we did.

172   Not really.

173   → BOOM!

44. WATER AND FIRE

Stag Do #2: Wales

MY GOOD FRIEND SAM WAS FINALLY TYING THE KNOT with his long-term partner, Jo. Sam didn't particularly want a weekend of strippers and guns, so instead the best man arranged a weekend of activities in the depths of west Wales. Knowing that the group was made up of 90% surfers, I was slightly apprehensive about what lay in store, but I gave myself a good talking to, determined to make the most of it. I was charged, pumped, and ready to engage. Well, that was the plan. The reality was slightly different.

We arrived at the campsite at around 10pm. Unsurprisingly, it was pitch black. There was no way we could set our tents up in the dark, so instead we decided to get drunk. Someone had already erected a colossal teepee that could easily sleep around twenty and, with no decent light to build our tent, they offered us a roof for the night. I was exceptionally grateful and squeezed myself into a spot right by the door of the tent — and for the next eight hours endured the 'drip drip drip' of rainwater onto my face. I couldn't move for the other bodies around me. I think I got around half an hour's sleep. Whilst lying there, it didn't take long for me to remember that I fucking hate camping.

The next morning, the best man announced the first of our activities: a trek across the countryside towards the beach. Of course, being completely unprepared, I had bought no wet weather clothes or any sensible footwear — so within the first hundred yards my feet were completely soaked, and my shoes covered in mud. I felt like the needy sibling as I trundled along at the back. After a short while, we made it to a remote spot where the best man asked us to place ourselves in chronological order according to how long we had known the stag. In position, we were asked to say a few words: how we knew him, lasting memories, wishes for the future. It was a lovely moment, often moving at times and I pondered to myself whether I would experience anything like this: surrounded by friends as we celebrated my life, and looked ahead to the future with my bride-to-be. I couldn't see it happening just yet.

Mass bromance over, we carried on towards the beach. We often had to negotiate some rather narrow pathways along rather big cliff edges, and I was fearful about my lack of sight and that I might suddenly put one foot out of place and end up at the bottom of the rocks, ruining the whole weekend for everyone. That never happened and, reaching our destination, I was stoked that I had made it. However this was to be short lived as someone announced that the next activity was for everyone to go Coasteering. A massive cheer went up.

"What's Coasteering?" I asked.

"We're going to put on some wet suits, get into the sea, climb over some rocks, explore some caves, and then climb up to a really high cliff edge, and jump into the water.

Coming?"

My belly hit the floor. I couldn't think of anything worse. Part of me so wanted to do it: to get involved, to be a part of the gang, but the practicalities of trying to get into a wetsuit — let alone negotiate a cliff face — rendered the dream impossible. I instead declared myself 'Official Photographer' for the weekend and got my camera out to prove it. I stood and watched in bemusement as these toned men shed their clothes and slipped into their wetsuits like it was a perfectly normal thing to do. I envisaged myself trying to do this and imagined it would be like watching a walrus put on a dress. I was better off taking photos.[174]

Back at the campsite and a massive BBQ was underway. This was more my domain. After filling our bellies with chicken and cider, the best man declared that it was time for the final ceremony. Sam the Stag was ushered over, blindfolded, and led around the campsite in total silence. After fifteen minutes of total silence, confused and no doubt mildly concerned, we positioned Sam in a spot and stood in a circle around him. The best man explained what he had to do: when ready, he was to walk forward, and touch the person closest to him. Sam tentatively did this. Each of us then took it in turns to wish Sam the best for his future and express what his friendship meant to us. It was an emotional experience, made even more so by the fact that these men who — only a

---

174   → And rather good photos they were too.

few hours before had been jumping off cliff faces — now had quivering lips and a tear in their eye. I didn't cry, of course: I don't tend to do things like that.

Emotionally uplifted, we made our way back to the campsite to indulge in more food and cider. Tim got on the bongos and made himself look like a garden gnome. By 2am it was decided that we should all try and squeeze into someone's car. Mayhem had finally taken over and I was glad to see it happen. I decided not to squeeze in and took photos instead. Why was it that I couldn't let myself go and take part in things like this? Was this just me or was it my hormones? Whatever it was, I didn't mind: I liked being on the outside looking in.[175]

* * *

Stag do's over, it was time for the weddings. Andy and Gail's was a sumptuous day, and I was honoured to be the one given the daunting task of controlling the iPod as the Bride made her way down the aisle. I had also been asked to compile a collection of tracks for the disco later that night. I'd concocted a range of ironic wedding classics and some pumping 90's dance hits. I even played 'The Birdie Song' — interrupting it with the sound of gunfire before moving into something more palatable. The older generations sat at the back, arms crossed and unimpressed.

Sam and Jo's wedding was a very different affair. We were back in the idyllic surroundings of west Wales, but this time we were 'glamping'. Oh joy, I thought to myself — more camping misery. Nothing could have been further from the truth.

---

175   → Definitely glad to be on the outside for this one!

These weren't tents we were staying in, these were palaces! I'd never experienced a yurt before, and it was magnificent: sheepskin rugs to sleep on, and a wood burner in the middle to keep us warm. Outside was a cooking area and space to sit and relax. This was bliss. After dropping our stuff off in our yurt, we made our way to the main reception area and indulged in another BBQ and lots of drink. A couple of hours later it was getting dark and cold. It had been a long day and I was ready to experience my sheepskin rug, and warm, cosy fire. I stood up, slightly unsteady on my feet, and shouted to the rest of the group that I was heading back. "Get the fire started!" someone yelled and I gave them the thumbs up as I stumbled my way across the fields.

I got to the yurt and pulled open the canvas doorway, master of my domain. "Right then," I said to myself and knelt down next to the fire. Newspaper and kindling had kindly been provided. I picked up a bit of each, looked at it and then realised I had nothing to light it with. I scrambled over to my bag and found a lighter. This was pretty much the only bit of light in the entire tent. I took a handful of newspaper and tore it up into small pieces and placed it in the stove. I carefully balanced some kindling on top — thinking that the newspaper would produce enough heat to set the dried wood alight. I made one final check to make sure everything was in place before running my thumb down the lighter and producing the magic of fire. I leant forward and gently started to burn the paper. It started to crackle and then fell on the floor. Eh? That doesn't make sense. I tried to pick it up but it disintegrated, and ash started to swirl around the tent. Perplexed, I moved to the other side of the burner and lit some more paper. Just as I was doing so, the door of the yurt flew open.

"Dan, what the hell are you doing?!"

"I'm trying to light the fire!" I retaliated.

"Well, why don't you try doing it IN the fucking thing then!"

Someone hit the light switch and illuminated the tent. I had, to my dismay, placed the wood and paper in the part of the stove that collected the charred wood and ash. They marched over and pushed me out of the way.

"See? Here's a handle, and here's a little door and here's where you make the fire!"

"Oh."

"You're a fucking idiot. Look at the place!"[176]

I had indeed made a royal cock-up: ash was now strewn around the tent, bits of last week's newspapers floating in the air. The smell of burning paper had penetrated everyone's clothing too. Four faces scowled at me as I sheepishly looked at the ground.

"I was only trying to help," I muttered under my breath, reverting to the mentality of a four-year-old. I was being told off and I didn't like it. But, more importantly, I was thoroughly disappointed in my own lack of man-skills. I decided that this was the last time I would do anything adventurous again — a declaration I was secretly happy to make.

---

176   → Yes. Look at it. I am so ashamed.

45. LIFE'S LITTLE
CHALLENGES

Back in Bristol, I opened my mailbox to discover two appointments from the hospital. The first appointment was for an MRI — yet again at 7.15am. The second was an appointment at something I hadn't heard of before: the Stroke Clinic.

The night before the MRI, I went to bed nice and early, determined to wake up fresh. Instead I ended up having a terrible night's sleep. When I finally managed to drop off, it felt like barely seconds had passed before my alarm shrieked its noise (I was secretly waiting for it — do you do that too?) and before I knew it, it was 7am. I jumped out of bed, chucked on some clothes, and walked at pace (I don't do running in the morning) to the BRI. I was ushered into the cubicle where I was given a gown and asked the standard set of questions. I replied "No" to all of them: not even really listening I had done it so many times before. A few minutes later I was called into the scanning room and placed on the bed. The procedure was explained to me again and I was gently pushed back into the scanner. I put the headphones on and was asked if I could hear their voice. I replied I could. I was told the scan was about to start and that I should stay as still as possible. I was already half asleep, so that wasn't going to be hard.

A couple of minutes into the procedure, the scanner stopped and I heard the click of the microphone.

"Mr Jeffries, are you wearing braces?"

"Erm... yes?"

"Did they not do the checks with you before the scan?"

"Yes. They asked if I had any metal fittings in my body, like metal plates in the head. I didn't think... oh dear."

"The braces are massively distorting the images. You really shouldn't be in the machine with any metal on you. We'll proceed, but the results are likely to be poor."

The clicks and whirrs started up again and I lay back, annoyed with myself and my own stupidity. Why had I said I had no metal on me? I only answered the questions I was asked and — in my opinion — there is a difference between there being metal *in* your body and metal *on* your teeth. As I slowly started to drift off again I chuckled as I had visions of this giant magnet grabbing hold of my face and yanking me up to the ceiling.

A week later I was back in the BRI and attending the second appointment: this one at the Stroke Clinic. I'd been referred to them because of the recent problems with my right eye, the fuzziness that was appearing and these strange, inconsistent 'visions' that would blur and distort my sight. Was this possibly connected to my heart in some way, or was it merely a simple case of retinal migraines? The consultant,

Julie Dovey, was great. I think she appreciated someone who had a good understanding of their medical situation (I think most doctors do) and — unsurprisingly — was intrigued by everything I had been through. She reviewed my blood pressure and pulse and these showed normal results, as did blood tests to check my glucose levels. In a letter to my GP she offered the following considerations:

Impression:

1. I do not think that Mr Jeffries symptoms are due to TIA [Transient Ischaemic Attack - in other words, a mini stroke] or cerebrovascular events [stroke, caused by disruption of blood to the brain].

2. I wonder whether he is getting retinal migraine symptoms. The other possibility is that his symptoms are related to cerebral AV malformation [the giant blood vessels] and pressure on the visual pathways within the brain. However I have reassured that as his symptoms have been going on for around 10 years and do not seem to be getting more frequent or more severe that they are likely to be benign in nature. He is clearly very worried about the possibility of losing his remaining portion of vision and is keen for further investigations.

Plan:

1. I will arrange for him to have an MRI and Angiogram to clarify the size and location of the suprasellar AV malformation.

2. I have also arranged for him to have an echocardiogram as a previous echo in 2007 showed mild to moderate aortic regurgitation.

3. I have arranged to review him in my clinic with the results of these investigations.

So that was the plan: undergo another MRI, angiogram, and echo. I hadn't had an echo since 2007, when they checked to see if my heart was okay prior to surgery and MRI's were now becoming standard procedure. I still didn't like angiograms though, and the thought of more hot dye being pumped through my veins filled me with mild dread, but it had to be done. I was obviously pleased to hear that it was unlikely to be stroke related, but I was still eager to know why I was getting these distorted images in my vision.

* * *

For the next few months, life carried on as normal. Well, as normal as it can do when you've got a mouth full of metal, and you're waiting for an operation to have your jaw broken and reset. I'd started to grow accustomed to my silvery friends — even though they caused me nothing but trouble. Not a day would go by without a clasp scraping my lips or a wire lodging itself in the wall of my cheek. Almost every week I was ordering in new packs of Brace Eze (I should have taken out shares I had gone through so much of the stuff). But I knew it was all for a good cause, so I was prepared to put up with the pain — even if it did make me look like a teenager in every photo that was taken.[177]

And even though my masculinity and self-image were being pushed to their limits, I still strived to live life to the

177   → Kiss me, kiss me!

full, or at least my interpretation of 'the full'. For example, I decided to experience Go-Karting. My past history with motorised wheels had not been good. When I was eight, I went to a country fair and decided to have a go on a mini motorbike. I was doing fine until I got confused between the throttle and the brake and went hurtling off into a bale of hay. Stunned and in pain, I put my hand out to push myself up — only to place it on the scalding hot engine. Not a good move. And then of course there was that car incident at Uni. Oh, and I went 'Ice-Karting' for a friend's birthday once — which is just as stupid as it sounds. Not only did I have no idea about how to navigate corners, I had to do it on ice. I only nearly killed myself twice, which I considered to be a result.

Thanks to the joys of the Internet, emails often would appear from one discount company or another offering me incredible deals on weekend breaks and bulk purchases of toilet rolls. This one for go-karting caught my eye. The track was only a twenty-minute drive away and so, with an air of bravado, I ordered four tickets and figured I would recruit some friends nearer the time.

I booked the racetrack for a Sunday morning in early December. I did this, of course, not knowing that the end of 2010 would bring some of the coldest weather in years. We arrived... or at least I think we did. The whole place was shrouded in freezing fog. Just getting to the racetrack was perilous enough as we negotiated the slippery footbridge to the warmth of the cabin. I would have quite happily stayed there as I couldn't feel my hands at that point, but I'd booked it so I guessed I'd have to get involved.

As per usual, I had come completely unprepared with no sensible clothing whatsoever. We each put on a pair of ill-fitting overalls and cautiously walked out towards our cars. As I got in mine, I felt a thrill of excitement course through my veins. This was now very real and, whilst I wanted to win, I also wanted to live — so I listened to the advice of the instructor very carefully. Confident that we all knew what we were doing, he pulled a cord that revved up what looked like some makeshift hairdryer, and away we went. I approached the first corner with a degree of trepidation, gently easing myself into the racing line. This was great! All the other cars were now out on the track and the race had begun: sixty laps of freezing-cold chasing. By the end of Lap 10 my face had turned to ice and by the end of Lap 20 I could barely feel my fingers. My feet felt like size 9 Viennettas as they tried to push down on the accelerator. Every lap was becoming more and more painful, but it didn't matter: I was driving and I was loving it.

Sixty laps later and we were back in the warmth of the office. We laughed about how difficult it had been to drive in sub-zero temperatures and exchanged stories about overtaking and crashing and trying to ram each other off the course. Covered in dirt and starting to regain sensation in our bodies we made our way back to Bristol, not before I took a few pictures as a reminder of my achievements. And of course telling Facebook about the day too. I was proper proud of myself.[178]

I wasn't quite so proud of some of my musical achievements, however. *CODE* was struggling. Because my *Accesso Rapido* EP was out at the same time as our next night, we thought it a good idea to get the label owner of Re:Sound

---

178　→ I love getting my helmet dirty. (Sorry)

down to play. He only lived in Birmingham and he was happy to oblige. I would then play after him, promoting the EP and all my other tracks too. And, once *CODE* was over, we would all head off to Lakota (one of Bristol's biggest clubs) where I was booked to play another set. I was naturally very excited to be top bill at CODE and to get the chance to play at Lakota afterwards. It promised to be a great night.

Sadly, it all fell flat on its face. Not only was it fireworks night, it was also pissing it down with rain. And I mean torrential. It soon became apparent that people weren't going to go to firework parties, let alone venture into town, and I got the feeling this would have been the case even if God himself had been spinning some tunes. Our guest sadly got to play to a near-empty club and by 1am the management decided to shut the venue — just as I was about to get on the decks. I laughed at the irony of organising a night where I was the headline DJ and still not getting to play. Never mind — Lakota was bound to be busy, so we made our way there.

As I walked through the entrance of the club, someone put their hand out and stopped me from going any further.

"I'm DJing in ten minutes!"

"No you're not. We're going to shut the room you're playing in. The club's dead. Sorry."

I'd given up hope by this point. Two bookings in one night and I got to DJ at neither of them. I turned round and made my way back home, dejected but strangely optimistic. This was the life of a small-time DJ sadly: a life where you were dropped without warning or recompense, but I wasn't going to let it bring me down. I still had my writing and my releases and that, at the end of the day, was going to be my legacy. We ran one more night but that was just as quiet. And so it was agreed between the promoters and the club that it was the end of the road for *CODE*.

I vowed never to promote another night again.

46. HIGHS AND LOWS

A COUPLE OF MONTHS LATER I WAS CONTACTED BY THE owner of a club asking me if I'd like to help promote and run a new night. Nooooooo! What had I said to myself? I balked at the idea at first but then — as always — it started to creep into my consciousness. So a few days later, myself and the other promoters involved met up and thrashed out some ideas. Someone joked that we could promote the night with a sort of 'lost dog' poster. We laughed at first but the idea started to grow. We called it 'Lost My Dog' — but no sooner had we come up with the idea than we discovered that there was a record label with exactly the same name. Determined to keep the concept, we cunningly shortened it to LOST! The talented Andy Basic (who was now very busy with a successfully expanding Slime record label) kindly created the poster for us and we stuck them up around Bristol. The posters were so effective that concerned pensioners would approach us, asking if we had found our dog yet. We smiled sweetly and told them not to worry: nothing had really been lost. They'd walk off, confused.[179]

We put a lot of effort into the design, layout, concept, and marketing for the launch night. We booked some big names and really went to town on the promotion. We brought someone to shoot a promo video and we even set a competition for people to win free entry to the night FOR LIFE! It was perhaps a tad optimistic to think that LOST! would run from now until the end of time, but we were hopeful. LOST! was born.[180]

And suddenly, music started to take off again. The beginning of 2011 saw what would be my final release on Slime, the catchily-titled *Jowump* EP. I loved this EP which featured four very distinct tracks: 'Jowump' (the name coming from a random vocal sample I had buggered about with), 'The Sirens', 'Popcorn', and 'Satisfaction'. All were different in tone and texture — yet it sounded like a complete body of work.[181] *Venue Magazine* gave it a great review and probably helped me to secure one of my biggest DJ bookings yet: supporting Felix Da Housecat at the Thekla. I'd been buying Felix's records since I was a teenager, with seminal tunes such as 'In The Dark We Live' having a huge impact on me, and now here I was DJing alongside him — I was somewhat star-struck. We had a nice chat just before he started his set (I had strategically decided to play a few of my own tunes just before he came on), and I was particularly impressed that he drank tequila straight from the bottle. During his set, I received some really nice compliments from the crowd, congratulating me on a great

179 → I guess you can see why.

180 → Check the promo video. You can really see my braces in all their majesty.

181 ♫

selection of tunes and that — sssh! — my set was maybe better than Felix's.[182]

* * *

It wasn't all glitz and glamour. The only glitz I was really getting was from my teeth and, having now worn braces for well over a year, my tolerance threshold was being pushed to the limit. Thankfully the time was fast approaching for surgery. In all honesty, I couldn't wait. I'd had enough of these chunks of metal digging into my face, making me look more ridiculous than normal, and I longed for the day when I could finally look in the mirror and not wince as a grimacing smile looked back at me.

In April 2011, I paid another visit to the Dental Hospital to talk with the team, including surgeons, about the final stages of treatment. I found the language of the dental world far more complex compared to that of eyes and brains, however I could tell that we were on the final straight. They wanted to keep the braces in for a further twelve weeks and during that time get some archwires fitted, to be used during surgery. It was also suggested that a final angiogram might need to take place to double-check the blood vessels around my jaw — just as a matter of precaution. I told them that I had booked a holiday in June and so it was suggested that July would be a good time for surgery.

Yes, you read that right: I had booked myself a holiday. For the first time since Tunisia I was finally going away. And this holiday was to be very different: I was going to Barcelona and

---

182   → But don't tell anyone.

the Sonar music festival. I'd heard so many good things about Sonar and Barcelona, and I couldn't wait to get over there and experience some sun and culture. I was going with a couple of friends whom I had met the year before at a nightclub in Bristol. It was after that night — and a little worse for wear — that we ventured back to mine and tried to write some music. One of them was strangely infatuated with just stopping a conversation... pausing.... and then saying "...Hello?", so we decided to record this a few times to see if we could use it in a tune. We programmed a drum loop and a lovely catchy bassline and then decided to call it a night. It would be a year and a half until '...Hello?' would finally get released.

A few weeks later, one of them mentioned that they were going to Sonar, and would I like to come? I hadn't been on holiday for ages, and with the promise of sun, sea, and synths, I made the decision that I would. Staged within a university campus, Sonar was a musical experience: experimental, familiar, cool. Perhaps a bit *too* cool for me. Everyone was tanned and trim, some men sporting the (in my eyes) brave yet ridiculous 'Shoreditch' approach to fashion: little brown shoes and trousers so skinny that a grasshopper would have trouble fitting into them. I was large, hot, and sweaty. But who cared? Sadly, I did.

The daytime artists weren't quite my cup of tea but the surrounding parties were: particularly the after-event at Sonar by Night — set in a huge industrial complex, with rooms so big you struggled to see from one end to the other. Whilst my friends went off to see Dizzee Rascal, I indulged in the twisted world of Aphex Twin. I made my way to the front of the crowd and watched this electronic genius create an atmosphere unlike anything else I'd experienced before.

Cameras would scan the sweaty crowd in front of him and twist and distort their heads, momentarily replacing their faces with his. It was truly an incredible experience and undoubtedly the highlight of the holiday for me. Well, that and almost getting myself killed.

Tim, a good friend of mine from back in Bristol was doing a bit of a world tour with his girlfriend, and it just so happened that they were in Barcelona the same time as me. We decided to check out the local water park. I was expecting it to be heaving — amazingly it was empty. I caught sight of a ride that looked fun and we made our way over. Just before we did, Tim tapped me on the shoulder and showed me a waterproof video camera he had brought with him. With a waterproof casing on it, we could film ourselves going down the slides. Amazing! We climbed up the ladder and, with not one other person in front of us, hurtled our way down. What I didn't realise was that we had picked one of the most brutal slides in the park: my stomach hit my chin with an almost ninety-degree drop. I smashed into the waiting water, gasping and struggling for air. BRILLIANT! I was nine years old again, and off we went to find the next one.

Having conquered and filmed almost every slide in the park, we decided to go on one last ride: the white water rapids. Tim and I positioned ourselves in one of the giant rubber rings: me facing backwards and Tim — camera in hand — filming all the action. I'm not sure the ride was designed for two blokes weighing thirty stone between them because, as it started to pick up momentum, the rubber ring began to swing viciously from side to side. Just as I was about to observe that it was getting a little hairy — BAM! — the ring flipped over and I was tossed out like a toy from a pram. My head smacked onto the chute, and for a moment I had no idea what was happening. I grasped for the ring but it was no good and I ended up on my back, sliding down towards an embarrassing exit. All I could hear behind me was Tim helpless with laughter as he tried to regain composure. My laughter was predominantly on the inside. We reached the end and plopped into the little pool of water, Tim still roaring his socks off. I decided I needed a lie down.[183]

Barcelona was at an end and it was time to go home. I was pleased that I had made the effort to get away, and that I'd managed to experience some amazing music, amazing food (the ice cream was worth the airfare alone), and that I'd gotten some culture too (seeing the Sagrada Família was truly jaw-dropping). But I was missing home. When I got back to my flat, I opened the post box to find another hospital appointment waiting for me. I somehow knew it would be there — why did this slap of reality always seem to happen on my return?

I'd been to see Andy Levy a few days before travelling to Barcelona. It was primarily a check-up to see how I was doing, and to also review the recent investigations by Julie Dovey and the Eye Hospital about the retinal migraines and mild chest pains. His letter to my GP surgery summed up the situation perfectly:

Just to let you know that I saw Daniel in clinic a few moments ago. As you know, he is blind in his left eye with a dense, right temporal field defect in the right caused by the somatotroph adenoma which has been beautifully controlled with transsphenoidal resection. He is due to

---

183 → Please don't laugh too hard. Oh, go on then.

have maxillofacial surgery in the fairly near future which he and I are looking forward to, and the only slight fly in the ointment are occasional episodes of blurring of the remaining vision in his right eye which has caused some concern but which Julie Dovey believes is retinal migraine, and an issue as to whether Daniel should be seen by GUCH team about his mild heart abnormalities. From my endocrine point of view there is not very much to do and I have just repeated his bassline hormones so that he is all set for surgery. He has an appointment to be seen by us in a year's time.

Oooh — GUCH. This was a new one. I picked up my laptop and did a quick search to find that it stood for Grown-Up Congenital Heart disease. I also found out that the BRI had a dedicated heart unit. Reassuring, I thought — but then thought, why do I need to visit a dedicated heart unit? I'm not that bad, am I? This was just a check-up, to see why my chest was beating a bit hard — there was nothing wrong with my heart.

There was another letter amongst the bundle of pizza offers and junk mail: the appointment for my jaw surgery had arrived. YIPPEE! Never had a person been so excited about finding out when someone was going to break their jaw and put it back into place. At last, I could finally get the smile back that had been robbed from me. At last, I could finally feel more confident about how I looked. The date for surgery was the 19th July, but before then there were a couple more check-ups to be made. Two weeks later I was sat in the now familiar surroundings of the Bristol Dental Hospital, joking with Farnaz about 'how time flies when you're having fun'.

She was happy with the work the wires had done and so were the rest of the dental team.

There were only two more things left to do before surgery:

1. Visit Southmead Hospital to have splints fitted
2. Have an angiogram.

Someone asked me if I had had an angiogram before. "Of course I bloody well have!" I felt like shouting, but restrained myself and nodded politely. They were a little concerned about the blood vessels around my jaw — blood vessels that were directly linked to the Wyburn-Mason syndrome. The angiogram would show them how big they were and how close they were to the surgery area. They advised that, if there were problems, they might have to consider whether surgery was really the best solution. I listened but I didn't hear.

On the 11th July, I visited Southmead Hospital to have the splints fitted. I had no idea what this involved. They probably don't tell you because, if you knew, you'd throw yourself under a bus. The whole procedure was horrendous — and this is coming from someone who's had meningitis. The purpose of having splints was so that surgeons would know where to position the jaw during surgery. Taking the moulds for the splints involved putting wads of putty in my mouth and getting me to bite down. Whilst it was setting, bits of putty would fall down the back of my throat, making me gag. I was powerless to do anything about it. And once the moulds had set, the dental technicians would put their fingers in my mouth and try to remove the mould without breaking it. My eyes were streaming as I gagged and choked on fingers and putty (not a phrase I thought I'd ever write!). Forty minutes later and it was all over. I felt violated.

And more violation was to come when, three days later, I underwent the angiogram.

"You're going to feel a warm sensation in your head," I was told, and by Satan's toenails he was right. I could feel the dye slowly trickling into my face: like someone turning on a hot tap of static. Every vein tingled as I stared dead ahead, my eyes trying to see a screen, wall, something, anything. Moments later the sensation was gone, and then another warning and it was back. I gripped the table as I anticipated more hot-face action. Why was I so afraid of this, after all I had been through? Angiograms in the chest were my only experience thus far — this was next level. Half an hour later and I was returned to the ward. I was then told I would have to lie flat on my back for the next four hours. FOUR HOURS?! That was probably the worst thing of all. It's hard to believe that lying flat could be so uncomfortable, but it was. God, I sound like a right whingebag. Sorry. Thankfully all my moaning ceased when I was told I could sit up and was handed a packet of biscuits. I'm easily pleased.

All of this discomfort was worth it though. In five days time I was going to have my jaw repositioned and I'd finally have my smile back. I spent the weekend indulging in good foods, knowing that eating would inevitably be a painful task once the surgery was over. I envisaged a couple of weeks of liquidised Sunday roasts — washed down with painkillers and antibiotics.

And so on the morning of Tuesday 19th July, 2011, I said goodbye to the dogs, locked up the flat, and made my way to the bus stop, wheeling my travel case behind me. Mum was going to come and visit me later that day (and look after the dogs), and work were aware that I was going to be off for a while. This was it. This was finally it.

I arrived at Southmead Hospital around 10am, well in advance of the operation taking place later in the day. I found the annex I needed and walked up to reception.

"Hi. I'm here to check in for surgery."

"What's your name?"

"Dan Jeffries."

"Ah, Mr Jeffries. Your consultant wants to see you before you check in. Let me tell him that you're here."

She picked up the phone and told someone on the other end that I was in the waiting room. A minute later and he was standing in front of me.

"Mr Jeffries — come to my office."

I followed him into a small room and sat down. There was an uncomfortable feeling in the air.

"Is everything alright?" I asked.

And then…

"Mr Jeffries, I'm sorry to have to tell you this — we're not going to operate."

47. HEARTBREAK AND HEARTACHE

"Excuse me?"

"We've looked at the recent angiogram results and there is a lot of vascular activity around the jaw area — no doubt connected to your Wyburn-Mason syndrome. If we were to operate, we would need to break the jaw around that area and there is real concern that the position of those blood vessels may be problematic. If a vessel is damaged in any way, the bleeding would be profuse and it could have serious consequences: potentially death. I have discussed this at length with my colleagues and it's not a decision we are taking lightly, but I hope you appreciate why we're taking that decision."

I looked at the ground, the impact of this information quickly sinking in.

"I appreciate that you're telling me this now, and of course I don't want to jeopardise my life in any way. I have one question though: why didn't you do the angiogram two years ago, before I had the braces fitted?"

"I don't know."

And with that I stood up, shook his hand, and left. Outside I lent against a wall and closed my eyes. Was this a dream? Was this really happening to me? I called a friend and vented my anger, disbelief and incredulity etched in my voice. Of course I didn't want to jeopardise my life, but why the hell didn't they look into this before I had my braces fitted? I hung up, took a deep breath, and called Dad.

"You can't risk your life, Dan. Maybe it's for the best."

And he was right. But deep down, I don't think Dad ever wanted me to go through this and thought that, in some way, I was perhaps becoming 'surgery addicted'. That wasn't the case, though I could see where he was coming from. I was deeply upset by their decision, but it wasn't like I was going to demand that they carry it out and to hell with the consequences! Make no mistake though — I was livid at this cock-up: a cock-up that had put me through the ordeal of wearing braces for nearly two years.

I left the hospital grounds and headed for the bus stop, my travel case unlovingly dragged behind me. On the bus I called Mum and Alix. The anger was building again with every person I told, but there was nothing I could do. I hung up the phone and updated Facebook — the only natural thing to do in order to get mass sympathy. It also reminded me that — now I wasn't having surgery — I could DJ at the Hijack Party that was on that weekend. Every cloud.[184]

Even though I was on 'holiday' for that week, I wasn't in

---

184 Let's not mention silver linings.

the mood to do anything. I tried to write music but I was in such a bad mood that everything sounded shit. Even my best friend, television, had nothing to offer me. I was — to put it mildly — pissed off, and justifiably so. One thing I did do was call the Dental Hospital to find out what the next steps were, and a week later I was back in the treatment room, discussing recent events with Farnaz.

I had two options. The first was to simply remove the braces. The other option was to keep them on in an effort to straighten my teeth some more, which in turn would marginally improve my bite. The impact was likely to be minimal and there were no guaranteed outcomes.

"How much longer would I keep them on for if we went down that route?"

"About two years."

I laughed.

"Absolutely no chance. I want them gone."

Farnaz nodded in agreement. She was, to her credit, incredibly sympathetic about my plight and apologised that this had happened. It wasn't her fault but I was grateful for her kind words. I asked if I could have a look at my medical records. I scanned through the earliest notes and there — in black and white — I could see the scrawl of handwriting stating that an MRI (not an angiogram) would be needed to check vascular activity. I felt my blood start to rise again, but I took a deep breath and endeavoured to keep it under control. What was the point of getting angry? What was that going to achieve? Two weeks later I was back at the Dental Hospital and those metal monstrosities that I had somehow grown to live with were finally being removed. Farnaz polished my teeth to erode the glue that had held those evil clasps for so long and I ran my tongue over the shiny new surface. I smiled. But it wasn't the smile I wanted.

Braces gone, I thanked Farnaz for all her work and we hugged, knowing what we had been through over the past two years. I was glad not to have to come back to the Dental Hospital: no more wire-tightening, no more lacerated cheeks. When I bumped into Farnaz a few months later, I was able to tell her that I had written a letter of complaint to the Dental Hospital. I had mulled over this for some time — did I really want the hassle? I decided that I did. The reply, to be fair, was sincere and apologetic and it offered to look into it further, should I wish. But really — what was I expecting out of this? Part of me was hoping that the NHS would pay my dental treatment for the next five years but I guessed that was unlikely. I digested their response and decided to do nothing more. This saga was over and it was time to move on.

* * *

Thankfully, life had some more pleasant moments to offer: and none were bigger than the arrival of my little niece, Evie. Our family has always found connections with the number 23 (I was born on the 2nd March, for example), but we couldn't figure out how twenty-three featured in Evie's birth. And then it hit me: she was born at 3:02pm. Tenuous maybe, but you can't deny the numbers. I visited Alix the next day and got to see little Evie close up. I'd never been this near to a newborn baby before and it really was a special moment. Part of me wished she was mine (obviously not mine and my sisters! You know what I mean), and it was a reminder that — at thirty-four — I was still single and, from what I could tell, unlikely to have children. Evie reached out and gripped my giant-like thumb. I was to be her Uncle Dan Dan: that's all that mattered.[185]

Back on more familiar ground, it was time for LOST! to throw a massive party — our biggest yet. We had booked an artist called The Advent and, if you know your techno (as I'm sure most of you do), you'll know he's pretty much techno royalty. I'd been listening to his music since I was a teenager and it was amazing to think that — not only would he be DJing at our night — but I would be DJing after him. We spent a lot of time and effort promoting our biggest event: huge posters, street acts, pre-ticket sales, press releases — the lot. Unfortunately, Motion (the biggest club in Bristol) had organised an event on the same night that saw the likes of Jamie xx gracing the decks — huge names in the house scene. We didn't stand a chance. We got a fair few people in but we had missed the student crowd. Perhaps The Advent was too niche a name, more appealing to the mid-thirties techno heads than eighteen-year old students. And considering most mid-thirties techno heads were now married with kids, it didn't take much to figure out why there weren't queues out the door. Sadly, we lost money. And the club weren't that happy either. A couple of days later I went in to see the manager.

"You need to be getting out there, going to all the other nights in Bristol, handing out flyers, making your face known."

Truly, I didn't. I was thirty-four with a full-time job. The last thing I wanted to do was undergo this faux-mission of shoulder rubbing, purely in the interests of promotion. I could tell the club didn't want us anymore — gutting really considering the amount of effort we had put in to the concept

185   → Bless.

and all thrown away because one event didn't quite hit the mark. I spoke to the other promoters and we decided to call it a day. I tried to keep LOST! going by moving to another small club in early 2012 but after two attempts we folded. The club were annoyed that our second night wasn't as busy as it should have been. I did point out that it was -8 degrees and Bristol was covered in snow, but that didn't seem to matter. And then, just as we were getting ready for March, they called us up a week before to tell us they were pulling the night. I tried my best to justify why they should keep us going, but they weren't having any of it. Bollocks to the lot of them. This really was the last time I was going to promote a night.

* * *

Maybe as a way to release some anger, I decided to get fit. I had joined almost every gym in Bristol with the full intention of actually using the place, but after a few weeks of testing it out I often found myself never returning and consequently wasting a whole year's subscription. I know I'm not alone in doing that. So instead I decided to work with a personal trainer. A private health clinic had opened up just around the corner and I'd arranged an appointment to see someone. I explained my previous medical conditions and what I wanted to get out of this ("Get rid of mah belly!") and he fully understood. The following week I had my first session and I felt ruined by the end of it — exhilarated but ruined. The next day every muscle in my body ached. In fact, they didn't stop aching until four days later, when it was time to do it all again. Within a few weeks I was starting to notice the difference: clothes were fitting better, belts needed to be done up tighter, and I definitely had more energy. I also coupled this with a new diet, one that I'd seen on TV (sounds disastrous already, doesn't it?). I'm sure you've seen it: it's based on pre-prepared meals and snacks that you eat throughout the month and, once it's all been consumed, you order a new batch in. It wasn't cheap but I figured that portion control was one of my biggest problems and having the right amounts of food would surely help. That was the theory. In truth, having four boxes of food in front of me was just as big a challenge, and I had to summon all my strength not to eat everything just because it was there.

The food, to be fair, was okay. Some meals were nice, some were just awful — leaving me in a quandary as to what I should eat. As is often the case, I started off well but slowly slipped back into a world of HobNobs and pasta (not together) and could see myself chucking the whole thing in. Someone then pointed out that calorie counting might be a better way to tackle this, so I looked into Apps on my phone and stumbled across *My Fitness Pal*. This became a total lifesaver. It's free, it's easy, and you get a thorough overview of what you've eaten and the exercise you've done — plus you can scan barcodes if you're unsure of the calorie content. It's a huge help and if you're struggling with managing your food, I strongly recommend giving it a go. Why not add me as a friend? We can be weight-loss buddies![186]

A few weeks into my training and I was really starting to feel the benefits: my stomach was flattening out and firming up, my arms were bulging where they should be, and my legs were strong like bull from highest mountain. Not only that,

---

186   Disclaimer: I may not always be using it.

my stamina had increased too — I could easily walk up steep hills without losing much breath, often leaving friends and family well behind. I was feeling good, like a new Dan was emerging from the cocoon: Dan 2.2, maybe.

But there was a problem. Whenever I went on the running machine, I would start to get a tight pain across my chest. After forty-five seconds of intensive running I would hit the STOP button, unable to continue. The look of concern on Stu's face was palpable — clearly he didn't want a liability on his hands. We tried it again in another session but the same thing happened. I wondered if it was the surface of the ground causing a harder impact or that my shoes weren't right (they were more designed for squash than running) and, interestingly enough, when we tried it on another running machine in a different room the pain didn't seem to manifest. I was still concerned though, and so was he, and we decided that the running machine just wouldn't be a part of our regime.

2011 was at an end. It had been another interesting year: full of incident and emotion. The disappointment at being told I wouldn't be having dental surgery was a particular highlight, as was the hot-face angiogram I had so thoroughly enjoyed. But then, I did get to go to Barcelona and had some great DJ gigs early on in the year, so it wasn't all bad. I decided that New Year's Eve needed to be something special. I was never a fan of going out to mega-raves surrounded by thousands of people I didn't know: I preferred my celebrations to be a little more intimate. And you couldn't get much more intimate than myself and three others. We had decks, lights, and a pumping sound system. I started mixing around 11pm and played some drum and bass, dropping a few of my own tunes that I hadn't heard for ages. By midnight, we moved into house and techno.

Around 4am a few more people turned up. I asked if everyone was happy with the music and was met with a resounding cheer. I guessed it was okay for me to continue. The next thing I knew it was 9am — I had been on the decks for over nine hours! I pulled back the curtains to see a dull, grey Bristol and immediately closed them again. A short while later a few more people arrived and another DJ relinquished me of my duties. I let out a huge sigh of pleasure: I hadn't played so long and so well in ages. It didn't matter that it was to a small room of people — the intimacy was what had made it so special.

2012 had gotten off to the perfect start.

48. LOVE, LUST AND EVERYTHING IN-BETWEEN

SHAKESPEARE ONCE SAID, "MAN MAY HAVE DISCOVERED fire, but women discovered how to play with it." Actually, that's not quite true — it was Candace Bushnell, author of *Sex and the City*, but it's something he might have penned, possibly omitted from Hamlet's dying soliloquy.

During the past few years, I had become very close with someone I met through a mutual friend in London. We clicked immediately. We seemed to just think the same things at the same time, share the same warped sense of humour, and said things to each other that we wouldn't tell anyone else. After months of sending emails and telephone calls and occasionally meeting up, I was starting to fall for her. But did she feel the same way about me? Experience told me that it was unlikely: I was best friend material not boyfriend material.

I was out for a meal one night with the family when my mobile rang. It was her. She had been through a traumatic time recently where she had lost a close friend. I made my apologies and popped outside. She was crying: clearly upset after recent events and was calling for some consolation. At one point the conversation became awkward, like she wanted to say something but couldn't.

"You know you can tell me anything. What is it?"

Silence.

"I think I love you. And I want to be with you."

Now it was my turn to fall silent.

"Are you serious? Do you mean it? Because I've felt like this for some time too. Do you really mean it?"

"Yes."

We ended our call and I skipped back into the restaurant, anxious not to get too hyped, but at the same time unable to hide my adulation. As soon as the meal was over, I called my sister to tell her the news. She was just as pleased — and shocked — as I was.

Over that weekend I tried to contact her but couldn't get in touch. I found this really difficult: I wanted to speak to her, to check this wasn't a dream. By Tuesday I had still heard nothing. And then I got a message on Facebook explaining that the phone call had been a mistake: that she was emotionally distressed after the loss, and that she wanted to try and work things out with her partner. I was devastated.

"In another lifetime and it might all be different," was the parting message. I couldn't understand it. Why not *this* lifetime? Why not *now*?

A few months passed as I let things cool down, but, as with most strong friendships, the bond started to form again and we began to talk once more. She had split up with her then partner and, in the light of recent activities, we decided that we both deserved a break, so we booked a room for two nights in a small hotel on the south coast. Now, it might be at this stage that you're thinking that I was setting myself up for a fall, but I didn't really think of it as anything more than a chance to have a bit of a weekend away together — a chance to rekindle our friendship. And besides, we'd shared a bed many times before. Y'know, as friends.

Having checked in we strolled around town, trying to find a specific restaurant that we had been recommended, but with my terrible sense of direction we practically ended up on the motorway. Finally we found somewhere to eat and, feeling full, felt the need to sit down and have a quiet drink. We spotted a secluded little bar with bizarre artwork adorning the walls. There was a special offer on: Jägerbombs, 5 for £10. We must have put away fifteen shots each. We stumbled back to the hotel, laughing and joking and fell into bed, still laughing about what we'd just consumed. I leant over and gave her a hug.

"No, no, no!" and she pushed me away.

I had once again reached the blurry divide.

More months passed. Relationships came and went (her, not me: never me). I'd often get phone calls complaining about boyfriend X or seeking advice about partner Y and I would offer impartial insights, all the while deep down resenting these strangers for being an intimate part of her life. Is that jealousy? I guess it is. I just knew that we were good together, that we were Yin and Yang. But if Yin doesn't feel the same way, what say does Yang really have?

April, 2011. I was headlining a night in Bristol and lots of my friends were coming to see me DJ — and she was coming too. I was excited. She came to Bristol the night before and we went out for food. The conversation turned to relationships and, in a rare moment of bravado, I told her that I'd always fancied her but was never brave enough to do anything about it.

"Well maybe you should have done. I was waiting for you to."

My heart sank. I'd missed my chance.

The next night we got to the club for about midnight. Everyone was there. I played for an hour and a half and it was a blinder, the last thirty minutes of the set dedicated to just my own music. At 4am we made our way back home. A friend of mine was staying over and, as he had an early getaway in the morning, we retired to my room. This time it didn't feel like the divide was quite so blurred, and we lay in bed, our legs rubbing against each other. Maybe it was the drink.

June 2011, and we were invited to a birthday. Well, she was: I was asked if I would like to be her '+1'. She was going to ask someone else that had been pursuing her of late, but she wanted to go with me instead. This stroked my ego quite nicely and I duly accepted. I booked a small guesthouse nearby, as there was a fair bit of travel involved. It was a lovely day and a great party but come midnight we decided to leave and head back to our hotel. We were feeling very merry and lay in bed for the night, cuddling and talking. I fell asleep.

At one point I woke up to find that she wasn't there. I was confused. Maybe she'd popped outside for some reason? In my hazy state, I fell back asleep.

An hour later I awoke to find her lying next to me, a half-empty bottle of whisky in her hand. She was pissed — seriously pissed. I sat upright and asked her what she'd done. She told me that she'd gone to the garage at the end of the road and bought a bottle of whisky. That I understood, but to drink half of it was next level. We made our way to breakfast but she was in no fit state to carry a plate, let alone eat what was on it. I tried to avoid a situation whilst we were surrounded by guests. It wasn't that I was concerned about what others might've thought — it's just that this was all new to me and I didn't know what to do. On the way home she repeatedly asked me if I loved her, to which I replied that I did — more to appease her than to finally declare my intentions. We got back to hers where she passed out in the lounge.

A few hours later and she'd sobered up and wanted a bath. I said that I was nipping to the shops to get something for dinner. On my return she called me to the bathroom. I gingerly knocked on the door and she told me to come in. As was to be expected, she was naked — but there was no attempt to cover up. I tried not to look but it was pretty hard not to. A thought flashed through my mind that — if I were a red-blooded male — I would jump in the bath and take her to soapy heaven. Instead I knelt next to her and massaged her shoulders upon request. I'm so subservient but that was close enough for me. Was this happening? Were we getting nearer? Were we falling in love?

That night we got into bed. I didn't quite know what to make of the past twelve hours. Again, I wanted to reach over and take her in my arms, kiss her deeply, and tell her that I wanted her to be mine. Instead I lay there, motionless. Moments passed. And then suddenly, she leant over, put her hand under the bed sheets, and grabbed between my legs.

"Come on then. Let's get this over and done with."

I froze. This was not how I pictured it happening. This was not the romantic explosion I had envisioned!

"I don't want to do this if you don't want to," I bleated out.

"It's going to happen, so let's just do it."

What should I do? My brain was telling me that this didn't feel right, that this wasn't the way it was meant to be — but my penis was telling me that this was what I'd been wanting, that this wasn't an offer I got every day. And so — after a millisecond of thought — I turned towards her and we made love. Or I think we did. I don't quite know what it was. Within moments of being inside her, she started to cry.

"This is so wrong," she whimpered. But at the same time she thrust back towards me and it wasn't long until it was all over. I came to realise that I'm a bit rubbish at this and probably a bit of a disappointment. I fell onto my back and she lay there, quietly sobbing.

* * *

The next day and I needed to head back home. We briefly talked about the night before but not much was said. I could tell from her body language that, for her, it was a mistake. On the train my brain was awash with thoughts: What had I done? Had I done something wrong? Was I out of line? Did I misbehave? Was that the end of our friendship? I concluded that it probably was all just a big mistake. So why did I feel so sad?

Months passed. Communication ceased. I didn't feel happy. It was like the promise of something had been taken away from me, and it's the one thing I'd been yearning for: a relationship. I wrote lengthy emails (hardly romantic I know) explaining my emotions, trying to make things work but I was rebuffed with an answer that I hadn't heard before: "I don't want a relationship because I fear it would ruin our friendship — one day we would split up, and we could no longer be best friends."

My brain could see the logic in this, but my heart was thinking: how do we know unless we try? Maybe it was the testosterone talking, maybe this *was* the best solution. But could we truly remain only friends? Once that divide is crossed, can anything be the same again?

The answer was no. In a moment of clarity and bravery, she told me that she had a problem with drink. I had, by that point, guessed as much. I would get random text messages that made no sense, phone calls with no one at the end of the line; I could see she was in need of help. I visited her on more than one occasion to make sure she was okay and — rightly or wrongly — we would sometimes end up in bed. I can't quite explain how I feel about this. Sometimes it was mutual, sometimes it was an offer I couldn't refuse, made all the more difficult by the fact that — when it happened — it was amazing. Yet all the while I knew it was under a foggy haze of alcohol.

I was having my own problems too: the 2.5mg Cialis I had been prescribed were not behaving as I had expected. Fine for a few minutes but then suddenly it would drop away. This only made matters worse — convincing her that I couldn't get an erection because I didn't find her attractive. Nothing could have been further from the truth. This intimacy was something I had been wanting for years, and not even the medication I was taking could help resolve my issues.

And then the next thing I knew, she had checked herself into a clinic for six weeks: six of the darkest weeks of my life. I thought we were really getting somewhere and then suddenly

— BAM — it was gone, and she's in a clinic that I don't know the name of and therefore have no way of getting in touch with her. And to make matters worse, an ex-boyfriend had become her new support mechanism and was visiting her all the time. He picked her up in his car (if only I could drive, dammit!), and took her home once she was better. They were back together, and I was off the scene.

After all this, we're still good friends. I think she's grateful to me for helping her through this very dark period of her life. Now on the proper medication, she's definitely doing much better and seems to be happier in herself — which in turn makes me happy too. I probably know her better than anyone else does: I know how brilliant her creative mind can be but I know all her foibles too. And they're pretty big. But, for whatever reason, I can't help but love her — even though I know it's no good for me. Some people think I like 'causes' but really I don't. Others think I aim far too high in the looks department, but I can't help what I find attractive. Perhaps, deep down, knowing that I'm not the best looking guy in the world encourages me to woo girls that most would deem out of my league. Is that it? Is it purely a trophy wife that I'm after? But beauty is in the eye of the beholder, right? Ah God, I don't know…

The truth is, I am totally comfortable in my own company and don't feel the need to force myself to have a relationship, simply because that's what society thinks I should do. I'm still looking though, still looking for someone to hold, someone to cuddle, someone to laugh with — and someone to look after. And hopefully that someone will want to do the same for me, too.

49. THE POWER OF WORDS

AND SO, DEAR READER, WE NEAR THE FINAL PHASE OF MY tale. If you're reading this on paperback then you probably know this already, simply by seeing how many pages are left. If you're reading the digital version, you're probably petrified that there are hundreds of pages to go. Don't worry: there aren't.

Whilst 2011 was primarily about love and teeth, 2012 turned out to be the 'Year of the Heart'. The investigations into my spiky vision had concluded that these were nothing more than simple retinal migraines — they were not the symptoms of heart or stroke issues. This was good news.

I was, however, still getting pains in my chest, something I had told Andy Levy about in 2011 and reported to my doctor too. Andy wrote to the GUCH team in mid-June, asking if they still wanted to see me as I had heard nothing since Julie Dovey's previous letter. Mark Turner, one the leading consultants at GUCH, contacted Andy in October with the following:

Thank you for your letter. I do not believe I received this referral from Julie, as I have never heard of this syndrome. I think he should be seen in a cardiology clinic and will be pleased to meet him.

And with that, an appointment was made for the 8th December. This would involve an echocardiogram and a consultation. I hadn't had an echo since July 2010, when I went to see Julie Dovey about the retinal migraines. The echos in 2007 and 2010 both showed that I had mild to moderate regurgitation and it was clear from the consultation afterwards that this was still the case. Indeed the consultant explained the findings of the echo in her letter:

Echo was performed today which demonstrated good LV systolic function with no LVH and no LV dilation (LVEDD 59mm, LVESD 42mm at upper limit of normal). The aortic valve was trileaflet with good leaflet excursions and no aortic stenosis. There was moderate aortic regurgitation seen. The right heart was not dilated with preserved free wall function with trivial tricuspid regurgitation with a BPD of the TR jet of 22 mmHg. Trivial pulmonary regurgitation and trivial mitral regurgitation and normal IVC diameter.

No, doesn't make much sense to me either. The important conclusion was this: they weren't sure where my chest pain was coming from. The latest echo didn't give them all the detail they needed and — considering my complex medical situation — they wanted to look at my heart in more detail. This would involve sending me for a transoesophageal echocardiogram, the next step up from the echo. A new one on me, they explained that it involved putting an ultrasound sensor down my throat to capture more detailed images of the heart. Sounded delightful — I couldn't wait.[187]

And I didn't have to. My appointment was made for 24th January. I arrived at the BRI with Mum, still my source of comfort and reassurance. If I'd had a partner, I would hope they would be with me too — but I didn't, so it was family all the way. I once again got into a rather fetching hospital gown and lay on the bed, waiting for someone to wheel me off. A nurse soon came over and inserted a cannula into my arm so they could give me sedatives — it was likely there would be discomfort when they inserted the tube into my throat. I hadn't eaten since midnight and I was more scared that I may actually eat the tube should it come to it. An hour or so later and a porter arrived — it was time. Mum kissed my forehead. This was only routine, yet something felt different about it. I was wheeled into a room where a team of consultants were waiting. They asked me to lie on my side (so the tube could easily follow the desired path), and a nurse squirted some spray into my throat to anaesthetise it. I felt a small dose of sedative trickle through my body.

"We're going to start putting the tube in now, Mr Jeffries."

At least that was their plan: my body had other ideas. As soon as the tube entered my throat I started to gag — badly.

---

187   → If you're still a bit lost by all my medical happenings thus far (and I really hope you're not otherwise I haven't done my job properly!) then it's well worth reading this letter, which summarises everything very clearly.

This was probably the most repulsive sensation experienced so far — far outweighing the surreal warmth of the angiogram and even the putty falling down the back of my throat. I coughed and choked and my eyes started to stream. I held my hand up as a sign for them to stop and they did, but they needed to try again and when I had composed myself they inserted the tube once more. Again I started to gag and then… well… I don't remember much else. They must have turned the sedatives right up because the next thing I knew I was back on the ward, nursing a mildly sore throat. I'm glad they knocked me out.

I lay on my bed, worn out and tender. Mum sat next to me reading her book. I felt pants. A short while later, the lady who had performed the TOE came round to check if I was okay. I asked her if the examination showed anything.

"Well, the ultrasound sensor shows that there is some aortic regurgitation taking place. Images show that it may be moderate to severe."

I'd heard it was mild to moderate — now it was severe?

"What does that mean?" I asked tentatively.

"It means you'll probably have to have heart surgery."

And with that, she walked off.

I lay there stunned. I turned to look at Mum. Disbelief was etched across her face. Heart surgery? Really? After all I'd been through, was I really now going to have to face heart surgery? We sat there in silence, trying to comprehend the situation. Someone brought me biscuits but — for once — they offered little consolation. A short while later we called Dad and Alix to tell them the diagnosis. They were just as shocked as we were.

That night, Mum and I went to a local restaurant where

I gorged on a sumptuously rich three-course meal, washed down with half a bottle of wine. Eating was my coping mechanism, and in hindsight it probably wasn't the wisest thing I had ever done: I was still under the effects of the sedatives and when we got home I started to feel a little worse for wear. As we said goodnight, Mum and I hugged each other just that bit longer than normal, scared more than ever by the news we had heard that day.

The knock-on effects of that comment had far more impact than we could have anticipated. It hit Dad particularly badly. He was deeply concerned that my heart was in trouble, that something drastic could go wrong at any moment. I had to do my utmost to reassure him that things were okay. It's amazing the repercussions such a small sentence can have. Even with a couple of big music releases coming up, I too was feeling the effects. Yes, even me: non-emotional Dan. And it all reached its peak on my 35th birthday.

50. SO LONG, OLD PAL

I DON'T KNOW WHAT IT IS ABOUT FOOD, BUT IT SEEMS TO PLAY a pivotal role at the key points in my life. Whether it was the Chinese meal at my graduation, the take-away whilst I nearly bled to death from my genitals, or the vomitorium-style feast after being told I would probably have heart surgery — food has always been there. And my 35th birthday was no exception.

The family had arranged for a dozen of our close friends to go out for a few drinks and then dinner at a fab Chinese restaurant — usually my favourite. The mood was good but as the evening went on — possibly as the result of too much wine and not enough food — I started to feel myself sink. Usually I was upbeat, positive, celebratory — but sat there at that table, the grim realisation of what had been said in that hospital ward was starting to penetrate my soul. And when I got up to make my usual after-dinner speech, I just stood there in silence. This wasn't me. I'd usually come out with an off-the-cuff quip or raise a toast to the chef, but instead… nothing. I looked around the room and sighed.

"I have of late — but wherefore I know not — recently lost all my mirth."

It may have been a bit grand to compare myself to Hamlet, but it was the only thing that came into my head. And it was true — I *had* lost my mirth. I muddled through the usual platitudes: sombrely thanking people for coming and reflecting on why… why… why me? Why was I the one to have to go through this? Hadn't I had enough?! I quickly realised I was letting things slip and did my best to turn it around, but it was no good. The mood had changed and I felt terrible for causing it. Later that night, Mum broke down in tears and wept uncontrollably for nearly an hour, shattered by the thought of me having to go through heart surgery. There was nothing we could do to console her and, whilst I don't doubt her feelings for one second, I think the food/booze ratio was probably partly to blame. The next day she was better, if not a little bit delicate, but it was clearly affecting us all.

* * *

In other news, March saw the release of two new singles: 'Matter' and 'Just Wanna Be'. 'Just Wanna Be' was originally written by a friend of mine who gave me the parts and asked me to turn it into something new. I duly obliged, creating one of my best tracks to date. 'Matter' was a very different beast: a heavy techno monster with a catchy bassline and dark twisted vocal hits, courtesy of yours truly. It reached No.1 on the Track It Down charts.[188]

I was also coming to the conclusion that, as much as I enjoyed working with labels, they weren't really doing much when it came to pushing my music. I did a bit of research and contacted some distributors to be told that I could setup my own label if I wanted to. This was great news: it gave me full artistic control of the output, the design, and the marketing. If it didn't succeed, I only had myself to blame. I settled on the name 'mu-sic', a subtle nod to my [sic] moniker. In hindsight, it was an awful decision because — when you type it into Google — it removes the hyphen and gives you 2,150,000,000 results. You live and learn.

Before I focused on my first release, I needed to ensure that I focused on my health. We had finally recovered from the initial shock of that announcement, but we also felt like we were in limbo as not much had happened since. In April I received a letter from Mark Turner, outlining where we were at:

Dear Mr Jeffries,

I enclose copies of some correspondence. Your transoesophageal echo suggests that the leak on your aortic valve may be a little more than we thought in the clinic. There was also a tiny hole in the heart which supports the fact that your other symptoms were to do with migraine.

I am going to request a cardiac MRI scan which can give us further information about your aorta, aortic valve

188 ♫

and heart in general. I noted you have had brain surgery before and would be grateful if you would let the MRI Department know if the neurosurgeons left behind any metalwork in your brain that could mean that an MRI scan is not possible.

I was pretty sure there was no metalwork in my brain, and the braces were long gone too, so the MRI could proceed. It was at this time that I decided to stop working with my personal trainer. My mind wasn't focused on it and, more importantly, I didn't want to risk complicating anything further by putting potential strain on my heart. I knew that being fit was important, but until this had all been resolved it just wasn't fair on him. It was a shame because I was trim and feeling fit, and I knew that a decline into food and lethargy would be inevitable.

One thing that I was noticing about the investigations into my heart in comparison to the brain tumour was the speed at which things were happening. When the tumour had been discovered back in 2007, it was only a few months between diagnosis and surgery — the process here felt very different. This was, I can't deny, frustrating. We all appreciated the need for the GUCH team to investigate thoroughly, but I was convinced that the various issues with my heart were severe enough to warrant surgery. In preparation for this, I did some research into aortic valve replacement and discovered, to my surprise, that it was a relatively common procedure:

'During surgery, a cut is made in the chest to access the heart. The heart is then stopped and a heart-lung bypass machine is used to take over the circulation during the

> operation. The aortic valve is removed and replaced with
> an artificial valve (prosthesis). The heart is then started
> again and the chest incision is closed.'

Strangely enough, the family were far more scared by the prospect of this than they were of brain surgery — which is pretty ridiculous when you think about it. Perhaps there is a *finality* when contemplating the heart. It is the organ that keeps us alive, after all — to operate on it felt like a last resort. I was fully prepared to be told that surgery was going to happen. Indeed, I was of the opinion that it *should* happen, that it would be better to have it done whilst I was fit and healthy rather than in thirty years' time when I wasn't. But of course, that decision didn't rest with me.

* * *

Sat at home one very ordinary evening, I suddenly felt something quite odd. I ignored it, thinking it was just a twitch. And then it happened again. And again. My heart was spasming. Every 30 seconds, I felt this fluttering sensation around the left-hand side of my chest. I wondered if it was just a muscle spasm, but muscle spasms don't last an hour, so I decided to give NHS Direct a call. It didn't take long for them to advise me to go straight to A&E, considering my previous medical history. I gave the dogs some food and walked down to the hospital. They checked me in and wired me up to an ECG. I called my sister and told her what had happened. Within an hour she was sat next to me — I was mightily impressed.[189]

---

189   Don't worry — Mum was looking after the baby!

She offered to stay over at mine and look after the dogs. I told her I hoped I would be out that night.

Typically, once I got to hospital the twitching stopped. Considering my medical history they decided it was probably best to keep me in overnight, just to be safe. By the morning their conclusion was that this was nothing to do with my heart but in fact an intercostal spasm of my chest muscle. In other words: a twitch. I thanked the nurses for their help and made my way home. As pleased as I was with the outcome, I was absolutely desperate for some sleep: all night long I had been subjected to the beeping and buzzing of machinery. In fact, one machine was so desperate to make itself heard that I took a video of it. How the guy sleeping next to it managed not to rip the plug out, I'll never know.[190]

I got home to find that Alix had scrubbed the flat from top to bottom. She loved doing this — I think it kept her mind off things. She wasn't so keen on mopping up gallons of Norman's piss, however. We reminded each other about the time when Alix was heavily pregnant and waiting to go into labour. Desperate for something to eat — but being pregnant and unable to decide on what she wanted — she eventually settled on a burger. She did her best to eat it but she just couldn't keep it down, and a few minutes later it was being puked back up into a washing-up bowl. In a bid to feel clean, she ran a bath and, having momentarily diverted our attention from the dogs, went back into the lounge to find Norman head first in the washing-up bowl and happily munching away. That dog had absolutely no sense of occasion.

After making sure I was okay, Alix returned home. I was

---

190 → Beep. Beep. Beep.

very grateful for all her help and support, and I was equally grateful for the peace and quiet too. Millie jumped up onto the sofa and looked deep into my eyes, making sure everything was okay. Norman tried to jump up but didn't get very far, settling instead for an intense session of bollock-licking.

I'd been watching Norman's steady decline for some months. After a recent visit to the vet, it was becoming clear that his time was nearing an end: his eyesight had gotten worse, his arthritis was causing him pain, and his back legs were so weak that they'd just give way underneath him. The decisive moment came when — calling him to give him his dinner — he ran straight into a wall and started barking. Norman no longer seemed to have any quality of life, and so it was time to say goodbye.

I spent days deliberating over whether this was the humane thing to do. Suddenly I was responsible for the life of one of God's creatures, and I now had the power to decide if he lived or died. I read about it online, asked others for their advice, and dreamt about differing outcomes. Eventually I called the vet and discussed with him what I had been thinking and he agreed, considering all his ailments, that it was the best thing to do. I made the appointment for a week's time and oh, how I regret doing that. For the next seven days, I would wake up and look at him, knowing that he was one day closer to death. I announced on Facebook that I had made the decision and received lots of warm support, advising me that it was difficult but the best thing to do.

And so, seven days on from that phone call, I walked Norman for the very last time. Millie came as well as I had been told that she should have her chance to say goodbye too. I'd been alright up to this point, but when they picked him up and put him on the table my lip started to go. They gently stroked his head as they gave him his first injection and he slowly started to drift away. He looked up at me as they administered the final shot and I watched as he lay back down, the final beats of life visible in his body. And then he was still. The vet said he would leave me for a minute and, as I held him in my arms, I burst into tears. I had never seen something die in front of me before — human or animal — and I was surprised at my own reaction. Not because I'm heartless, but because I always thought I was strong. But now I had witnessed the death of a creature that I had looked after for the past seven years. Sharon put her arm on my shoulder and I hugged her. I picked Millie up to say goodbye to her lifelong companion. She sniffed and then kicked her legs — a sign that she wanted to get down. It appeared that she was completely unaware of what had happened, perhaps a bit too old now to be fully affected by the separation.

Outside the vets, I called Mum to tell her it was over — bursting into tears as I did so. She loved Norman just as much as I did, so it was hard for her too. Back at home I packed a bag so I could head down to Weston for a couple of days, temporarily forgetting that someone was buying a computer from me that morning. As he turned up minutes later, he found me sat on the sofa, sobbing like mad. Poor sod — I bet that wasn't quite what he was expecting.

A couple of weeks later and I gathered a group of friends up on Brandon Hill to say goodbye to Norman. I was determined to give him a proper send off. I'd paid to get his ashes returned and, once up on Brandon Hill, made a speech about the good times we'd had, showing pictures of him that I'd collected over the years on my iPad. Finally, I turned around, looked at the landscape of Bristol in front of me, and scattered his ashes into the breeze.

It was the end of a very long chapter in my life — one that saw me caring for an elderly dog often at the expense of my own existence. But he was worth every minute.

Goodbye, Norman. In Heaven you can eat as much puked-up burger as you like.[191]

191   → *sniff*

51. STRESS

THE FLAT WAS NOW STRANGELY EMPTY WITHOUT THE rasping cough of Norman.

Millie — bless her cotton socks — seemed to be rejuvenated by the whole experience. She clearly wasn't mourning his absence: in fact, it was as though it had given her a new lease of life. Her newfound independence made her happier, tougher, more confident. She no longer barked at other dogs — something she used to do just because Norman did. She wallowed in the attention that she would get whenever I walked her round the park and particularly if I took her into town. She was an instant hit with the ladies — something I was quietly jealous of. But she was getting old too and I could no longer let her off the lead as she had a habit of running away. Indeed, one Sunday morning she decided to break free and run as fast as she could to wherever there was a road. The trouble was, the more I chased her, the faster she ran until she found herself in the middle of Jacob's Wells Road, coincidentally just outside my old school. Mercifully, as it was Sunday, the roads were quiet, but I still had the fear that something bad was going to happen. I stopped, held my hand out, and pretended it contained a delicious treat. She looked at me and I turned around and started to walk away — I had read that this was what you needed to do, and I just hoped to God that it would work. Suddenly, I could hear the scratching of claws on the pavement behind me and I spun around to see her there, staring at me with those big, loveable eyes. I bent down as if to give her the treat and scooped her up in my arms, scowling at her for almost giving me a heart attack. She sniffed my face and licked my chin. You've just gotta love dogs.

If Millie wasn't going to give me a heart attack, maybe the exercise tests that I was about to endure would. July saw me back at the GUCH clinic for a further ECG, echo, and consultation. This time, Dad and Alix came along. Mum had decided that — like Dad when I was younger — her non-attendance seemed to bring the best news, and so she waited at home for the call.[192]

After the tests, we had a long and detailed discussion with the consultant. Before we were told any results, I was keen to stress how upset we had been by the comment made back in January, that I would "probably have to have heart surgery". He apologised for this, stating that it shouldn't have been said. Our minds were rested. He then went on to explain that, in light of recent test results, the team were still trying to assess whether my leaking heart valve was either moderate or severe

---

192   Family superstitions are something special, aren't they?

— as the echo and the MRI were showing contrasting results. In his letter to my GP he wrote:

> *I explained to them that although he may need a surgical intervention to his aortic valve and ascending aorta in the future, first he would need a thorough assessment and team discussion. His TTE, TOE and cardiac MRI examinations did not fully agree on the severity of the aortic regurgitation [the leak] and the degree of the left ventricular dysfunction. Also he is not terribly symptomatic from this point of view.*

To help with the diagnosis, the GUCH team wanted me to undergo a series of exercise tests. This was to give them a better idea as to what was causing the chest pains, and to monitor how my heart coped under extreme physical pressure. Finally, he recommended that I should start taking some medication known as ACE inhibitors, which would help protect the heart and relax the blood vessels. Things were moving forward — but we were still none the wiser as to whether I would need surgery.

Early September, and time for my cardiac exercise test, also known as a Stress Test.[193] I arrived at the hospital with a pair of running shoes and some gym gear. The consultant in charge explained the procedure: they were going to attach an ECG to my chest, and then monitor my heartbeat as I first walked, then ran, on a treadmill. The test would last for as long as I could keep running. I hadn't done any serious physical exercise since I last saw my personal trainer, so I was both intrigued and anxious about the results. They asked me

---

193   They do come up with some cracking names!

to take off my shirt and ECG pads were placed all over my body. This has never been an easy thing to do as I'm a rather hairy being, and the pads often failed to stick. I feared they would stick even less when my body was covered in sweat.

All wired up, I stood on the treadmill and suddenly felt very hot. I looked up to see that my head was almost touching the ceiling. Halogen lamps beamed down onto my face and it was like being in a sauna: I was sweating before I had even begun![194]

"Ready?"

I took a deep breath and nodded. It was easy at first, just a gentle walk, but every thirty seconds they would start to increase the pace. Within five minutes, I was jogging pretty hard. After ten minutes I was running like Mo Farah needing the loo. I finally stopped at 11 minutes and 8 seconds, which I was pretty pleased with. As I sat on the floor, gasping for air, they informed me that they had accidentally stopped the test halfway through. I laughed.

"I don't need to do it again, do I?" I asked in mild panic.

Thankfully I didn't: they had managed to record the results manually.

A week later and I was sitting in a consultation room opposite Andy Levy, Dad and Alix by my side. Andy started off by apologising for the "probably" blunder, and then proceeded to apologise about the dental work I'd undergone too, feeling responsible because he was the one who had recommended this. We reassured him that he was not responsible and that, unfortunately, these things happen. Andy then looked at the results from my Stress Test, impressed with the findings. Dad

---

194   I wonder if this was intentional? If so, they are evil.

got down to the nuts and bolts: was I going to need heart surgery?

"Oh, I don't think so," he said. "You look like you're doing pretty well to me."

The relief in the room was palpable. This was just the plain and simple language Dad and Alix needed. I sat there and took it all in, not quite so sure.

Consultation over, we made our way outside. Alix was almost skipping with elation, Dad overjoyed at the news he'd just heard. I, on the other hand, felt confused, and was struggling to show the same sense of relief that they were. Was I confused or was this just a personality trait? Or was I just letting Dad and Alix have their moment while all of the above sunk in? Out in the open they turned to me, smiles beaming across their faces, but these soon fell away — they could see that my face didn't show the same. Alix, awash with emotion, grabbed me by the shoulders and shook me.

"What's wrong with you?! Why aren't you happy?!" she wailed, tears welling up as she desperately tried to elicit some emotional response.

This was very difficult. I had gone into that consultation convinced that Andy was going to tell me that I would be having heart surgery. In some ways, I was disappointed to be told that I wouldn't. Some part of me, for whatever reason, believed that it was better to have heart surgery now than in twenty, thirty, forty years time. My heart had a leak, and it was only going to get worse — let's fix it now while I'm young and healthy. I wasn't going to deny Dad and Alix their moment, but the truth is I'm not as outwardly emotional as they are. It's very different when *you're* the one experiencing the conditions every day, when *you're* the one who is aware of how your body feels, when *you're* the one who has to think about your own future. I tried to express this as best I could, conscious that I didn't want to upset anyone even more.[195] Of course I was pleased about the news, I just wanted to hear it from the GUCH team as well. We made our way to a cafe and sat quietly for a moment, contemplating what we had just heard. Lunch was ordered and everything was back to normal. Maybe I was tired but maybe that's just an excuse.

195   And once again, putting my own feelings on the back-burner.

52. 183%

T HINGS WERE, AT LAST, FINALLY DRAWING TO A CLOSE. ALL that remained now were a handful of tests: an angiogram to further explore my heart, an MRI to do the same, and a Cardiopulmonary Test to see how my lungs, heart and muscles reacted to exercise. I also had an MRI booked in to see if any nasty pituitary tumours had grown back in the last twelve months, but I wasn't so bothered about that.

Mark Turner's letter to my GP explained the plan of action:

> We felt that he should come back for a further MRI with late gadolinium enhancement assessment and a multi-phase angiogram to look to see if there is any evidence of arteriovenous malformations that would be falsely elevating his cardiac output and causing a high cardiac output, that could be an explanation for his dilated left

ventricle. However I think the most likely thing is that he has moderate regurgitation. Dr Hamilton has kindly agreed to perform some further volumetric assessment to see if a different method of measurement will change the MRI assessment of severity of the aortic regurgitation. If all this is normal I will probably arrange an exercise test, which could be a cardiopulmonary test, to reassure us that we do not need to intervene at this stage.

I received a copy of this letter just after it had been written but decided not to share it with the family.[196] My intentions were honourable: I didn't want it to raise false hope. That final statement — *we do not need to intervene* — was key, and the MRI, angiogram, and exercise test would provide the definitive answer.

The MRI and the angiogram took place in October and December. The MRI was a walk in the park, the angiogram — for once — not too bad either. It was purely around the chest area, so no hot static in the face this time. The exercise test took place in mid-November. This was a Cardiopulmonary Test — different to the Stress Test I had undergone earlier in the year. I arrived at the hospital (yes, running shoes and shorts at the ready) and discussed the procedure with the consultants. They explained that they would wire me up to an ECG (more chest hair shaving), put a blood pressure cuff on me, a saturation probe, and a soft rubber face mask with a turbine to measure the expired gases. It looked like I was about to undergo training for NASA. My mission: to walk and then run up a treadmill for as long as I possibly could.

196   Sorry folks.

The test started at a gentle walking pace with no uphill climb, but after a few minutes they started to crank up the resistance and the incline until it became unbearable. The team stood around me, shouting encouragement like I was a champion boxer being slaughtered in the twelfth.

"Come on Dan! Climb that treadmill! Don't let it beat you!"

I pushed myself harder and harder as they urged me to use every last bit of strength and oxygen to climb what was now feeling like a vertical wall. After twelve and a half minutes, I was done. I stumbled off the treadmill and fumbled my way towards a chair. My legs were like jelly. I was exhausted but charged — something I hadn't felt since my last session at the gym. I looked up and saw the team analysing the results.

"How did I do?" I panted.

"Very well. Looking at your Physical Capacity parameter, you're 183% of the normal result."

"And that's good?"

"Very."

They gave me a towel and pointed me towards the showers. 183% of the normal result. Wow. That's almost twice as good as they had expected. I was chuffed. I might be a bit overweight (or 'clinically obese' as they called it, but let's not worry about that right now) but it appeared I was still pretty fit too. [197]

* * *

Christmas. There was more of an air of calm around the family

---

197 → No, I don't know what most of it means either, but I'm guessing anything over 100% is good.

table that year. Dad and I spoke about what a 'challenging' year it had been, mostly in relation to my health (no surprises there then!). But we also spoke about how it looked like there was a light at the end of the tunnel. I reminded everyone that I had an appointment to see Mark Turner on the 10th January, and that this would probably be the day we'd find out if they were going to perform a heart-valve replacement.

"Merry Christmas!" I joked and made a toast to the future. Speeches over, it was time to get down to some serious drinking. It was Christmas Day after all.

* * *

January arrived. Consultations were running behind schedule. Dad and Alix paced around the hospital: their way of keeping their minds occupied. Terrible daytime TV quietly churned away in the background. I liked to watch the medical teams in action, admiring this intricate ecosystem at work. Suddenly, Mark Turner appeared and called out my name. We stood to attention. Showtime.

The first thing he told us was that the results from the MRI scan weren't available yet. Great. Was this going to be a wasted journey? He discussed the results from the Cardiopulmonary Test, and he was very pleased. I said I was too, still beaming over my score of 183%. Dad asked if there was perhaps some link between the acromegaly and the damage that had occurred to my heart valve. Mark thought this was more than possible. He then went on to explain that heart valve replacement — should it be needed — was an exceptionally common operation and the risks were low. I could see the relief in Dad's face. Alix squeezed my hand.

We finally discussed the elephant in the room: would I need surgery? The answer was no. Well, not yet. There was no immediate risk to my heart but perhaps in the future, the option could be explored again. Mark Turner's letter summed it up perfectly:

> *Given that the most obvious explanation for something is often the one that is true, I suspect that he actually has moderate aortic regurgitation. If we see progressive left ventricular dilatation in the presence of moderate regurgitation then we do recommend aortic valve replacement, but if we find an alternative explanation for the left ventricular impairment, and there is no progression on medical therapy, then we would not be intervening for a moderate level of aortic regurgitation.*

> *[We have] truly excellent information to guide our decision making from the cardiopulmonary tests, so it may be that this will help us make a judgement. Therefore I think there is an outside chance we will be offering Daniel an aortic valve replacement, but this is certainly not imminent.*

And that was it. A year of worry and anxiety culminated in the decision that we all wanted. I say all: the decision that the *family* wanted. I was still in two minds. If I was likely to need the valve replaced, why not do it now? But I had to listen to the experts. Some weeks later it slowly started to sink in that not having majorly intrusive surgery wasn't such a bad thing after all. Maybe I *was* a little 'surgery addicted'. Who knows?

Two months later and Ian invites me to his birthday meal and the rest, as they say, is history. I'm glad Danielle casually said, "You should write a book" because without that seed, these pages probably wouldn't exist. I'm glad they do — and I hope you've enjoyed the flowers.

ME, MYSELF & EYE

A MEMOIR

EPILOGUE

So that's it. That's my story! The tale of Dan is told. If you've made it this far then kudos to you — and thank you for sharing the journey with me. You've clearly put a lot of faith in someone that's never written a book before, and for that I'm truly grateful.

So, where am I at now?

I'm pleased to report that things have generally settled down, but there have been some interesting developments too. Let's start with the most important thing: health.

You'll be relieved to know, I'm sure, that very little has changed since those final meetings with the GUCH team just over two years ago. I had my bi-annual review just the other day, and it's all looking good. They're going to increase my Ramipril to 5mg just to support my heart muscle a little, otherwise everything's still the same. I decided to ask whether surgery two years ago would have been the solution, as I was young and able to handle it. The consultant stated that it was kind of like 'replacing one disease for another'. That might sound extreme, but I understood what she meant: it comes with its own set of issues. Valve replacement, whilst a common procedure, should only be considered when that becomes a better solution than leaving the heart to do its natural thing. In a weird way, it was somehow comforting.

Every ten weeks I still have the testosterone injection and that'll be the case for the foreseeable future.[198] I now have annual or bi-annual check ups with the Endocrinology team. Interestingly, I told Andy Levy that I was writing a book and sent him a couple of chapters for him to read. He really liked it, and then told me that he had been working on an App called *Clinically Speaking*.

"What's that about?" I asked.

"It's a library of video interviews with patients I've recorded over the years, discussing how their illnesses had affected their lives. We sometimes forget that the life story can tell us more than the diagnosis."

"Wow. That sounds like a really exciting project."

"It is. Fancy doing an interview?"

As I'm sure you can guess — not being one to turn down some free publicity — I was there in ten minutes. Much to my surprise, I visited the website a couple of days later to discover that — shock! horror! — I was now the 'poster boy' for the website too! How was I supposed to respond to that, considering my dysmorphophobia and all? I smiled on the inside. Once again: happy to be the face that launched a

198   Ironically, I totally forgot to go to my appointment last week, and now have to wait two weeks until I can have the injection. In those two weeks, I finished the book. Coincidence? *(Dan: No!)*

thousand ships, not happy when I have to talk to the Captain's daughter.[199]

So what about my eyes? They are, after all, the organs that started this whole thing off.

Thankfully there's been very little change in my sight. The left eye is still blind (that's never going to change), and the right eye hasn't lost any more sight. However, I still get retinal migraines — and a couple of them have been severe. A few months ago I was on a train heading back to Bristol when I casually looked out of the window. A glimmer of light seemed to catch my eye and I immediately knew that something was going to happen. However, what I didn't expect was a total loss of vision. A grey cloud descended across my eye, and for a couple of minutes I was totally blind. Understandably, I momentarily shat my pants but, after rubbing it and biting my lip in quiet desperation, my sight slowly started to return. I've never experienced a migraine as bad as that, and total loss of vision was incredibly scary.

So.

Eyes: check. Brain: check. Heart: check. Teeth: Oh dear.

Yup, out of all the things to cause me the most trouble, my teeth have definitely come up trumps. Remember in the opening prologue how I said, "I like these. Teeth don't thin"? How wrong I was. Over the past couple of years, the left hand side of my mouth has progressively gotten worse and worse — not surprising when you consider that I can't eat on the right. In the last few months, I've had two large fillings and a root canal. Only the other week I went to the dentist to have

---

199   → If you've got an interest in all things medical, I really recommend checking out the App. There are some truly fascinating stories and conditions on there. My video is actually one of the free ones. Now you have <u>no</u> excuse!

some work done on the lower right molar — the only molar I have left down there. After giving me two huge injections she had barely touched the tooth before I was wincing in pain. Her verdict? The pulp of the tooth was completely gone: it would have to be removed. I almost cried. How was I going to eat now, with a mouth in constant pain, an impossible bite on the left, and no teeth on the right? I sat in the dentist's chair and looked crestfallen. She rubbed my arm in sympathy.[200]

"But what about your music?" I hear you cry. Well, I'm still writing and still releasing, though it's quietened down of late. I'm not writing the bouncy techno that I once was and I've moved towards a deeper house sound. I've also created a new persona and it is... wait for it... Balls Deep! It's definitely a name that divides opinion. I felt like I wanted a new identity for this new sound and I happened to hear it mentioned somewhere. It also reflected a change in my life: I was no longer [sic] — I was virulent, alive, *a man!* Perhaps I'm totally misguided, but it works for me. I've had a couple of releases to date under this name and I've setup my own label too: *Protect and Serve*, so that's pretty exciting. I never want my music to take a back seat, but my creativity comes and goes in waves. I think I can be excused over the last couple of years: been a bit busy writing a book, you see.

Oh, and I'm running another night. HAHAHA![201] No, I am! It's called *Heist* and we're theming it around 1920's gangsters.

200   I have to tell you that, just before Christmas, I made the decision to ask her out. I felt a bit of a bond had formed between us (no dental jokes, please), so after having a filling and using the cunning ploy of giving her my number in a Christmas card, I stood up, wished her "Merry Christmas", gave her the card, and practically ran out of the surgery. The next few weeks were agony (not because of her work) as I eagerly awaited my appointment. She thanked me for her card. And that was about it. Ah well. At least I tried.

201   No, seriously — I am.

No Lego heads or lost dog posters this time. I swore I wouldn't do too much in the planning and preparation but of course I ended up doing totally the opposite. Mercifully, our first night was a complete success, all thanks to the months of hard work we put into making it something a bit new and original. I don't know what it is with me and new projects — I just can't help myself. Maybe they're my children: I'm involved in the conception, birth and growth and, inevitably, their departure. I know the day will come when I stand at the doorway, a tear in my eye, and say farewell to this creature that I've nurtured. So far, *Heist* is a little toddler — let's hope it stays that way.[202]

And speaking of children…

Almost had you!

Sadly, I have little to report when it comes to love, sex, and everything in-between. That's not to say I haven't been trying. Since my early excursions into online dating, new technologies have sprung up. *Tinder* now exists which, in all honesty, makes the whole process even more humiliating. I didn't really get *Tinder* when it first started (I now realise it's like *Grinder* for heteros), and so, when I decided to join, I made Herman Munster my profile picture. Not sure that was wise. Otherwise there have been a couple of blind dates, but that's about it. The tumbleweed still rolls.

As much as I love the concept of having children I am — if the real truth be known — very mixed about the whole thing. Some natural instinct deep inside me wants to continue the Jeffries' legacy, but another voice points out all that I have around me: absolute freedom and creativity. I get my parenting kicks once every couple of weeks when Evie comes to visit, an

---

202 → Plus I get to make little videos like this.

experience that is both exhilarating and exhausting. I love the pure energy that only a three-year-old can have, but by 9pm I totally understand why parents walk around like the living dead, and thus I am in utter awe of those who dedicate their lives to their younglings. But as nice as it is to hand Evie back, I still yearn to know what that unparalleled bond would be like.

The other big news is that I've left Access To Music. It had been a fantastic twelve years but the time had come to move on to pastures new. I'm incredibly proud of all that I achieved whilst I was there, and there's no denying that it was a difficult decision to make. I'd formed some brilliant friendships over the years and, whilst everyone was sad to see me go, I reminded them that leaving a job isn't what it was like ten years ago. Now when you say 'I'll keep in touch' you can actually mean it! The joys of social media.

And so, on my final day, myself and the Curriculum and Quality team ventured out to one of the nicest restaurants in Birmingham where we dined on incredible steaks and gallons of wine. Speeches were made, tears were shed, I even read a section from this book! There was an undeniable sense of unrealism about the whole thing. Isla cried, and even I got dewy-eyed. I don't think we could quite comprehend that this was happening. I was ATM furniture: a stalwart, a cushion. And now it was time to go.

One of the most touching things I received was a card conceived and created by Kate, who must get special mention for this. During my final years at ATM, I had become really interested in a new educational concept — Digital Badges — and Kate hand-made a card covered in them. It is truly a work of art, and hence gets its place in this book.[203]

The more observant amongst you will have noticed the first badge says, 'Award Winning Dog'. And it was true — Millie *had* become an award-winning dog!

Watching *Crufts* in 2014, I had seen a competition called *Scruffts* — the non-pedigree version of the dog show. One of the categories was for *Golden Oldie* and Millie — now sixteen — seemed to me a prime contender. I looked into the regional heats, only to discover that the nearest one was in Plymouth. I weighed up whether I thought she was fit enough to make the journey and came to the conclusion that she was: she was an *epic* Golden Oldie.

In the summer of 2014, accompanied by my delightful friend Rosie[204], we made our way to the event. Nature had decided that it was going to be one of the hottest days of the year and, once we arrived, it was evident that the dogs thought it was too. Dozens of different breeds lay in the shade, gasping for water. Millie coped pretty well, clearly psyching herself up for her big moment.

And within an hour, that big moment arrived. We stood next to five other dogs and their owners, each of them grooming and preening over their pride and joy.

"How many times have you competed?" one of them asked me.

"Never," I replied.

It therefore must have made them all the more sick when we won! After parading up and down the exhibition space and having had a thorough examination[205], we waited in

---

203 → She knows me so well!
204 Delightful yet massively hung-over.
205 Millie, not me.

anticipation to find out who was victorious. When the judge approached me and Millie, I nearly fainted. I think the grin says it all.[206]

A few weeks later I received a letter with details about the *Scruffts* semi-finals. To my amazement, it was being held at Earls' Court! Now *this* was the kind of stage I was after! It felt like forever until the big day arrived, but it eventually did — conveniently on Remembrance Sunday. Unsurprisingly the train up to London was packed, as were all the tube stations we had to negotiate. Millie still trotted on diligently beside me, unperturbed by the thousands of pairs of feet galloping past her.

When we got to Earls' Court, we had minutes to spare until we were on. After some hunting I eventually found the ring where *Scruffts* was being held, but had no idea where to go. Another lady — clearly in the same predicament as me — thought it was down the left hand side, and so we quickly made our way there. As we approached, it was clear we were in the wrong place, as a big sign said 'NO ENTRY!' Just as I was about to turn around, I could see all the other dogs and their owners walking into the ring. 'Fuck it,' I thought and ducked under the barrier, pulling Millie behind me.

"YOU CAN'T COME THIS WAY!" screamed a security guard, like I was jumping the fence at Glastonbury.

"My dog's meant to be on show!" I yelled back, and I ran onto the ring. The woman behind me did the same.

An official approached me and asked for my name.

"You're in the wrong spot. Come with me," and she promptly positioned us in our correct place in the line. You

206　→ What a winner.

could tell we were novices.

Mum, who had come with us, took her seat. I waved and watched as she tried to operate the ultra-complicated camera I had recently bought. And then before I knew it, the judge was standing in front of us, and the compere for the show was introducing Millie to the world.

"And next we have Bernard, a twelve-year-old Alsatian..."

I glared across the ring at the compere who had her head buried in her notes.

"No, no, NO!" I mouthed at her, shaking my head — utterly embarrassed that the wrong credentials were being read out. The judge didn't even appear to be listening.

"And who's this?" she asked, bending down to give her a stroke.

"This is Millie. She's seventeen."

"Seventeen?!" she exclaimed, as if dogs that old didn't exist. She smiled and moved on to the next one, and I carried on listening to the wrong information being read out.

Alas, Millie didn't win. She was, in all honesty, probably too old, and the judges were no doubt fearful that she may not make it to the *Crufts* finals, which were taking place mid-March.

And sadly, their fears were right. In the last week of February, I made the agonising decision to put Millie to sleep. Her health had steadily been declining, and during that last weekend it had gotten to the point of no return. She was drinking like mad — a sign that her kidneys were really on their way out. And when — after she had a wee in the flat and her back legs gave way — I knew something had to be done. I looked at her lying in her bed, the fire completely gone from her eyes. I felt the inevitable was imminent and decided that,

Monday morning, I would take her to the vets.

It didn't take long for the vet and I to concur that it was time to say goodbye. God knows I didn't want to, but I knew that to prolong her agony would be even crueller. The vet asked me if I wanted to stay. I thought about it for a second but I just couldn't bring myself to watch her go, as I had done with Norman. I gave her one last hug, left the room, and went outside and wept.

Outside I sat on the wall, tears streaming down my face. I knew I was doing the right thing, but it didn't make it any easier. I had to remind myself that I had given her eight years' of love and care and affection — eight years she might never have had had I not taken her from the Dogs' Home. And I had to remind myself that *my* life was changing too: that Friday would be my last day at ATM, that Monday was my birthday, and that Wednesday I was starting a new job. It felt like the closing of some massive chapters and the start of a whole new book. I sniffed and smiled and wiped the tears from my eyes — in many ways, Millie was giving me the freedom to live.[207]

Mercifully, that week was incredibly busy for me. I had a couple of days holiday, which I spent with the family in Weston and the Friday was my last day at ATM. After a fantastic meal and emotional farewell, I got so drunk that I couldn't face the train journey home (back to an empty flat), and so crashed on someone's sofa. Finally arriving home on Saturday morning, I opened my postbox to discover the usual junk mail and one hand-written envelope. I guessed it was a birthday card: it was in fact a hand-drawn picture of Millie, sketched by Rosie's sister, Flo. I was stunned. The likeness was incredible and the

---

207 → My lip still trembles every time I look at old pictures. But here's my little homage to one of the greatest dogs that ever lived. RIP Mills.

words inside the card moving and emotional. I gulped and looked across the room to her empty bed. The cold reality of being on my own washed over me and I placed the picture next to all the birthday cards I had received, a reminder of the wonderful friends and family that surrounded me.[208]

And that was exemplified on the following Monday when, dear reader, I reached thirty-eight of Her Majesty's glorious years. For once, I decided to make a proper day of it: personal shopper at Debenhams (where I spent £400 on new clothes), lunch at Browns with Alix and Sharon, spa session (annoyingly closed for refurbishment), and then food and drinks with friends. It was exactly what I needed after the emotional roller coaster of the week before.[209]

Compared to where I was in 2007, I feel pretty damn good. New job, new clothes, new friends. Okay, so I need to lose a few pounds and my hair's getting thinner and I'd still like to write more music, but all in all I'm pretty pleased with where I am right now. In spite of all the things I've been through — Wyburn-Mason, nosebleeds, acromegaly, meningitis, braces, leaking heart valve — I genuinely don't think I've had that bad a deal. As I look back at my journey, I feel almost blessed in some ways to have been given such a *smorgasbord* of rare conditions. "I'm not like anyone else," sung Ray Davies, and I now understand why. Not only that, I look at the world around me and see pain and heartache and inoperable illnesses, and then I consider that I've got a family that love me and a network of friends that care for me. Somehow, I've been blessed with being funny, compassionate, and creative and

---

208 → The likeness is just uncanny.

209 → Burgers and cake were exactly what I needed too.

that, I have found, is enough to get you through the hardest of times.[210]

I have to confess — I never thought I'd get this far. I started writing *Me, Myself and Eye* in August, 2013 and I'm writing these final thoughts in March, 2015. That's pretty good going if you ask me. I've had spells where I didn't want to write a single word, and other times when I couldn't stop myself. I'm used to that though: it's just like writing music.

Writing the book on Google Docs has been an absolute revelation. Gone are the days of typing, printing it, posting it, and then waiting days for a response. Instead, I can edit some work I did the night before whilst waiting for a train. Or at the doctor's surgery. Or on the loo.[211] I've been able to share chapters online with close friends and family, making sure they're happy about the bits I've written about them. Some of these people are on the other side of the world. Imagine trying to do that via snail-mail?

And then of course there's been the editing process. I've had an amazing right-hand man working tirelessly by my side, cajoling me when I needed it, questioning words and phrases that perhaps didn't quite make sense, making sure it all flows as it should do. But all the time he's never watered down the intentions of the book, and so to Bayu I am eternally grateful.

Erm... I think that's about it. Oh, one last thing. I want to thank everyone that's been involved in the writing and creation of this book, from friends who became 'reading guinea pigs' to the consultants and specialists who gave me medical advice, to everyone who's contributed to the

---

210   I guess I should add 'confident' to that list as well!

211   Caution: do not edit very long chapters whilst on the loo or you'll end up with piles. So I hear.

Kickstarter campaign (don't worry — your moment's coming soon), and to my family who have had to endure the whole ordeal with me, from start to finish. Thank you.

And of course, thanks to you for indulging me and coming along for the ride. I know I'm hardly Mother Theresa, but if it's helped you on your own personal journey even just a little bit then I'm super-pleased I could be of assistance. However if you found it too long, too sordid, or too medical: tough.

Sordid and medical is just how I like it.

If you enjoyed this book please consider giving it a review. More information and links to online ebook stores can be found at **www.memyselfandeye.co.uk/review**

KICKSTARTER HEROES

AT THE START OF 2015 I HAD THE CRAZY IDEA OF LAUNCHING a crowdfunding campaign in order to raise awareness (and some funds) for *Me, Myself and Eye*. I'd contributed to a couple of successful projects in the past and had seen how involved people feel when they're part of something new. I figured that if I was going to try and raise funds, people kind enough to pledge would want something back — even if it's just a 'Thank You'.

I decided to go with Kickstarter — being one of the most successful crowdfunding websites out there — and set about devising my campaign. I recorded a video with the wonderful David Martin from CompanyX and spent a good week editing it down to a 4-minute masterpiece (my words). Then it was time to write the blurb, devise the pledges, and get as much media coverage as possible. BBC Radio Bristol, the Bristol Post, and Made in Bristol TV all covered the story. We raised £3,501, £501 over the target (the £1 was from my good friend, Kate, who upped her pledge just to upset my OCD balance. It didn't work.)

So — as promised — the following list of names are all the people that pledged their support and their hard earned cash to the campaign, to make *Me, Myself and Eye* the reality that you hold in your hands.

Without your love and kindness, this book wouldn't exist. You're amazing.

Marc Allen
Heber Alves
Sean Atkinson
www.flightradar24.com
Daniel Ayres
Alison Babington
David Babington
www.improveinternational.com
Ursula Bailey
Ayesha Begum
www.lechladekhushi.co.uk
Simon Bos
Margaret Bourne
Roger Bourne
James Brown
Dave Bruton
Dani Carpenter
Al Carter
Thomas Chapman
Andy Cooke
Gail Cooke
Janet Croucher
Merv Cullen
Bob Cutler
Cilla Cutler
Peter Cutler
Costas Efthymiou
Jean Gill
Pat Goodrich
Carol Hampton
Colin Harrison
Jono Heale
www.acscustom.com
Dominic Herring
Alix Jeffries
Chris Jeffries

Evie Jeffries
Sue Jeffries
Zoe Johnson
Jeremy Krantz
David Martin
Isla McMenemy
Dale Newland
Jenni O'Connell
Roy Pawley
Sharon Pawley
Shirley Pawley
Nicola Pengelly
Simon Ridge
Matthew Rowse
Richie Royale
Stuart Seymour
www.motiv8personaltraining.co.uk
Greg Shaw
Irene Sloan
Paul Sloan
Tim Stephens
Ross Stringer
Avril Sugg
James Teri
Pete Thain
Ian Townsend
Jan Warner
Kate Webber
Teri Welch
Chris Williams
www.thatbritguy.com
Fiona Williams
Anna Wills
www.annawillsmusic.com
Sarah Wolsey

ACKNOWLEDGEMENTS

A S WITH MOST THINGS IN LIFE, IT'S ALMOST IMPOSSIBLE TO complete any project without the love and support of those around you. It goes without saying that my immediate family — Mum, Dad, and Alix — have been amazing during what must be a difficult and challenging period, yet an exciting one too. You don't know how nerve-wracking it is to give your mum a copy of the first draft, knowing that, at some point, she's going to read Chapter 37. Mercifully their feedback was always honest and positive. Many thanks to Sharon too, for her positive support and help in general. And of course, huge thanks to Evie. Just because.

Feeling almost like he is family, Bayu must get huge thanks as my copy editor. When we initially spoke about the project, I thought he would be writing the book for me. After reading the first couple of chapters I had drafted, he said, 'You don't need anyone to write this for you — you're writing is perfectly OK'. He's been an amazing support in dotting every i and crossing every t, even when I thought the t should be dotted and vice versa. He's pushed me to clarify every statement, ensure there are no contradictions, and cut out some of the excess that was inevitably going to happen (yes — there were edits!). I think we can both agree that we've had great fun along the way, and I've found a firm friend for life. Hartelijk bedankt! And thanks to Demi at The Writing Company who put me in touch with him in the first place and for believing in the project too. It's been a brilliant collaboration and this book wouldn't be the award-winning memoir it is without his help. Presumptive I know, but you live in hope.

Special thanks must go to the following people too for their involvement throughout the writing of *Me, Myself and Eye*: Andy Levy for his kind words, support, and occasionally cynical view of the publishing world; Sabine Torgler at www.englishfornurses.org for doing an amazing job deciphering and translating some particularly difficult medical records; Rosa Watkins and the Pituitary Foundation (www.pituitary.org.uk) for their support with the project and the brilliant work they do; Richard at Tangent for believing in the book and the whole concept surrounding it; Michelle Harris for her amazing PR work, even with a ten-month-old baby hanging off her neck; Jane Reece and The Folk House for running the memoir writing workshop that really got my creative juices flowing; Dani Carpenter for her expert advice and guidance when it came to the complex world of marketing; D A Allen for her sage advice and guidance; David Martin at CompanyX (www.co-x.co.uk) for his amazing work on the cover, artwork, and promo video and especially his tolerance when I wanted the tiniest bit changed; Paul Drummond (www.pauldrummond.co.uk) for producing a fantastic eBook and wanting to be involved with something new and unique; Grace at Novel Nights for her kind support and feedback; Jenni O'Connell for digging out some fantastic photos and taking the time to send them to me (anyone with kids that can do anything is right up there in my estimations). And if I've missed anyone out then my heartfelt apologies — it was amazing at the time.

I think that's it. You can go home now. Nothing more to

see. Well, not until *Me, Myself and Eye: The Senior Years.* Pre-order your copy now: available at all good virtual bookstores — in 2045.